DOG EARED

Also by W. Nikola-Lisa

PRIMARY GRADES

America: A Book of Opposites

Bein' With You This Way

Can You Top That?

My Teacher Can Teach...Anyone!

One Hole in the Road

Setting the Turkeys Free

Shake Dem Halloween Bones

Summer Sun Risin'

INTERMEDIATE GRADES

Gaya Lives in a Blue House

How We Are Smart

The Year With Grandma Moses

Till Year's Good End

Tangletalk

MIDDLE GRADES AND UP

Dear Frank: Babe Ruth, the Red Sox, and the Great War

Dragonfly: A Childhood Memoir

Hey, Aren't You the Janitor?

The Men Who Made the Yankees

Shark Man

Praise for W. Nikola-Lisa's *Dog Eared: A Year's Romp Through the Self-Publishing World*

"By the time I had read ten pages, I knew I wanted to finish the book. By the time I had read fifty pages, I knew I couldn't put it down."

–WILLIAM B. BEIN

Award-Winning Business Writer, Consultant, and Chicago-based Entrepreneur

"In this charming, unorthodox, and personable memoir, W. Nikola-Lisa uses the seemingly mundane task of cleaning out his office as a clever frame for reflections upon everything from his love of Robin Hood to the self-publishing process, taking readers on an enjoyable journey that every book lover will relate to—and every author, indie or otherwise, will learn a thing or two from."

–BROOKE WARNER

Author of *Green-Light Your Book*

"A quirky, informative, and highly absorbing journey into the world of self-publishing, told by a master storyteller. If A. J. Fikry were to self-publish a book about self-publishing, this would be it."

–HOLLY BRADY

Publishing Strategist and Former Director of Stanford Publishing Course

"A fun, yet thoughtful, romp through the self-publishing process interwoven with the journey toward becoming a writer. Part self-publishing how-to, part memoir, part travelogue, this story unfolds with a storyteller's precision that includes involving vignettes, surprising historic asides, and personal observations. A treat for anyone who loves books, reading, and the publishing world."

–MARLENE TARG BRILL

Author of *Bronco Charlie and the Pony Express*
Recipient of the Beverly Cleary Children's Choice Award

DOG EARED

A Year's Romp Through the Self-Publishing World

W. Nikola-Lisa

GYROSCOPE BOOKS
CHICAGO

Published by Gyroscope Books
Designed by Six Penny Graphics

For orders by U.S. trade bookstores, retail outlets, and public libraries, please contact the Ingram Content Group: Tel: Retail (800) 937-8000; Libraries (800) 937-5300; or visit www.ingramcontent.com.

Author: Nikola-Lisa, W. [American, b. 1951]
Summary: The author's yearlong office-cleaning project turns into a romp through the world of books. The loose collection of essays touches many themes, including the author's writing and publishing experiences, the challenging world of book promotion, and the ever-changing world of digital and print-on-demand publishing.

Library of Congress Control Number: 2017907533

ISBN: 978-0-9972524-4-6 (paperback)
ISBN: 978-0-9972524-5-3 (e-book)

Printed in the U.S.A.

So many books, so little time.

–FRANK ZAPPA

Contents

Part III

Part IV

Reb Zebulun told Naftali, "When a day passes, it is no longer there. What remains of it? Nothing more than a story. If stories weren't told or books weren't written, man would live like beasts, only for the day."

Reb Zebulun said, "Today we live, but by tomorrow today will be a story. The whole world, all human life, is one long story."

–Isaac Bashevis Singer, *Stories for Children*

When I was a college student, in the midst of great turmoil and angst about my future, I fell asleep one night after finishing a biography about the eccentric inventor Buckminster Fuller. At the end of the book, Fuller described how, at every moment, awake or asleep, we are hurtling through space, on an infinitesimally small but dynamic planet, adrift in a sea of great cosmic events. As I fell asleep that night I couldn't help ask: *What keeps us from falling off the Earth? Gravity alone cannot possibly explain it.*

In the middle of the night I awoke in a cold sweat with the answer to my question: *Story! That's what keeps us from falling off the Earth.* Without our cultural stories, and the personal stories we tell each other, we'd simply fall off the Earth and cease to exist.

–W. Nikola-Lisa, *Personal Notes*

DOG EARED

Part I

I should be writing this entry on the first day in March, but it's leap year so I'm not. I'm writing it on February 29, 2016. Every four years a day is added to the shortest month of the year in order to keep the Gregorian calendar aligned with the Earth's revolutions around the Sun. The question is: Why?

1 | Hole in the Head

ANYONE WHO KNOWS ME knows that I never make New Year's resolutions. I mean, never. I'd rather wrestle a wild boar knee-deep in mud than make a New Year's resolution. *Why?* Simple, most people don't keep them. So why make them? They're useless. So it was quite a surprise this year when I announced to my wife in late December that I was going to make one.

"Starting in January," I said with firm conviction, "I am going to remove all of the books in my office, wipe each one clean, and then—after culling out those that are no longer of interest—shelve them in a new and more accessible order."

"Sure you are." My wife shrugged and walked away.

"No, really, I am," I replied, raising my voice as she disappeared into the next room.

I anticipate the project lasting most of the year. My office isn't large, but three of its four walls sport floor-to-ceiling bookshelves. And since the ceiling height of our little Victorian farmhouse is 10 ½ feet, that's a lot of shelf space, and by extension a lot of books. If my wife were a tweeter, she'd probably tweet "OMG" in response to my proposed resolution.

Impractical or not, I am resolved to carrying it out. After all, I haven't touched three-quarters of the books I own since we moved into the house some twenty years ago. The idea of removing each book, wiping it clean of dust and grime, then replacing it thoroughly stirs my imagination. I've already begun to imagine all of the books that I will rediscover. Books that have meant so much to me, have shaped my early intellectual life, but are now all but forgotten. Books I bought with the firm resolve to read but for some reason or another have never cracked open. Books that were gifts from friends and loved ones, that contain hope and promise, but whose message has been buried by the passage of time. The prospect of discovery is endless.

But, first, I should tell you, so you don't work up an unrealistic sense of anticipation, I don't consider myself a bibliophile, that is in the technical sense: one who loves and collects rare and exotic books (with or without unusually fine bindings). I have very few books that fit into that category. I also don't have any first editions (at least, any that are worth mentioning). Moreover, I'm not a collector of fine literature; you'll find very few books by Shakespeare, Dickens, or Dostoevsky; no volumes by Keats, Wordsworth, or Coleridge; and not a lick of Longfellow or Thoreau.

So, you might ask: What *do* you have on those bookshelves?

Well, besides a gallery of family photos that takes up one row of adjoining bookshelves (a relatively new addition, I might add), and a stash of personal notebooks, you'll find an eclectic collection of fiction, memoir, biography, nonfiction, essays, reference books, and books for children of all ages. And all of it combined is precisely what I want to write about: that and my own work, which reflects my transition from a traditional author to a non-traditional or self-published author.

But first...*it's Inventory Counting Day!*

EVERY AUTHOR KNOWS THIS because it's part of the annual federal income tax preparation ritual. After all, it's January, the start of the New Year, and as most authors know it's time to count last year's inventory. I usually start this ritual on December 25, Christmas Day, since my wife and I are "pedestrians" (our oldest daughter's term for people who believe in God, but don't affiliate with any particular religious organization). Yep, that's us: pedestrians (which means that we also have a little more time on our hands on Christmas Day since we're not celebrating anything except a little peace and quiet). Still, since it seems a bit sacrilegious to begin Inventory Counting Day on Christmas Day, I've decided to start the ritual after the New Year.

Inventory Counting Day begins by rounding up a few items—pad of paper, calculator, ink pen and marker, post-it notes, Scotch tape, and a flashlight. Okay, paper, pen, marker, and calculator I get. But what about post-it notes, Scotch tape, and a flashlight? Post-it notes because I mark each box of books with its contents—book title and number of books. Scotch tape because I don't trust the glue on the post-it note (even though 3M introduced "Super Sticky Notes" several years ago). Flashlight because half of my inventory is tucked inside an attic crawlspace where there's no light whatsoever. (When my wife sees me heading for the crawlspace she says what I really need is a miner's hat, and she's right because not only is it dark in the crawlspace, but the ceiling is low and I'm always bonking my head.) Oh, one more tool of the trade—an electric screwdriver. It turns out that the workmen who insulated our crawlspaces last year screwed the entry doors to them shut in order to block any unsuspecting drafts. They did such a good job that I need an electric screwdriver to unscrew their thick two-inch screws.

So I'm headed for the crawlspace with everything I need. The only thing is I shouldn't be headed there at all. Since I didn't take any inventory out of the crawlspace last year it should be exactly the same. *Right?* Well, yes, technically, except for the fact that I lost my inventory sheet over the course of the year and have to start from scratch this year. The running joke in our house is that I'm incredibly organized, that I know where everything is, and it's true, more or less. You see, I rarely lose anything because I know, for a fact, that it's "in my office," which as everyone in my family knows is a euphemism for…*He's gone and lost it again!*

But I know where the crawlspace is, and I'm headed that way. But what irks me is that I shouldn't have to do this silly exercise at all if I hadn't changed accountants (I had to: the last one I had went on vacation and never returned). My new accountant took one look at what I had been doing—or not doing—and said that I really needed to count my inventory every year and not just rely on last year's sales numbers. It's all about accounting for "shrinkage," which means things—inventory—go missing and should be accounted for. So, I'm counting. Well, actually I'm unscrewing the screws that hold the attic crawlspace's door in place. Three screws, that's all, and I'm in. But it's always the last screw that gives you the most problem. But, then *presto!* It gives way and I remove the door, only to be greeted by a dozen or more boxes of books.

Now this should be a rather easy task; after all, I did label the boxes last year. Unfortunately, the boxes are stacked three or four high and I can't actually see the post-it notes affixed to them. That means I'll have to remove some boxes and climb over others to get at the ones in the back of the crawlspace. Not what a sixty-something-year-old wants to be doing on a cold January morning. But what I find both delights and depresses me.

I'm delighted to find two boxes of an early book of mine titled *Tangletalk.* It's an absolute favorite of mine, published almost twenty years ago. I still enjoy reading it at author events, and to know that I have over eighty copies left makes me extremely happy. It's the only book of mine that I published some time ago that I don't discount (the thought of selling out of it is just too much to bear). When it went out of print and the publisher offered me the remaining copies at a steep discount, I jumped at the chance to buy them—and have never regretted the decision.

On the other hand (and this is what depresses me as I stare at the contents of the attic crawlspace), I counted not one or two or even three boxes of my first out-of-print book. I counted seven boxes of *One Hole in the Road*, a counting book for young readers. *Seven boxes! My God, what was I thinking when I bought them?* And this is not all: there are more copies lining the shelves of my office downstairs. Indeed, what *was* I thinking, that I'd make a killing? Technically, at $1.00 a copy, I could make tenfold my investment. Only there's a reason a book gets remaindered—*IT'S NOT SELLING, IDIOT!* And it's *not* selling (even with illustrations by Dan Yaccarino, one of my favorite children's book illustrators). So, as I climb over boxes, pulling them apart, trying to read my scrawl on various post-it notes, I read over and over again: *One Hole in the Road, One Hole in the Road, One Hole in the... Head!*

But I was new to the publishing game, a greenhorn. *One Hole in the Road* was an early book of mine, and the first to go out of print. So, like any greenhorn, I jumped at the chance to buy up the publisher's inventory—*everything*, lock, stock, and barrel. And that's why I have over three hundred copies of *One Hole in the Road* at home twenty years after it was first published.

2 | This Is Going to Be Fun

OKAY, ENOUGH OF INVENTORY Counting Day. Let me tell you why I became a writer. It's 1976. I've just graduated from the University of Florida with a master's degree in education and I'm headed to Montana with my wife and newborn daughter.

Why Montana? Because several years earlier my wife and I spent a winter in Bozeman, Montana, with my wife's high school boyfriend's older brother and his family. (My wife's high school boyfriend was there too, but only for a couple of weeks; he slept on the floor next to our bed.) We liked Montana, and we liked Bozeman (though I didn't particularly care for my wife's high school boyfriend). So, after I graduated from the University of Florida, we packed our belongings and headed west. It took three-and-a-half days to drive from Florida to Montana and for the entire trip our dog—a mixture of Siberian husky and Norwegian elkhound—slept curled up in the front passenger-side foot well. Great for us, but not for him: he emerged with a crook in his back and couldn't walk in a straight line for almost three weeks.

We settled in Bozeman where I began work as a teacher in a local alternative school, which was housed in the residence of a prominent Bozeman family (he taught photography at the university; she ran the alternative school). We deemed the school a success when we had six or seven children signed up for the year (three from the director's brood and several more from the neighborhood). The director held music classes on the first floor and art classes on the second floor; I taught math, science, and literature in the attic. Lunch was in the kitchen or, on warm sunny days, in the backyard.

It was during this time that our second daughter was born, which meant that I was a teacher during the day and a father at night. And that's exactly how I developed an interest in writing books for young readers. I was always making up stories, singing silly songs, and creating puppet shows with a homemade theater in our living room. I also read to both of our children from books we checked out of the local library or received mail order from our book-of-the-month-club subscription. It was a happy time at home, but at work things were not going so well (there was never a clear boundary between the director's home and the school, which made for some awkward moments). So I began to look for another teaching job.

It was while driving the Herbie Bus for Bozeman's summer activities program that I got to know one of the local schools. When I had the time I used to wander around the school, which was one of our stops each week, dreaming of teaching there. I dreamt of teaching second grade in my own room and with my own students. By the end of the summer my "dreaming" turned into a regular meditation because I had found a room that really spoke to me. It was large and spacious, but not well lit (only two slivers of windows framed the double chalkboard at the front of the room). What you noticed first, however, when you walked into the room was the garish orange carpet that covered the concrete floor. Carpet notwithstanding, the room spoke to me. When I got the chance, I stood in the middle of the room and said over and over again: *I want to teach second grade in this room at this school. I want to teach second grade in this room at this school. I want to teach second grade in this room at this...*

Now, I'm not superstitious or anything, but it must have worked because when a job suddenly opened up right before the school year began I landed an interview and was offered the job on the spot. The "job" was to teach second grade. Now all I needed was the room with the garish orange carpet. But that seemed somewhat of a remote possibility because as we walked around the school the principal mentioned that the other teacher he had hired earlier that day came from another school in the district and had first choice of two available rooms.

The first room he showed me was quite small, wedged between his office and the gymnasium (probably an afterthought during a school expansion project). The only thing that it had going for it, besides a beautiful old hardwood floor, was a bank of windows that faced south, flooding the room with sunlight. The other room was in the new wing. It was large and roomy, not too well lit, and it came fully carpeted (with a garish orange carpet). Of course, I imagined that the other teacher would fall in love with *my room* the way I had during the summer. But to my surprise, she chose the smaller, brightly lit room, leaving me with the room of my dreams (you know, the one covered with that God-awful orange carpet).

For the next five years I taught second grade at Irving Elementary School just down the hill from Montana State University, and I had a blast. The "blast" started the moment the principal told me—after I tried to tell him how I wanted to teach—that he didn't care how I taught as long as parents didn't complain.

That was music to my ears. Yes, the light bulb went on big time. I remember thinking: *This is going to be fun!* And it was because I followed my imagination, rather than the prescribed curriculum. I taught using a literature-based thematic approach, which I had begun to explore at the alternative school. With literature at the heart of the curriculum, I began to collect books, lots of books, which I kept in piles on my work desk in the back of the room. I had books to help me with my lesson plans. I had books to give to individual students. I had books to read aloud after lunch. I had all the new books that had just arrived at the library. And I had books that ultimately influenced my writing. These fell into two distinct groups: those incredibly beautiful books that you drool over because they are so well written; and then—like the orange pile carpet in my room—those God-awful books that make you shake your head, wondering how on earth they ever got published.

At some point, I remember thinking that my writing (which I had secretly been doing for several years) fell somewhere between those two piles of books. That thought not only motivated me to write, but it also gave me the courage to start submitting my work to editors. After a number of false starts, dozens of manuscript submissions, and encouragement from several local authors, I sold my first book—*Night Is Coming*. It was 1988. But I was no longer married. No longer teaching second grade. And I was no longer living in Bozeman, Montana. I was starting a new life as a junior faculty member at a private college in Chicago, Illinois, where I had moved in 1986 with my soon-to-be second wife.

3 | Kiss of Death

ALL RIGHT, ENOUGH PROCRASTINATION. It's time to start cleaning bookshelves. But where should I start? Isn't this always the question? Even though I haven't cleaned my office bookshelves for a decade or two, still it's not rocket science. And just like Inventory Counting Day, I'll need several things to complete the job: a six-foot ladder, a bucket of soapy water, a vacuum, and two rags (one to clean shelves; the other to dust books). But first, let me give you a quick tour of my office.

My wife calls it "The Cave" (not only because it's small, about 7' by 13', but also because it's dark). What makes it distinctive is that three of the four walls have floor-to-ceiling bookshelves. With a ceiling height of 10 ½ feet, that's a lot of shelf space. The ceiling height also explains why I use a six-foot ladder to get to the top shelf and not the easier-to-carry kitchen stepladder.

The room has three doors and a seven-foot-tall, double-hung window that faces the next-door neighbor's brick wall (which explains why my office is dark). The one wall that is free of bookshelves—the north wall—has two worktables, one on either side of a two-drawer filing cabinet. Then there's my office chair (no high-back, ergonomic, good-for-the-back chair for "active" sitting; just a straight-backed wooden chair my wife found in the alley).

But enough of the furniture; let's return to the bookshelves and how I plan to clean them.

First of all, I set up the ladder at the start of a row of shelves and slowly climb to the top of the ladder, pull out a couple of books within reach, and place them on the little paint-can holder that flips out from the backside of the ladder. When the mound of books on the paint-can holder that flips out from the backside of the ladder is sufficiently high, I begin the long journey down the ladder, taking several of the books from the top of the mound with me. It's practice for what I have to do next: climb the ladder with one hand while grasping the handle of a bucket of soapy water with the other.

For this phase I haul a bucket of soapy water up the ladder, place it on the paint-can holder that flips out from the backside of the ladder, and clean as much of the shelf I can reach. Climbing the ladder with the bucket of soapy water is by far the most dangerous part of my bookshelf-cleaning project. In fact, it's probably the most dangerous thing I'll do all year, which tells you a lot about my life or my age—or both. Of course, I don't clean the shelf with the bucket of water: I clean it with a rag that I immerse in the bucket of water, careful to wring out as much excess water as possible so as to not dampen the shelf excessively. This action is repeated the full length of the bookshelf with several time-outs in order to replenish the bucket of soapy water and to get a new rag. (It also gives me a chance to catch my breath.) The amount of grime is unbelievable, twenty-years-worth unbelievable. But once I've finished this unpleasant and quasi-dangerous task, I have a genuine sense of accomplishment—as well as several stacks of books on my office floor.

Now for the fun part—cleaning each book by hand. I used to do this while perched at the top of the ladder, but that was when

I was younger and more agile (and could better suppress my fear of heights). Now I clean each book while standing squarely on the floor of my office. This is the part of the bookshelf-cleaning project that I look forward to the most: gently dusting off a book as I turn it over and over in my hands, then cracking it open and leafing through it before retracing my steps back up the ladder to shelve it. The cleaning process is always the same: less physical than emotional, because in the process of cleaning a book I get to reacquaint myself not only with the contents of the book, but also with an earlier part of my life when the book meant so much to me. It's like thumbing through an old family photo album that you haven't looked at in years.

IN THE DIGITAL AGE it's quite easy to lose track of the physicality of a book—how it looks, how it feels, how it smells, how it sounds. It's not that I'm a Luddite, a holdout against the constant stream of digital books available on the market; rather, as a writer brought up in the pre-digital age, I still have a healthy appreciation of the physical book. I buy both—e-books and physical books—I just buy more physical books (though that might be changing in the future: it'll be a heck of a lot easier to move an e-book library to the nursing home than a library of physical books).

E-books, of course, have their place. And it's easy to see how they've impacted me, particularly my book-buying habits. When I buy a physical book, I'm much more discerning in what I buy: aside from intriguing content, the book has to delight my senses, which usually means a hardcover book with an alluring dust jacket, exquisite endpapers, engaging front matter, attractive interior design, a unique blend of font styles, and, last but not least, pleasing paper stock.

Case in point. Several years ago I bought Witold Rybczynski's *One Good Turn: A Natural History of the Screwdriver and the Screw.* I found it in one of Daedalus' book catalogs (if you don't know Daedalus, you should as they offer an odd assortment of remaindered books at quite affordable prices). Rybczynski's book on the history of the lowly screwdriver caught my eye. I mean, how on earth can you squeeze a book out of that—a screwdriver, for God's sake? Well, Rybczynski more than did: it's as much a history of human tool-use as it is a history of the Western World, with some interesting side adventures along the way (like a quirky discussion about 16th-century armorers' tools).

Daedalus offered Rybczynski's book as a paperback, which I'm not opposed to buying (not only am I not a purist book collector—hardcover first editions and all that—but I figure at my age a paperback has as good a chance of outliving me as a hardcover). Rybczynski's book was all it was advertised to be: an exceedingly entertaining and informative book for such a slim volume. Several years after purchasing the paperback, however, I stumbled upon the hardcover edition while scanning the shelves of a local used bookstore. I immediately fell in love with the hardcover edition. Everything about it beckoned me: its cover, endpapers, selection of fonts, interior design and organization, but especially its thick, deckled paper stock. I didn't equivocate: I bought it on the spot even although I had the paperback edition sitting on my bookshelf at home.

I buy a lot of books on the spot, sometimes forgetting that I have a copy at home. I buy books partly because I enjoy reading them and partly because I enjoy writing them (which means that I need them, need to surround myself by them: it's how you learn the craft). But I shouldn't be writing books in the first place, at least according to my astrological chart.

Your astrological chart?

Yes, doesn't everyone have one? Of course they don't, but I do. And what I learned from it almost ended my career before it even began. But I didn't realize it at the time. After I published my first book, several years after the astrological chart reading, I sold six or seven books over the next five years. It was a great feeling and I was thinking like, "Okay, this is it. I'm on my way." When four of those books came out in the same year—1997—and I still had another two in the pipeline, I was definitely feeling, "This is it, I'm on my way."

Over the next ten years I published another dozen books, bringing my output to an even 20 books in almost as many years. Now, most people would say that I was a success, and I suppose—by most standards—you could say that I was, except for the fact that I bounced around from one publisher to the next, never really feeling that I had a solid home. More than that, selling a manuscript was always a chore. You'd think that after 20 books it would get easier; well, in my case, it didn't.

Then, in 2008, I hit the wall. It was the same year that the market crashed, bringing almost everything to a halt. After floundering for a year or more, I decided to turn my writing ship in a new direction—toward the world of self-publishing. By coincidence, just as the market crash was dragging the economy down, the do-it-yourself world of self-publishing was on its way up. By 2010, the self-publishing world had in place all of the mechanisms a writer needed to produce, promote, distribute, and sell a book worldwide (thanks to Amazon, the bane of independent bookstore owners).

I jumped into this world with both feet, publishing *Dragonfly: A Childhood Memoir* that year. I chose this particular piece for two reasons. First of all, I couldn't stop thinking about growing up in Texas at the hands of a cruel stepfather. Secondly, I didn't think the piece would sell. I saw it as a place-marker, a book project to entertain me while the market righted itself and I got back on track publishing with traditional publishers. But it didn't work out that way because the market didn't right itself overnight. Not only were editors not buying projects, they were slowing down production on the projects they already had in the pipeline. I heard this story from editors over and over again. So the following year I decided to publish another book on my own.

I approached it the same way that I approached *Dragonfly*. I looked in my files and asked a very simple question: *What won't sell?* Again, I thought these self-publishing projects were place-markers, minor distractions until the market turned around. Since I keep a lot of writing notebooks, I naturally turned to them for inspiration. What I landed upon was my travel journal, which contained a collection of humorous stories about my visits to schools, libraries, and bookstores. *Hey, Aren't You the Janitor?*—the title of the file (and resultant book)—reflects one of these stories.

I was scheduled to give an author program for kindergartners at a local school. Three classes of six-year-olds had assembled in one room, waiting for me. I knew they were waiting for me because when I entered the room I noticed that they, or at least a teacher, had written a welcome sign on the chalkboard—*Welcome Author and Storyteller W. Nikola-Lisa.* Beneath the sign there was another clue that they knew who I was and what I did—several of my books lined the chalk rail.

So, I assumed that the kids were primed and ready to meet the author. Thinking this, I started the program with a rousing "All right, kids, who knows who I am?" (I figured they knew, and if they didn't, at least I could point to a few clues to help them remember).

A boy in the back of the room shot his hand up; he didn't hesitate at all, he just shot his hand right up. So I called on him.

"All right, who am I?"

"Aren't...you...the janitor?" he replied, haltingly.

"Well, not exactly," I said, "but it's a good guess." *(And a great title for a book,* I thought.)

Now, you're probably thinking: *What on earth does this have to do with your astrological chart?* Everything. You see by the time I self-published my third book, I was totally hooked on being a self-published author. Why? Simple: I found that I really liked being in charge (my wife could have told you that). It goes back to the astrological chart reading that I had when I was in graduate school. After telling me this and that (all things that I already knew about myself, like "You'll have more than one child." *Well, duh, I already had two!)*, the astrologer looked me in the eye and said, "When it comes to writing, you have every writer's destiny mark except one."

"And that is?" I said, leaning forward.

"Contact with publishers."

Contact with publishers! Talk about the kiss of death. I mean, a writer without publisher contacts might as well hole up in an insane asylum and scribble notes on paper napkins. I was distraught, mortified, crushed, but undeterred (that's how it is when you're young and ambitious). It also explains why I spent the next twenty years bouncing from one publisher to the next, a dozen or more, until I discovered the DIY world of self-publishing.

4 | Junior High Math

IT'S ALMOST THE END of January and I haven't climbed to the top of my ladder yet. I keep looking at my bookshelves, but I haven't been sufficiently motivated to start the laborious task of removing, cleaning, sorting, and re-shelving all of the books in my office.

Procrastination runs deep in my family. I usually know when my wife is in procrastination mode: she cleans the house sorting through things she hasn't touched in years. That's when I know she's getting ready to start a new project. I'm kind of the same way, but in this case, when the actual project *is* cleaning, I'm at a loss as to how to procrastinate, which means that often I find myself standing in the middle of my office staring up at the books on my bookshelves. But it's time to start. How else am I going to write about my yearlong office-cleaning project?

It shouldn't be that difficult. As a child I was really good at taking things apart. Unfortunately, I couldn't always get them back together again. Take my father's train set. My father died when I was just shy of my third birthday, so I really don't remember him that much. But I do remember his train set. That's because my mother gave it to me once I was old enough to appreciate it (I guess, in the world of model train sets, it was pretty expensive). I was about ten years old when she gave it to me. She made a big deal of telling me about the train set and how much it meant to my father. But I guess I didn't listen that well, or understand the importance of what she told me, because as soon as she left my bedroom I started to dismantle it.

That's right, I took it totally apart—tracks, train cars, bridges, switching stations, everything. When the parts lay in so many piles on my bedroom floor, I started to string the tracks around my room so they resembled a miniature roller coaster. After stringing up the last set of tracks, I took a set of wheels (which I had pried loose from the undercarriage of a train car) and sent it screaming down the tracks. I did the same with another set of wheels. And another. And another. It was great fun, until my mother walked in, surveyed what I had done, and started screaming at me. I really didn't understand why she was so mad: it was a lot of fun playing with my new model-train-set-turned-roller-coaster.

Anyway, as I stare at my bookshelves, I'm starting to think that the best approach to my yearlong office-cleaning project might be the take-everything-apart approach. I decide to remove all of the books on all of the bookshelves on one wall of my office. And the easiest wall to start with is the east wall. Why? Simple: it's the one with the least amount of shelf space and, by inference, the least amount of books.

The bookshelves are wedged between two doors—one that leads to the kitchen and one that opens into the living room. There are seven shelves total, with each shelf measuring three feet across, for a total shelf space of twenty-one feet. Each of these shelves is filled with books that stand upright, side-by-side, fore edge in. I say this because the next thing I want to do is to calculate how many books I have on the seven shelves before I take them down and dust them off. Let's see: seven shelves, each one three feet long. That's a total of 21 board feet of shelf space (or 252 inches).

The next calculation is spine width. I need an average spine width in order to obtain a divisor, which is then divided into the dividend. Uh-oh, this is starting to bring back memories of junior high school. Isn't that when we learned about divisors, dividends, and quotients (as well as factors, products, remainders, and a host of other mathematical terms)? Luckily, the books on these shelves are all about the same width, because they're all the same type of book—mostly fiction, with some biography, memoir, and nonfiction sprinkled throughout. In terms of spine width, most of the books range from three-eighths of an inch to an inch-and-a-quarter wide, with the majority measuring five-eighths of an inch.

Let's use that number—five-eighths of an inch—as our divisor, except now we have to convert the fraction to a decimal. (Ugh, more junior high math.) We can make this conversion in two ways, one longer than the other. Let's start with the longer method, the one I learned in 5th-period algebra class.

Step 1 - Find a number you can multiply by the bottom of the fraction to make it 10, or 100, or 1,000, etc.

Step 2 - Multiply both the top and the bottom number of your fraction by that number.

Step 3 - Then write down just the top number, putting the decimal point in the correct position (one space from the right-hand side of the number for every zero in the bottom number).

Let's try it for ⅝. To make 8 a multiple of 10 we'll have to multiply it by 125 (8 × 125 equals 1,000; anything less leads to a fraction). Then we multiply 5 × 125 to get 625. Finally, we move the decimal point three digits to the left (because there are three zeros in 1,000) to get our answer: 0.625, which reflects our average spine width as a decimal.

Now, the easier method: divide 8 (the divisor) into 5 (the

dividend) and you should get—yep, you guessed it—0.625 (the quotient). Why didn't they teach us *that* in junior high?

I now have all of the figures I need to calculate the number of books on the seven bookshelves on the east wall of my office. The equation being: 252 divided by 0.625, which equals 403 (or 400, if we round down). Four hundred books—that's not so bad. But let's extend that a bit, to cover my entire office. All we have to do is multiply that number by 6 (because there are six more sections of bookshelves in my office approximately the same dimension). Let's see, 400 times 6 equals 2,400. By the time I conclude my office-cleaning project I will have taken down, culled through, cleaned, and reshelved about twenty-four hundred books.

Wow! I better get started—and soon.

But I don't. Instead I check my email (I told you procrastination runs deep in my family). After scanning a few business-related emails, I see a note in my inbox from one Robert Goodman. *Robert Goodman?* Let's see, my sister's first husband's last name was Goodman; but he was Steve, not Robert. The email says that he's been looking for me for years. At first I thought he might be with the FBI, but it turns out—after we speak on the telephone—that we attended the same high school, we even played varsity baseball together. (He reminded me that one day we crashed into each other chasing a fly ball. After one of us threw the ball back into the infield, we continued to argue over whose ball it was while the coach yelled at us from the dugout.)

Yes, now I remember—Bob Goodman. We used to go surfing together, although he didn't surf. I'd surf and he'd hang out on the beach. And we were in a lot of the same classes together. This is where things get a little fuzzy. I don't remember much of my high school years. Bob, on the other hand, remembers everything (probably because he returned to the school after he graduated from college to work as a dorm monitor).

The only teacher I remember, besides our English teacher who could recite *Froggie Went A-Courtin'* and several other ditties with aplomb, is Commander Adams, our geometry teacher. I remember Commander Adams because he treated his students like naval cadets. He was strict, and I mean *strict*. You didn't dare take your eyes off of him while he was teaching. If you did, you paid for it. He'd walk up to you, slap your desk with his ruler, lean over, and say something like, "You asleep, cadet?" It wasn't the embarrassment that I hated. It was the fact that he snorted when he talked, spraying small bits of nose material at you.

Yes, I remember Commander Adams.

And I remember Bob Goodman.

Fortunately, I also remember that tonight is the Chicago Writers Association's annual book award ceremony, so, sorry, I've got to go upstairs and get ready.

5 | An Award, Sort Of

THE CHICAGO WRITERS ASSOCIATION'S award ceremony is held each year at the end of January at a local independent bookstore. I always look forward to this event, and this year more so because my book—*The Men Who Made the Yankees*—received an honorable mention in the "non-traditionally published non-fiction" category. The book came out last summer, just before the application deadline for the book awards. Last summer: now *that* was some summer. It was some summer because I did something that I had never done before: I hired a publicist. I had a little extra money from a family inheritance and thought, *Well, if ever there was a time to blow a couple of grand, this is it.*

And blow a couple of grand I did. I can't say that it was a total bust though. I learned an awful lot. First of all, I learned that you don't need a publicist; that is, if you're willing to do a lot of the leg work yourself, which I was. What I couldn't do by myself was get the list of contacts that my publicist got (at least not without blowing another grand or two). After signing her contract, she sent me a small book filled with people that she said she was going to contact, and then urged me to do the same.

Wait, isn't that why you're paying her?

Yes, but after a few weeks of working with her, we were a team, we were tight; we had each other's back (until she had blown though my small fortune; then I didn't hear from her again).

But while I had her attention she got me a number of gigs on sports talk radio throughout the summer. I talked to radio announcers all over the country who were either local sports enthusiasts, ex-minor league players, or, in one case, an ex-NHL player from Canada. I talked to anyone interested in *my story*—the origin of the New York Yankees. I thought I had a pretty good slant too, tying the origin of the Yankees to the rise of the American League. No one had ever done that before. Most stories about the Yankees start at three different places: 1903, when they came to New York as the Hilltop Highlanders; 1913, when they adopted the Yankee moniker while sharing the Polo Grounds with the National League Giants; or 1923, the year they moved into Yankee Stadium, claimed their third American League pennant, and won their first World Series title.

Yes, I had a good story. And since it was summer—when professional baseball permeates everything—the book generated a lot of interest with the live sports talk radio crowd. But, then, this is their business: fill up airtime with relevant content. And, at the time, I was relevant content.

But I had a dilemma: everyone wanted me to use a landline phone and not a cell phone for the interview because landline phones generally get better reception. It was a dilemma because I like to pace around my office and flail my arms when I talk. Cell phone, no problem (just use my ear buds). But landline? I didn't have a headset (and I wasn't about to buy one for a few radio interviews). So, after thinking about it, I came up with a solution: I would duct-tape my handheld landline phone to my head. Yes, you heard me correctly: I would duct-tape my phone to my head. That way I could pace up and down the length of my office and flail my arms all I wanted to. Luckily, I came up with the solution before my publicist called with her first lead.

Publicist: "Hey, WGN wants you."
Me: "What? WGN? Isn't that Cubs radio?"
Publicist: "Yes."
Me: "They want me?" (Remember, I live in Chicago. I used to grade papers in the leftfield bleachers when we first moved there. I was there when Steve Bartman caught the foul ball that Cubs' leftfielder Moisés Alou should have caught in Game 6 of the 2003 NLCS. Yes, I know the Cubs—and I know WGN.)
Publicist: "Think you can handle it?"
Me: "Ah, yeah, sure."
Publicist: "Good, because they want you *now*."
Me: *"Now!"*
Publicist: "Yes, there's a rain delay in Colorado, and they need to fill airtime."
Me: [*gulp*]
Publicist: "Hang up and keep your line free. They should be calling you in five minutes."
Me: "Five minutes!" (It turns out that she was right. In five minutes the phone rang. It was WGN. It also turns out that five minutes is just about enough time to duct-tape a handheld landline phone to your head.)
Telephone: *B-r-r-n-g. B-r-r-n-g.*
Me: "Hello."

Voice on the Telephone: "Hey, WGN here. We're on the air at Coors Field in Denver. We'd like to ask you a few questions about your book, *The Men Who Made the...*"

SO THAT WAS THE start: on the air with five minutes notice and I'm talking to Cubs' announcer Steve Stone. But that doesn't tell you why I joined the Chicago Writers Association, which is really what I want to talk about. I joined because I was mad at the SCBWI.

What on earth is the SCBWI?

By anyone's reckoning, the Society of Children's Book Writers and Illustrators is the largest, most influential, professional organization for writers and illustrators of children's books, and I was mad at them because I thought they were too cozy with leaders of the industry (publishers, editors, art directors, and the like). The result of this coziness is most visible in the SCBWI's PAL policy (PAL, as in *Gee, aren't we great pals?).* But PAL, which stands for "Published and Listed," is a decidedly *unfriendly* policy, especially for independently published children's book authors. Here's why: PAL authors get to do things that non-PAL authors don't. They get to list their books in certain SCBWI registries. They get to sell their books at certain SCBWI events. They get to submit their books to several SCBWI book award contests. Non-PAL authors don't (or at least they hadn't been able to until recently).

And what really burns me up is the fact that non-PAL members pay the same membership dues as PAL members. That really gets under my skin. But first: how do you become a PAL author? Easy, at least that's what the SCBWI website says. Just have your book, article, poem, short story, illustration, photograph, film, and/or television show for children published by one of the organizations listed in the SCBWI Market Survey and you're in. Oh, and if your publisher isn't listed in the survey's drop-down menu, no problem, simply enter the name of your publisher in the space provided and, just like that, you'll be added as a full member. *Easy?* Right. *Fair?* You bet.

Wrong. Read the fine print, dummy. A publishing house must meet the following criteria to qualify for PAL status:

1. The author/illustrator shall not have paid any money or consideration for the publication of their work in any format. This would eliminate all vanity publishing and subsidy publishing.
2. The publisher (whether traditional or new media) must have a professional editorial process prior to publication, at no charge to the author/illustrator.
3. There must exist a means of broad distribution to the retail customer.
4. The publisher must publish works from more than one author and illustrator, or family. Thus, if there are several illustrators but only one author (or vice versa) it will not qualify.
5. The publisher must have published at least one prior list, or in the case of a digital publisher, have been in business for a minimum of one year.
6. The publisher, whether traditional or new media, provides a means of marketing at no cost to the author/illustrator.

In other words, *self-published authors need not apply!* And that's me (as well as a slew of other people). So I'm hot under the collar. I'm steaming. I'm really mad and ready to write the SCBWI's Board of Directors—and I did, several years ago. I wrote and told them how unfair it is that I pay full membership but *don't* get full benefits—because I'm not a PAL author (actually, I am, just not completely). To my surprise, I got a response. Rather quickly too: *Hold on buddy. Be patient. We're working on it.*

So I do, I hold on and immerse myself in other things (which means I completely forget about my letter and the Board's response). Then, several months later, the SCBWI's Board of Directors makes an earth-shattering announcement:

Hurry! Hurry! Read all about it!
SCBWI announces the first-ever Spark Award
for non-traditional publishing!

Yep, that's right. Self-published authors just got an upgrade: now we're called "non-traditional publishers." I was ecstatic, euphoric: they listened (or maybe I was just riding a wave that had already crested). Anyway, now self-published authors...I mean, non-traditional publishers could get their due: their own book award from the SCBWI, one of the greatest, most generous, outstanding organizations in the entire world (okay, maybe it's a bit over the top, but then again I've been a faithful member for over thirty years).

But I didn't apply. I couldn't. I didn't have an independently published book ready to go by the application deadline. But I was working on one: my fifth, called *The Men Who Made the Yankees.* It was a classic "labor of love," over a decade in the making (think Kadir Nelson's *We Are the Ship*). I wasn't quite finished with it to make the 2014 Spark Award application deadline, but once it came out (one day after the cut-off date), I raced to the post office to put in my application—but not for the Spark Award.

The application I was hurriedly mailing was for the 2014 Literary Classics Book Award. If you're not familiar with Literary Classics, it's a new organization that caters to the needs of self-published authors. And it's not alone in this capacity: it turns out that due to the rise of non-traditionally published books an entire marketplace of fee-based services exist to "service" this new sector of the publishing industry. Along with editorial, design, and marketing and promotion services, you can also buy book reviews and awards.

Reviews? Okay, I've heard of that (even Kirkus Reviews, one of the most esteemed book review agencies in the business, offers book reviews for a fee). But awards—isn't that going too far?

Well, you really can't buy an award from a reputable organization (though you can purchase award stickers online from some disreputable businesses). What you can do is throw your hat into the ring—for a fee. In other words, a handful of literary organizations are quite happy to take your application (and your accompanying application fee) on the promise that you *might* win an award. And, if you do win, here's what you get: a glowing review, a brief mention on their website, and a handful of silver or gold medallions to stick on your book. Remember, that's *only* if you win. Now, let's do the math: $75 application fee (standard charge) times 3,500 applicants (a fairly typical amount, though I've heard that some awards garner more than 5,000 entrants) equals (I think you better sit down for this one) a cool $262,500. Yes, folks, that's a little over a quarter of a million dollars.

Guess who gets the *real* award?

Anyway, as P. T. Barnum once said, there's a sucker born every minute. And I guess I'm one of them, because I dug into my pocket and shelled out $150 (that's right, I entered my book in not one, but two categories), then I waited. And, lo and behold, the next thing I knew, I won. But before I could pop the cork on a bottle of champagne, the phone rang. Nope, not at 5:00 a.m., when authors and illustrators get word that they've received the BIG awards—the Newbery and Caldecott Awards—my phone call came around 6:00 p.m. when Lin Oliver and Stephen Moser, co-directors of the SCBWI, called from the SCBWI's Los Angeles office (or their neighborhood bar) to inform me that *The Men Who Made the Yankees* had won the 2nd annual Spark Award for non-traditionally published nonfiction. (You got it: even though I missed the deadline for the inaugural award, I didn't sit around eating bonbons; I entered *The Men Who Made the Yankees* in the 2nd annual SCBWI Spark Award.)

Pop. Fizz. Clink. Gulp.

After a glass or two of champagne, I told my wife that everything was cool between the SCBWI and me. Yep, I was no longer mad at them. I *was* mad, just not at them.

I was mad at the Chicago Writers Association. I'm mad at them because at the awards ceremony, which I attended earlier this evening (and even got dressed up for), the moderator only mentioned the awardee and the runner-up for each category. There was no mention whatsoever of anyone who received an honorable mention, which means *me* (and I was all set to stand up and take a bow).

Oh, and what about the Literary Classics Book Award? Well, lo and behold, I won that too. Not the whole thing, mind you, but I did receive a gold medal for the best book of nonfiction published by an independent author.

Wow! Book Awards! They're definitely worth it—if you win, that is.

6 | Sign of the Twins

BOOKS HAVE ALWAYS MEANT a lot to me, though it took me a while to realize this. I began life with a gun, a bicycle, and a fishing pole. I grew up in rural America—southern Texas—where trees were my books, nature my library. My family, though educated, was not interested in books: we had very few of them at home (*Reader's Digest* and *TV Guide* were pretty much it), and the library was something that I had heard about, but had never visited. But then I didn't want to: I only wanted to hunt and fish and ride my bicycle. And I did so for most of my childhood.

It was while serving after-school detentions in high school that I first discovered the library. That's because detentions were served in the library in the small, private high school I attended in Florida. It was a cavernous room filled with study carrels in the center and bookshelves around the perimeter. I tried to sit near the edge of the room, where the detention teacher—who would have rather been anywhere else in the world than in the library monitoring us—couldn't see me. In doing so, I unwittingly placed myself in close proximity to the room's primary inhabitants—books. Invariably, my eyes wandered (after all, there's just so much homework you can do without taking a break), and more often than not my eyes landed upon a nearby shelf of books. I don't have a strong memory of actually picking out a book and reading it, or even just leafing through one. What I do remember are the shapes of books—their varying heights, thicknesses, designs, and distinctive lettering. In an odd sense, my lifelong love of books emerged from my early attraction to their physical beauty.

Although I read many books in high school (we had to: it was required), it was not until my girlfriend gave me a book by the German-born Swiss writer Hermann Hesse that I started to pay more attention to the contents of books, what was between the covers. The book she gave me—sadly, right before we broke up—was Hesse's *Narcissus and Goldmund*, which chronicles the pull within each of us between the life of the mind and the life of the senses—between intellect and spirit; science and art. As a double Gemini, I have always felt this relentless pull: it's basic to the Sign of the Twins (apparently doubly so in my case)…

> "Why, yes," Narcissus continued. "Natures of your kind, with strong, delicate senses, the soul-oriented, the dreamers, poets, lovers are almost always superior to us creatures of the mind. You take your being from your mothers. You live fully; you were endowed with the strength of love, the ability to feel. Whereas we creatures of reason, we don't live fully; we live in an arid land, even though we often seem to guide and rule you. Yours is the plentitude of life, the sap of the fruit, the garden of passion, the beautiful landscape of art. Your home is the earth; ours is the world of ideas. You are in danger of drowning in the world of the senses; ours is the danger of suffocating in an airless void. You are an artist; I am a thinker…"

Narcissus and Goldmund spoke to me in a way that no other book had up to that point in my life, but Hesse's storytelling wasn't enough to pull me into the world of books completely. It was intriguing, perplexing, even tantalizing, but I was a child of nature serving out my high school years in Florida and all I wanted to do was go to the beach. And I did, all the way through high school and well into my first two years in college. I attended the University of Florida, which was only seventy miles—72.9 to be exact—from St. Augustine, known for its long stretches of pristine beach. Being that close, I tried to get to St. Augustine any way that I could: I hitchhiked, took a Greyhound Bus, rented a van, and even rode on the back of a motorcycle clutching my surfboard (of course, we never made it; we didn't even get out of town).

I did this—and a lot of other things I'd never done before—while trying to keep up my studies at school. It's the Gemini thing: we lead a double life, always pulled in more than one direction. While I was trying to live the carefree life of a beach bum, I was also trying to excel at school—as a student of comparative religion. No, I didn't go to college intending to major in religion; it just happened, more by default than anything else. I thought I'd be an English major, then a psychology major, then a philosophy major, then a history major, then a [blank] major (substitute any number of disciplines for the blank and I probably tried it).

If it isn't obvious yet, I was on a quest—like most young adults—trying to find a major that would allow me to read, and think, and talk, and dream. But every major I tried on, like a new shirt or pair of jeans, just didn't seem to fit. You see, I didn't like anything that had a methodology that you had to learn first, and all of the majors I tried seemed to be predicated upon learning an underlying methodology. The methodologies had funny names, too (analytic, clinical, quantitative, positivist); all, that is, except one—comparative religion. Faculty in the Religion Department had no interest in methodology. In fact, you were encouraged to read, and to think, and to dream, and to discuss—in seminar-style with a dozen or so other students—the insights you gleaned from your reading, and your thinking, and your dreaming. Not that it was easy; quite the contrary: we read an exorbitant amount of books, wrote lengthy papers, and took excruciatingly difficult final exams. But I didn't mind: I had found my major; I had found a home. Foolishly, I thought that my parents would approve since they were ardent churchgoers, but they scoffed at the idea. But nothing they said deterred me and I persisted, even flourished…

> Goldmund stood looking at his friend, the determined face, the goal-directed eyes; he had the unmistakable feeling that they were no longer brothers, colleagues, equals; their ways had already parted. The man before him was not a dreamer; he was not waiting for fate to call to him. He was a monk who had pledged his life, who belonged to an established order, to duty; he was a servant, a soldier of religion, of the church, of the mind.

Not only had I found my calling in life—or so I thought at the time—I had also found the library. I had been going to the main campus library sporadically ever since arriving on campus, but only because I had heard that that's where you could pick up girls. Urban lore, I'm sure, because it never happened to me. What did happen was that I began to explore the library. I mean, here was a seven-story building filled with books. That's it, just books. Now that impressed me. It totally piqued my curiosity so that on my visits to the library (which were becoming more frequent than my sojourns to the beach), I began to wander around each floor, poking my nose in every nook and cranny.

My favorite spot to study in was the large reading room on the second floor of the main library. It's an historic room with its spacious ceiling height, large multi-paned windows, detailed murals, and an assembly of reading tables and study carrels. Yes, I was slowly becoming the monkish Narcissus, knowingly or not, pushing Goldmund aside. A split was inevitable. It came unexpectedly on a Sunday morning in late October during my third year in college. By this time I had bought an old van and could go to St. Augustine anytime that I wanted to. But the beach scene had become tiring; it no longer held the magic that it did when I was younger. Still, I went, which only hastened my existential crisis.

I had driven to St. Augustine late Friday afternoon. I went by myself, which I did sometimes, and slept in my van in the parking lot of Anastasia State Park, just north of the pier. I surfed all day Saturday, trying various places along the State Park's beaches: the waves were so-so, occasional swells, not too much, but the sun was out and the water refreshing. When I woke up the next morning the ocean was flat and glassy, not a wave in sight, so I packed up and headed back to Gainesville.

It was midway between St. Augustine and Gainesville, on a deserted stretch of road just west of the city of Interlachen, that my interior struggle abruptly came to the surface. I knew that I couldn't go on—living a carefree life of the senses while trying to cultivate my newfound life of the mind. Something had to give, and it did, there in the middle of nowhere with only an occasional car whizzing by. I pulled onto the shoulder of the road, took my surfboard out of the back of the van, walked to the closest tree, and shoved my board into the lower branches. Then I got back into the van and drove away.

Looking back, I often wonder who found my surfboard. It must have been an odd sight—a surfboard stuck in a tree beside a deserted strip of county road in the middle of nowhere. What would they have thought? Did it fly off of someone's van and land in the tree? Was it stolen? And who on earth was its owner?

Its owner? He was being sucked into the world of books, the world of ideas, the world of study carrels, term papers, and final exams. He—that is, me—was leaving a part of himself behind in order to evolve into the person that he knew he would become someday. It would just take a few more years—along with a marriage, two kids, a divorce, another marriage, and a move to Chicago—to complete the transformation.

7 | *Il Dunce*

WE'RE ALL FAMILIAR WITH it: that incredible and enduring icon of Italy—*Torre Pendente di Pisa*, a.k.a. the Leaning Tower of Pisa. It is the *campanile*, or freestanding bell tower, located behind Pisa's Cathedral in the Piazza del Duomo. Was it built with a tilt on purpose—perhaps to attract tourists, which it certainly has over the centuries? Or, was it one big goof-up? After all, construction on the tower began in 1173 when building techniques were still evolving.

In any case, it tilted, almost immediately. In 1178, after construction had progressed to the second floor, the tower began its slow incline to the right (or left, depending upon where you're standing). The reason: not only was the marble foundation only ten feet deep, it was set in weak, unstable substrata. In short, the tower was doomed from the start. The only thing that saved it was greed and hubris. It turns out that the Republic of Pisa liked to fight with its neighbors over trade routes and political prestige. Because of this, construction was halted for almost a century allowing sufficient time for the underlying soil to settle, which most certainly kept the tower from toppling over.

In 1372, one year shy of the structure's bicentennial, the tower was completed. That's the year that the bell-chamber was added (the bells—seven in all, comprising a major scale—would take another three centuries to be hung, with the last and largest bell installed in 1655). But all of this is prologue to one of the most distinctive tourist attractions in Western Europe, which should have toppled ages ago, had it not been for the Italian government (and the U.S. military that spared it from bombardment during WWII even though they knew the Germans were using it to spy on *their* neighbors).

For several decades after the War the Italian government, recognizing the tower's powerful attraction as a tourist destination, tried in vain to stop the tower from tilting. They closed the tower to tourists. They removed the bells. They girded the tower with cables. And just to be safe they evacuated all of the residents in the path of the tower (in case their efforts failed and the tower suddenly collapsed, as the Civic Tower of Pavia did in 1989).

Finally, the government assembled a consortium of engineers, mathematicians, and historians and took them to the Azores (I guess they needed to get away for a while), where they decided to straighten the tower to a safer angle. Over several tasty margaritas (or whatever they drink in the Azores), they planned to remove 1,342 cubic feet of soil from underneath the raised end of the tower. The alcoholic-induced plan worked because when it was all said and done the tower was straightened by almost 18 inches, returning it to its 1838 position, which meant that the Leaning Tower of Pisa could be opened for business once again. And it was, on December 15, 2001. By the end of the decade, a team of engineers declared the tower stable, and that it should remain that way for another 200 years. *Ka-ching. Ka-ching.*

IT TURNS OUT THERE are leaning towers all over the world: some of them, like the Leaning Tower of Pisa, the result of bad judgment; others, built on purpose. And one of them (one of the "on purpose" towers, that is) is in my backyard. Well, not literally, but close. It's a couple of townships over. If you were walking along West Touhy Avenue in 1934, you might stop to watch workmen put the finishing touches on the Leaning Tower of Pisa.

The Leaning Tower of Pisa? Isn't that in Italy?

The original, yes; but industrialist Robert Ilg of Niles, Illinois, built a pint-sized tower (actually, it's a half-sized replica) that year as part of IlgAir, a recreation park Ilg began in the 1920s for employees at the Ilg Hot Air Electric Ventilating Company of Chicago.

Some say the tower was to celebrate the 600th anniversary of the original tower's construction. Let's see: 1934 minus 600 equals 1334, which makes no sense at all because the last architect to work on the tower was Tommaso Pisano, who worked on the tower from 1350 to 1372, the latter date marking the tower's official completion date (unless you count completion from the installation of the last bell in the bell chamber; then 1655 is your magic number). But all of this really doesn't matter because a more plausible theory exists. The theory postulates that the real purpose of the Leaning Tower of Pisa in Niles, Illinois, was to store water for the park's public swimming pools.

In either case, residents of Niles, Illinois, don't have to worry about the tower falling over (in the same way that residents of Pisa, Italy, had to). The reason is twofold: not only had building techniques improved considerably by 1934, allowing for such an off-kilter building to rise over a public space, but also, and more importantly, the city of Niles became the first city in the United States to offer free ambulance service to its residents. It did so in 1946, anticipating—possibly—a building collapse or two.

But neither of these towers concerns me right now. What concerns me are the piles of books lining my office floor, what my wife calls *my* Leaning Towers of Pisa (smirking when one of them occasionally falls over). The towers represent the contents of the bookshelves from the east wall of my office. You know, the one that I had counted earlier, coming up with 400 books, plus or minus.

Half of them decorate the perimeter of my office, scattered here and there in precariously arranged stacks. The stacks are not thematic, however, as I had first imagined. When embarking on my yearlong office-cleaning project, I thought that as I took books off of my bookshelves I'd arrange them thematically into separate piles: ancient history, medieval Britain, legends and fables, art, music, literary criticism, etc. Not so the books from my east-wall bookshelves: these are arranged by trim size.

Trim size?

I knew that would catch your attention. You see, over the last few years I've become quite interested in the trim size of books. The reason: as a self-published author I have to be cognizant of the trim size of a book because not every trim size is "standard," which means that they may or may not be available in various bindings: paperback, case lam, saddle-stitch, cloth, and so on. This is important information because I usually publish a book in three editions—paperback, e-book, and hardcover—using three different companies. I do so because each company offers unique promotion and distribution opportunities that the others don't. But they also don't share the same standard trim sizes (of course, here we're talking paperback and hardcover, and not e-book). So I have to be mindful of the trim sizes that they share in common so the transition from paperback to hardcover is seamless.

And that's why the piles of books on my office floor are arranged by trim size. But there's another reason: I got it in my head several months ago to arrange the books on these shelves by height. I just wanted to see what it would look like to arrange a shelf of books by height, rather than alphabetically by the author's last name or by theme. (Think of it as a variant of the train-set-turned-roller-coaster experiment.) The exercise, arbitrary and nonsensical as it is, has proved to be rather useful: in the process I culled out books that fit every standard and not-so-standard trim size published by Ingram and CreateSpace, two of the print-on-demand publishers that I use for my self-published books. The books in this group are measured, labeled, and shelved on a separate bookshelf (on the west wall of my office, which we'll get to later). Whenever I start a new project, I first consult this set of books, along with Ingram's *File Creation Guide*, in order to help determine which trim size might work best for the particular project I have in mind.

And, yes, like many things in my office—and in my life—I could go on and on. But I can't right now. I have to get ready for a trip to Florida.

HISTORY IS FILLED WITH coincidence: here's one involving the Leaning Towers of Niles and Pisa. As Robert Ilg's workmen were putting the finishing touches on the Leaning Tower of Pisa in Niles, Illinois, in 1934, making sure that the tower leaned at exactly the right angle, workmen in Pisa, Italy, were doing the opposite. Under the direction of Prime Minister Benito Mussolini, head of the Italian Fascist Party, workmen were frantically trying to straighten the tower. Apparently, Mussolini, a.k.a. Il Duce, thought the leaning tower an embarrassment to Italy and ordered it straightened. To do so, Mussolini ordered several hundred holes—361 of them to be exact—drilled into the foundation of the tower. That was step one. Step two involved filling the holes with cement, a whopping 90 tons of it, all in the hope that the weight of the cement would wrench the tower back into its original upright position. Unfortunately, not only was Mussolini a bad dictator, he was also a terrible architect. When the cement was poured, instead of forming up in the holes, as Mussolini had expected, the wet cement flowed right through them, settling in the clay substrata beneath the tower, causing it to tilt even more, leaving us to wonder if Il Duce was a misspelling. Might the correct spelling be *Il Dunce?*

8 | Booze, Bikers, and Bimbos

I'M HEADED TO FLORIDA because I've signed up to be a vendor at the annual conference of the Florida Library Association. This year I'm on a mission to promote my latest book, *Shark Man*, a novel for the middle grade reader. More than that, however, *Shark Man* is a surfing adventure based on my experiences growing up on Florida's east coast. Remember *Dragonfly*, my memoir of growing up in Texas under the regime of a mean stepfather? *Shark Man* is the sequel. But instead of writing a memoir, I decided to write a novel, distilling a dozen years of surfing on Florida's beaches into one summer, making up my own cast of characters and plot to go with it.

And what better way to promote *Shark Man* than to attend the Florida Library Association's annual conference. But I wouldn't be going at all had it not been for a change of venue. The FLA usually meets in Orlando, which is ground zero for Florida's tourist trade. *Orlando?* It's not my favorite Florida city. I have a very low tolerance for crowded restaurants and hotels decorated with fake palm trees. Even more, I can't stand the endless lines of screaming kids who pull their parents around from one glitzy tourist attraction to the next. No, give me a sleepy coastal town where I can walk the beaches in the morning, read a book poolside in the afternoon, and eat at a seaside café in the evening. That's the Florida I remember, and enjoy. Not Orlando. And that's why I'm headed to Florida in a couple of weeks, because this year the FLA is not meeting in Orlando: it's meeting in Daytona Beach.

Daytona Beach. Oh, yeah, baby, sun-drenched beaches here I come. I haven't been to that part of Florida since I was in college. I was a "Gator," a University of Florida Gator. When we had a break from school, my friends and I would jump in my van and head to St. Augustine to check out the waves north of the pier. If the waves were good, we'd stay; if not, we'd head south to Crescent Beach. Again, if the waves were good, we'd stay, tent camping in the dunes or, if there were too many no-see-ums, crashing in my van. We'd surf till we dropped and then return to Gainesville. But if there weren't any waves, we'd keep driving south, with stops at Flagler Beach, Ormond Beach, and, finally, Daytona Beach (if it was a longer break, we'd try to make it all the way to Cocoa Beach, Florida's east-coast surfing capitol).

That's right, Daytona Beach, the land of hard-packed, white-sand beaches populated with skimpily clad, bikinied girls. You'd think that it was a great place for a bunch of surf bums to have a good time, I mean a *good* time; but it wasn't. Daytona Beach, like most Florida towns, is extremely conservative, made even more so by the presence of the Daytona International Speedway.

The two—cars and beach—go way back. Once the pioneers of the auto industry set their eyes on Daytona's long stretches of hard-packed sand beaches, they flocked there from all corners of the nation to race their souped-up cars (nope, it's not a typo: I looked it up; "soup" is slang for fuel, jet fuel in particular). And it wasn't about racing each other; it was about setting the land-speed record. The first mention of such a record in the greater Daytona

Beach area appears in 1903 when Alexander Winton eked out a win over H. T. Thomas, traveling at a scintillating 68.198 miles per hour. The following year William K. Vanderbilt beat Henry Ford's land-speed record, zooming along at a cool 92.29 miles per hour. No wonder they call the greater Daytona Beach area the "birthplace of speed." But it all came to a grinding halt in 1935 when Malcolm Campbell topped 276 miles per hour. After city fathers found a few dead seagulls, several flattened crabs, and a couple of upturned tourist umbrellas littering the track after Malcolm's run, the birthplace of speed headed west—to the Bonneville Salt Flats.

But not everyone moved west. A year after Campbell set the land-speed record auto enthusiasts raced stock cars up and down the newly designated Daytona Beach Road Course. Within a decade, the races became commonplace, and then institutionalized when Bill France founded the National Association of Stock Car Auto Racing (you and I know it as NASCAR). But that wasn't the end of it. After another decade passed, France and his backers built the Daytona International Speedway, which replaced the old beach road course (and put Daytona Beach on the map forever).

Speedweeks (nope, again, not a typo) is still held in early February. That's when over 200,000 racing fans flock to Daytona Beach to attend a week or more of stock car racing hoopla, including the season-opening Daytona 500. Of course, cars are still allowed on the beach; they just can't go over 10 mph (which allows just enough time for inattentive sunbathers, snoozing seagulls, and three-legged crabs to get out of the way).

But Daytona Beach isn't just about cars; it's also about their two-wheeled counterpart—motorcycles. Yep, bikers have long claimed Daytona Beach their home-away-from-home, returning to the city every spring for an annual rally. In fact, bikers have been coming to Daytona Beach almost as long as their four-wheeled counterparts. The first Daytona 200 for motorcycles was held in 1937, one year after the first stock car races on the beach and twenty-one years *before* NASCAR's inaugural Daytona 500. Californian Ed "Iron Man" Kretz, Sr., riding an Indian Sport Scout, won the race, with an average speed of 75 miles per hour. Today, Bike Week (finally, a conventional spelling) draws thousands of motorcycle enthusiasts to the greater Daytona Beach area for a week of world-class motorcycle events, including street festivals, concerts, rallies, bike races, manufacturer showcases, and much, much more.

But that's not all Daytona Beach has to offer. In this volatile environment you have to throw in a few frat boys and sorority girls arriving each spring from colleges and universities as far north as Amherst, Massachusetts. Of course, I'm talking about spring break. Just as Orlando is ground zero for the tourist trade, Daytona Beach has long been ground zero for the spring break crowd. Spring break in Daytona Beach is like staring at an ant colony without the queen to organize it: just swarms of half-drunk, sunbathing college kids out for a good time. Now, take a giant swizzle stick and stir all of these elements together and it's a toxic mix—booze, bikers, and bimbos (definitely not your typical surfer's paradise, especially surfers with hair down their back and weed in their trunk). So my friends and I only visited Daytona Beach if the waves were *really* good (and all of the aforementioned parties were out of town). Otherwise, we avoided this high-octane cocktail at all costs, preferring our relaxed and idyllic college campus in central Florida instead.

BUT I'M OLDER NOW, and I'm not looking for the same experience that I was when I was a young adult (nor do I have weed in the trunk anymore). So, I'm off to Daytona Beach, but not before I check the official Daytona Beach Spring Break website, where I find out that spring breakers won't be in Daytona Beach until the week *after* the FLA conference. Terrific. I'm going. And, besides, I notice that there are a few Starbucks on the beach road. I mean, it can't be all that bad.

In my professional career, I've attended a lot of conferences, but most of them as a session speaker or an invited author. This time I'm going as a vendor. Yep, I'm going in the most crass way possible: as a salesman hawking my own wares. But I don't mind; in fact, I look forward to it. It's all part of my transition from traditional author to independent author/publisher. If there's one thing I've learned about self-publishing it's that you have to think like a publisher. And publishers want to sell books. No, publishers *have* to sell books or they don't survive. So I'm headed to Daytona Beach in late February as a vendor. But before I leave, there are several things I need to do.

The first thing I need to do is to create an advertisement for the conference program to announce that I'll be at the conference with my new book. I'll do the same for the Florida Reading Association's annual conference later in the fall (I just won't be attending it, budget considerations and all that).

Next, I need to send out letters to every single elementary and middle school within twenty-five miles of the conference hotel. The message is simple: *Hey, I'm coming to Daytona Beach with my new middle-grade novel, Shark Man, and I'd be happy to talk to your students. Call now for information on availability and my discounted fee.* I also need to send out a letter to every public library within twenty-five miles of the conference hotel with a similar message.

As the conference gets closer, I'll send out a second round of letters, hoping to increase my chance of getting invited to a school or library.

Finally, I need to order a ton of books to take with me. I've decided to use the old Barnes and Noble sales approach: create buzz by mounding up huge stacks of *Shark Man* on my sales table. I can see it now: people crowded around my table, wondering what all the stacks of books are. People are talking, browsing, buying. Yes, I'm starting to get psyched. I can't wait for the conference. I can hear the cash register already…

Ka-ching! Ka-ching!

But first, I've actually got to get to Florida. It's not as straightforward as you think. It's not just a quick drive to Daytona Beach and back. No, it's a bit more complicated than that. In a nutshell, I've got to pick up my sister in northern Alabama, drop her off at our stepsister's campsite near Panama City, drive to Daytona Beach for the conference, then pick up my sister in Pensacola (where she's moved to visit an old friend), drop my sister at her home in northern Alabama, then head back to Chicago.

And all in ten days or less—w*hew!*

The car's packed. I kiss my wife good-bye, climb into our trusty Subaru (which, at twelve years old, isn't so trusty anymore), and I'm off, well, almost…

I forgot sunscreen.

9 | Down a Quart

I SHOULD BE WRITING this entry on the first day in March, but it's leap year so I'm not. I'm writing it on February 29, 2016. Every four years a day is added to the shortest month of the year in order to keep the Gregorian calendar aligned with the Earth's revolutions around the Sun. The question is: Why?

It's all in the math. It takes the Earth a little over 365 days to circle once around the Sun (365 days, 5 hours, 46 minutes, and 45 seconds to be exact). It's important to be exact because if you left it at 365 days, you'd lose almost six hours each year. At the end of a hundred years, you'd lose almost a full month (twenty-four days, again, to be exact). So, every four years we add an extra day to make up the difference, which means that the next leap year will be in 2020. Just think presidential election cycle: when America picks a new president, the whole world leaps (and holds its breath).

But not every four years. If that were the case then we'd be following the Julian calendar (named after the Roman general Julius Caesar). The Julian calendar had only one rule: any year divisible by four was deemed a leap year. But this approach produced too many leap years. So, fifteen hundred years later the Gregorian calendar (named after Pope Gregory XIII) booted the Julian calendar out of office, making the Gregorian calendar the internationally accepted timekeeper.

The Gregorian calendar has two very important rules. The first rule you know: the year has to be evenly divided by four. The second rule you don't (probably because it was dreamed up by an obscure theoretical mathematician): if the year can be evenly divided by one hundred, it is *not* a leap year, unless the year is also evenly divisible by four hundred; then it *is* a leap year. I know your head is spinning. Mine, too. But, don't worry, those calculations won't happen again until the year 2100 (and again in 2300 and 2500, *ad infinitum* to use a rather well-wrought—albeit obtuse—mathematical term).

But this is not what this entry is supposed to be about. It's supposed to be about my arrival in Daytona Beach, because on February 29, that's exactly what I did: I drove into Daytona Beach late in the afternoon with the Beach Boys blaring on my car's radio. But first, let me backtrack a little.

After leaving Chicago, I arrived at my sister's house two days later (I could do it in one long, thirteen-hour day, but it's a much nicer drive spread over two days). I'm not there long, only over night. In the morning we head out for a six- or seven-hour drive to Panama City. That's where our stepsister, Wendy, is spending the winter with Charlie, her husband of forty odd years. Wendy should have showed up in *Dragonfly*, my childhood memoir. After all, the mean stepfather in *Dragonfly* was none other than Wendy's natural father. But she and her two sisters—Jeannie and Debbie—don't make an appearance; it was just too complicated to explain the details of every single relationship (and besides, they were my stepsisters, not my natural sisters).

I'm sorry Wendy doesn't make an appearance because in getting to know her over the last few years I learned that she experienced as much of her father's wrath as I did. It appears he had it in for the extremes: me, the youngest boy; Wendy, the oldest girl. But Wendy doesn't like to talk about those dark years too much (unlike me who could go on forever). Instead, she and Charlie have created a large and loving family. The neo-Freudians among us would say that we create what we lack in childhood: Wendy created a large and loving family, the one she never had but always wanted, while I created books because I don't remember having any as a child. But none of this is spoken; it all remains "between the lines."

I head out bright and early the next day, leaving my sister with Wendy and Charlie, and head toward Daytona Beach. It's a good eight hours or more to Daytona, easily done in one day. And immediately I start to kick myself that I didn't plan on two. That way I could have stayed overnight in St. Augustine, my old surfing haunt. But when I get to St. Augustine, via I-10 and I-95, it's mid-afternoon and I want nothing to do with my old haunt. It's crawling with tourists (February is still high season for snowbirds down for the winter). Traffic through Old St. Augustine is at a standstill. Sailboats keep the drawbridge up way too long. And the beach, once I finally get there, is unrecognizable. Where the local surf shop used to snuggle up against the pier with nothing else around, now there are condominiums as far as the eye can see. The sight pains me, and I want to get as far away from it as possible. Soon I find myself on the beach road heading south. I pass Butler Beach, Crescent Beach, then Matanzas Inlet. Soon I hit a lonely stretch of highway south of Palm Coast, around Painters Hill, and all my memories of living in Florida as a teenager and young adult come flooding back all at once, overwhelming me. I didn't think this trip would be an emotional journey, but for a brief moment it is.

And then I hit Ormond Beach, just north of Daytona. The condominiums reappear, along with dozens of garishly painted strip malls selling the most useless items known to man. I pull into a parking lot to get my bearings. I'm looking for directions to the Airbnb I rented for the next few days. It's in a quiet residential neighborhood on the west side of the Halifax River. I find it, take Route 40 west over the river, and turn left onto Highway 1. As I head south through a congested commercial strip, I notice something: signs welcoming motorcyclists to Bike Week—a lot of signs. Although I checked the official Daytona Beach Spring Break website, I didn't check the dates for Bike Week. I don't know, I just didn't think about it.

I guess I should have, because… Yep, you guessed it: Bike Week runs from March 4 to March 11. It's the end of February so technically Bike Week doesn't start for several more days. But it's a big event and there's a lot to set up. That means of the more than 500,000 bikers expected (you heard me right, over half a million bikers), a good 100,000 of them are already in town. And I can vouch for it after playing trivia at the Daytona Taproom with a bunch of bikers from South Dakota while munching on a quarter pounder topped with mushrooms, Swiss cheese, and hemp seeds. I guess even bikers like to eat well.

AFTER AN EARLY DINNER (and the weirdest trivia game I've ever played: "Who was the first biker to cross the Mohave Desert?" and "How many inches is it from the ground to the top of a Honda Valkyrie's handlebars?"), I find the Airbnb. It's not that difficult, thanks to my iPhone's GPS and Google Maps (which I print out ahead of time just in case the woman in my iPhone doesn't know exactly where I'm supposed to go). The house is in a sleepy residential neighborhood with its neatly kept carpet-grass lawns, palm trees surrounded by woodchip mulch, open-air carports, and the perennial Hibiscus bush with its lush red flowers sticking their seductive red-and-yellow tongues out at passing pollinators.

My hosts are Ken and Ruth. I meet Ruth. She greets me with a smile, guides me through the ropes (where to park, how the A/C works, when *not* to be loud, etc.). I thank her and retreat to my room, which turns out to be a mother-in-law apartment with an entrance at the back of the house, guarded by the family cat, a large Siamese with a low, gravelly meow (which I learn the following morning around 5 a.m.).

Once settled, I hunker down and begin to plan my conference experience. Being a vendor is a much harder task than being a conference participant. There are rules, lots of rules. So I sit down at a table by the window and start to plow through a brochure in my packet labeled "Vendor Rules and Regulations." As I study the regulations, the whine of motorcycles fills my ears, though I just think it's my tinnitus flaring up. But I know better, because it's not just Bike Week; it's the 75th anniversary of the first motorcycle rally ever held in Daytona Beach. In 1941, four years after Ed "Iron Man" Kretz, Sr. won the first Daytona Beach motorcycle race, the city officially opened its arms (and cash registers) to bikers from all over the nation—and they've been coming ever since.

And they're coming now, one after the other, so much so that by the fourth day of my visit the area is buzzing with the hum of Hondas, Harleys, Indians, BMWs, Yamahas, and Triumphs racing up and down the streets of Daytona Beach and neighboring seaside townships. Well, not exactly racing; more like strutting, sashaying, and parading than anything else. But that's in the streets. And I'm not in the streets most of the time: I'm in a beachfront conference hotel. I'm a vendor at the annual Florida Library Association's annual conference. I've got badges, ribbons, table decorations, giveaways, books, lots of books, tons of books, especially my latest book—*Shark Man*.

And I've got a great location. Let me say that again: *I've got a great location.* Front and center. When you walk into the exhibit area, there I am—the first table you meet. Unbelievable. Incredible. Fantastic. At least that's what I thought when I saw it. Then I realized that most people entering the exhibit area don't want to be greeted by a smiling author-turned-bookseller. They want to survey the scene first, get a read on things, and know what they're dealing with before they commit to a plan of action. So when they enter the exhibit area, they don't look at me or my carefully arranged display of books. They avert their eyes and look at anything else *except me*—and then they turn left or right and begin to saunter down the vendor aisles.

After two days of this, I'm exasperated (actually, I'm ready to kill). I think of all sorts of ways to get the conferees' attention: lasso them, hook them with a gaff, start singing the National Anthem, or throw things—books—at them. *Anything to get anyone's attention!* But I don't. Instead, I lose interest in the conference and let my focus drift. It drifts to the guy next to me. He's a quiet, older man dressed in rumpled clothes behind a not-too-exciting table set up, but everyone, and I mean *everyone* (especially the folks with all the ribbons dangling from their conference badge) stops at his table to say hello *and* give him a hug.

"Who is this guy?" I wonder over and over again. Well, it turns out that he runs a wholesale company that supplies most of Florida schools and public libraries with books. *Setting up a new library? Just give us a call and come on over to our warehouse. We'll even put you up in the area for free*. Yep, he has it down. He has just the right low-key, soft-sell approach that draws people to him like moths to a flickering porch light.

Meanwhile, nobody's stopping to check out *Shark Man* (and I've got a hundred or more of them stacked up on my table, along with a couple of posters, bookmarks, and a few other freebies). Eventually, I give up trying to promote my title and start talking with my neighbor who, although low-key and soft-spoken, is magnanimous, offering me a ton of advice about how to get my book into the Florida school and library market. His advice makes the entire trip worthwhile.

ON THE MORNING OF my departure, three things happen…

First. The raspy-voiced Siamese cat that likes to hang outside my window startles me awake at 5 a.m. Her voice is a cross between a carnival barker and the mechanical sound of a barbershop pole. Once awake, I gather my stuff in an attempt to get out of town before too many more motorcycles arrive.

Second. I finally meet Ken. He's a slightly built man with thin graying hair. I meet him as I back out of the driveway. I stop, roll down my window (A/C is a must even in February), and say hello. We chat for a minute or two and just before I drive away he says, "Sounds like you're down a quart." "What?" I reply, still half asleep. "Yep, hear that low raspy sound?" (I think he's talking about the cat outside my window.) "It sounds like you're down a quart of oil." I smile, thank him for the advice and drive away, but as soon as I'm on the main highway—and out of eyesight—I stop at the nearest gas station and check the oil. Ken's right. I'm down a quart, exactly a quart.

Third. After adding a quart of oil to my car, I get on the road, happy to be free of my conference responsibilities. I like road trips, always have. And now my road heads west across the Florida panhandle to Pensacola, where I'll pick up my sister before heading home. As I leave the greater Daytona Beach area behind me and hit the open road, I notice something: every fourth car is a Florida State Trooper heading *toward* Daytona Beach. Makes sense: with half a million bikers descending upon the area, there's bound to be a ruckus or two.

But none of this concerns me now. The only thing I can think of is Gainesville, my old college town.

10 | Temple of the Universe

INSTEAD OF TAKING RTE. 40 through Ocala National Forest, which would have been the more scenic route, I drive north on Rte. 1 to the town of Bunnel and turn left onto Rte. 100. This takes me to Rte. 17, which follows the St. Johns River into East Palatka. On the other side of the bridge in the main part of town, I turn onto Rte. 20, which takes me due west to Gainesville. It was on this stretch of road, just west of Interlachen, that I jammed my surfboard into the lower branches of a tree and left it.

It was also on this stretch of road, though a bit closer to Gainesville, that I rolled my van. Well, I didn't roll it: my friend did. By my junior year in college I had acquired a van and with the help of my stepfather (that's stepfather #2; not the mean one from Texas), I had converted it into a real surfing van, replete with wood paneling, double bed, and a great eight-track stereo system. Three of us headed to St. Augustine on a quiet Saturday morning but the waves were terrible. We spent the night in the parking lot at the entrance to Anastasia State Park, harassed by no-see-ums all night. In the morning, instead of heading south to Crescent Beach and points beyond, we decided to drive back to Gainesville.

I drove for half an hour or so, but I was too tired to continue so Eric took the wheel. On the way back I woke up once and all I did was put my seatbelt on and then fell back to sleep. Since this was in an age when we didn't wear seatbelts regularly, waking up to put mine on was somewhat of an anomaly. In this case it was more than an anomaly: it was an otherworldly act that saved my life. Several miles east of Gainesville Eric fell asleep at the wheel and lost control of the van. The sharp swerve of the van woke me with a start, but all I could do was watch as we careened off the road and catapulted into a small stand of pine trees where we came to rest—upside down.

As we hung upside down in our seatbelts, a man from a nearby gas station ran up to Eric's window and yelled, "It's going to blow up!" Then he ran away. We didn't wait around to see if the van would blow up: we unbuckled our seatbelts and crawled out of the van, calling for Ken who was riding in back. Fortunately, he had scrambled out a back window and was standing around half dazed. We staggered toward the road and sat down on a log as a platoon of emergency vehicles arrived on the scene. Fire engines, ambulances, and police cars came racing from all directions with their sirens raging. Traffic stopped as people poured out of their cars to see what had happened.

As several firemen tried to pry open the van's front doors, a lone highway patrolman walked up to us, looked us over, and asked, "Is that your van?"

"Yes, officer," I stammered, barely able to speak.

"Just the three of you in it?" he asked.

"Yes."

He stood there shaking his head, repeating over and over again, "You don't know how lucky you are. You don't know how lucky you are."

Yes, we were lucky. But then again, maybe it was more than dumb luck. Maybe, just maybe an angel had appeared just in time to guide us through the ordeal. In any case, we were alive; shaken, yes, but alive. As for seatbelts, I was like Saul on the road to Damascus: a true convert.

AS I THINK ABOUT this earlier incident in my life, Rte. 20 merges with University Ave., the main artery that runs into Gainesville and in front of the University. But, like St. Augustine, it is utterly unrecognizable. Forty odd years of gentrification has laid down a solid veil of trendy chain stores, making Gainesville—like so many other sleepy college towns—"Anywhere, U.S.A." It is not the Gainesville I remember—until I see several campus buildings in the distance.

The first one—Heavener Hall—seems familiar, but I can tell from the construction that it is rather new, even though it is built in the same Collegiate Gothic style as the others around it. Besides, there wasn't a building at the corner of 13th Street and University Avenue when I was a student. There was only a foot-worn path that weaved its way through a small grove of trees. Besides being a shortcut from 13th Street to University Ave., it was a place—very visible and very public—where students gathered to protest the Vietnam War. It was here that large, hand-made banners decrying the war dangled from trees (only to be ripped down at night by ROTC cadets and frat boys who supported the war). Today most of the trees are gone, replaced by the University's official welcome sign, a large wrought-iron arch with the words *University of Florida* emblazoned on it.

The next two buildings I do recognize: Matherly Hall and Anderson Hall. It was at Matherly Hall that I took a survey class in geography, which almost convinced me to major in the discipline. Not that I liked—or even understood—geography; rather the instructor used to slip a photo or two of himself surfing somewhere in the world into his daily slide show. I don't know if it was to get people like me interested in majoring in geography, or just to wake us up from his mind-numbing lectures about cuestas, contour lines, and the lithosphere.

My memory of Anderson Hall, one of the oldest buildings on the UF campus, is associated with one of the first majors I declared: English Literature. I chose it after dropping the math and science classes that I had signed up for on the first day of freshman registration. What else was I to do with my parents standing on either side of me? When they left, I returned to the Registrar's Office and dropped everything, signing up for liberal arts classes, intent upon being an English Lit major. But when faced with the tedious dissection of *Tess of the d'Urbervilles* and *The Picture of Dorian Gray* during my first semester, I bolted, convinced that I was totally unfit for life as an English Lit major.

My memories of the next building are just as strong: Smathers Library (a.k.a. Library East) is where I spent many an hour reading and studying, and generally dreaming about my future. I decide to stop and see the library in person, so I pull into the visitors' parking lot, lock my car, and, with a campus map in one hand, walk toward the brick structure. Named after George A. Smathers, a former Florida senator, the library is not one building; it is a complex of buildings with a diverse set of collections. I studied at Library East because two years before I arrived at the University it became the Undergraduate College Library, after the completion of the Graduate Research Library—Library West—in 1967.

Since most of my memories are associated with Library East, I walk past Library West, shaded from the sun by the open-air walkway that connects the two libraries. I had traversed this path many times as a student, going from Library East where I studied to Library West where I took many of my religion classes. But it was Library East, which opened in 1926, that I was most interested in, especially the cavernous Grand Reading Room on the second floor (today it's the Special Collections Research Room).

As I climb the stairs to the main entrance of the reading room, I am flooded with memories of my time spent in the building: I studied in the Grand Reading Room, at one of the many circular tables clustered in the middle of the room surrounded by magazine racks and tall wooden bookcases. The vaulted ceiling, buttressed wood beams, and three-tiered glass windows often transported me back to my high school "detention days" spent in a similarly elegant room filled with books and magazines. But what really captured my attention was the large mural on the north wall that stretched above the Reading Room's main entrance. Completed in 1953 by Hollis Holbrook, the University's first art professor, the mural is appropriately named "A History of Learning in Florida." It is more than a snapshot of the State's history of learning, however; it is a window into the past, my past spent in Library East as a serious undergraduate student.

After I exit Library East, I follow a brick path lined with flowerbeds to the Plaza of the Americas, a large grassy quadrangle designed by Frederick Law Olmsted, Jr., in 1925, the year before Library East opened its doors to faculty and students. I find a sun-drenched bench in the Plaza, sit down, close my eyes, and try to summon some of the experiences I had here: sunbathing on the lawn, playing Frisbee with friends, listening to Nate and John, two musicians who frequented the Plaza, yelling anti-war slogans during one of the many anti-war rallies held in the Plaza, and, of course, reading and studying on a bench by myself on a warm sunny afternoon.

After a while, I stand up and walk to my car. Although I am reluctant to leave, it's time to hit the road again. As I drive out of the parking lot, I notice a two-story commercial building across the street. My mind begins to race as I recognize the building: it housed Great Harvest, the natural foods restaurant that I worked at during my junior and senior year. Great Harvest was on the second floor of the building, above a flower shop, an alternative bookstore, and a take-out Chinese restaurant. I had many fond memories of Great Harvest: busing tables, running the dishwasher, and taking care of the "sprout room." Not many restaurants had a sprout room, but Great Harvest did and I was its keeper, making sure that the racks of sprouts and thick tufts of wheat grass were moist and aerated.

LIKE EVERYTHING ELSE, GREAT Harvest is gone and in its place is Grog House, advertised as Gainesville's number one college bar with the "cheapest drinks, best music, and the most fun!" But the number one college bar in Gainesville during my college days wasn't Grog House; it was The Library, where students and faculty congregated after hours. If you told your friends—with a wink and a nod—that you were going to "the library," they knew exactly where to find you. Of course, in my case, when I said I was going to the library, I usually was—at least by the time I was a junior. By then I was all Narcissus: the B's and C's I'd received during my first two years—during my Goldmund days—were replaced by A's. Yes,

I was hooked on books, writing, and the discourse that accompanied them.

I was also hooked on religion. Although my declared major was comparative religion, I concentrated on Eastern religion much to the chagrin of my advisor, who wanted me to be more ecumenical in my studies. ("Shouldn't you be taking classes in Western religion?" was his constant refrain.) But I was interested in Buddhism, especially Tibetan Buddhism, Tantric Buddhism, and Zen Buddhism. Like other "liberal hot spots"—Berkeley, Boulder, Amherst, Madison, and the like—Gainesville was a magnet for the alternative crowd with its mix of Hippie culture and adherents of Eastern religion.

Yoga groups abounded. There were the laid-back followers of Paramahansa Yogananda, the Indian guru who introduced yoga and meditation to millions in the West. There were the more regimented and uptight followers of Maharishi Mahesh Yogi, who founded Transcendental Meditation. And, of course, there were the feverish Hare Krishnas, members of The International Society of Krishna Consciousness, who beat their drums and clanged their bells while chanting "Hare Krishna" over and over again in a feverish, almost frenetic trancelike state.

And then there was Mickey Singer, who founded Temple of the Universe, a spiritual retreat center fifteen miles northwest of downtown Gainesville near the town of Alachua. Unlike the often-exclusive groups that invaded Gainesville in the 60s and 70s, Singer welcomed anyone of any faith who sought the Truth in a sincere manner. So we went, gathering at the Temple on Sunday mornings with people from all walks of life, all religious persuasions who believed fervently in Singer's mission: "To provide an environment in which men and women of any religion or set of beliefs can come together to experience the love, peace, and bliss which exists within all beings."

Like the Hare Krishnas—who rarely frequented the Temple—we beat drums, shook bells, strummed guitars, played flutes, and raised our voices in unity—young seekers of the Truth, innocent and blind, as gullible as we were infallible, intoxicated with the serum of Life and Love and Innocence. Perhaps that's why I really majored in comparative religion: it spoke to me in a way that no other subject matter did.

11 | Silver Lining

IT ALL SOUNDS SO idyllic, so calm, so peaceful, but that was Gainesville when I was an idealistic youth. By the time I roll into Pensacola to pick up my sister, my mindset has swiveled 180 degrees: I'm tired, I'm hungry, and I'm terribly annoyed by all of the traffic. And, to make things worse, I make a strategic mistake.

Several miles before the exit I'm supposed to take to get me to my sister's friend's house, I see a highway sign informing me that the exit is under construction. I glance at the map on the seat next to me and see two other exits that might help me avoid the construction, but erring on the side of caution I don't take them. I take the exit that my sister told me to take, and it is a mess, a big mess. I wait on the exit ramp the better part of an hour as the line of exiting cars inches up to the main road. By the time it's my turn to enter the highway, I'm not only tired and hungry, I'm lightheaded, almost giddy, and a bit turned around. I can't seem to figure out how to get to my sister's friend's house. I creep through a couple of neighborhoods, looking for her house, but I just can't seem to make sense of the house numbers. They don't seem to be consecutive. I'm really frustrated and downright mad. *Man, could I use some Mickey Singer now!* Finally, a half hour later, I see my sister and her friend waving at me.

Sister: "What are you doing?"
Me: "I couldn't find the house. I've been driving around in circles."
Sister: "I know. You passed us twice and didn't see us."
Me: "What?"
Sister: "Yeah, we waved at you, but you drove by. Then you stopped, got out of your car, and looked around—and you *still* didn't see us."
Me: "The house numbers just didn't make any sense to me."
Sister: "Apparently."
Me [fiddling with the side panel]: "Something's wrong."
Sister: "What are you doing?"
Me: "I'm trying to close the windows."
Sister: "Are they stuck?"
Me [getting really flustered]: "I don't know, they won't close."
Sister: "What's wrong?"
Me: "How do I know?"
Sister's friend [approaching]: "Do you want to park in our garage? It looks like rain."
Me: "Sure."

After my sister's friend pulls her car out of the garage, I pull mine in. I try the windows one more time, but none of them will close. I'm tired, hungry, and extremely frustrated. A glass of wine puts me in a better mood. After dinner my sister and I go out into the garage to try the windows again. While I fumble with the car manual, my sister sits down in the driver's seat, looks around, and presses a button. The windows go up.

Me [dropping the manual]: "What did you do?"
Sister [grinning]: "Pushed this little button."

Me: "What is it?"
Sister [still grinning]: "The window lock button."
Me [storming off into the house]: "*Argh!*"

If there is a silver lining to the evening it's what happens next: my sister's friend and her husband start to ask me about the library conference. One thing leads to another and before you know it I've got all of my books spread out on the kitchen table. While I arrange them, they start naming nieces and nephews, and several friends, who might like one as a present. When it's all said and done, they buy more books from me than the conference-goers do during my two days as a vendor at the Florida Library Association's conference in Daytona Beach. It's quite a silver lining (with real silver lining my pocket for the trip home).

Part II

It's a beautiful day in April, chilly but clear. Clumps of snowdrops and crocus flowers poke through thin layers of winter mulch. A circle of daffodils joins them. Nearby, last year's stand of false indigo and Joe-Pye weed sit idle, waiting for the heat of summer. Only the hardy kiwi vine stretched across the front fence and several spirea bushes in the tree lawn show any interest in putting forth a spray of greenery.

12 | Shake, Rattle & Read

THE TRIP TO CHICAGO is a blur. I drop my sister off at her house in northern Alabama, then head north to Chicago, which is two more days of driving. All in all, I spend eight out of ten days driving. It's a whirlwind trip, and when I get home I'm tired, really tired, and feeling a little bit like my dog did after spending four days curled up in the foot well of our car. Not only can't I think straight, I can't walk straight either. I'd just driven over 3,000 miles in ten days, pretty much by myself.

"Well, what did you think?" my wife needles me. "You're not eighteen anymore."

"I know, I know," I say, as I curl up on the couch.

But this isn't the end of my *Shark Man* promotion timeline. It's only the beginning: I still have work to do. Not only that, when I walk into my office the day after my return I'm faced with several piles of books on the floor and a ton of unopened mail on my desk.

Where to start?

When in doubt, make a list. That's my motto. And so I do. At the top of the list I write: *Deal with piles of books on office floor.* I write that because right now I've got as many books on my office floor as I do on my bookshelves. As I mentioned earlier, I've always been good at taking things apart, but not so good at reassembling them. When I was young I used to take my bicycle apart on a regular basis. All of my friends did. On a warm summer day we'd meet at a friend's house, pliers and wrenches sticking out of our back pockets, and spend the morning taking our bikes apart. Then we'd swap parts and put them back together.

I was really good at the take-your-bike-apart portion of the morning, but not so good at the put-it-back-together portion. I remember once, after we had made our swaps and put our bikes together, we built a ramp in the driveway. It was a small ramp, nothing that you could get hurt on even if you slid off the side of the ramp. Everyone did fine until it was my turn. I jumped on my bike, raced down the driveway, hit the ramp full speed, and took off. It was while suspended in midair that my assembling talents—or lack thereof—were put on full display: my front wheel fell off as soon as I was airborne. I guess I forgot to tighten the nuts that lock the wheel onto the frame. When I hit the driveway pavement the front fork, which was now exposed, dug into the pavement sending me catapulting over the handlebars and into the grass. Luckily, I was pretty good at tumbling in gym class, so when I hit the grass I just did a forward roll and came up without a scratch. Everyone started yelling and cheering, thinking that I had done it on purpose. "Do it again," they shouted. *"Do it again!"*

Nope, once is enough.

TODAY MY OFFICE IS like that reconfigured bicycle—just not all there yet. What is there on the floor are piles of books from the top shelves of the south wall of my office. Before I left for Florida I managed to take down all of the books on four six-foot lengths of bookshelves, neatly stacking them into piles, each topped with a post-it note indicating the general subject matter of the books in that pile. Fortunately, I had cleaned the shelves before I left, so they were ready to be reloaded. All I had to do was haul the already dusted books up the ladder and arrange them on the shelves, culling out books that I didn't want to retain.

Simple? Well, it seemed like it—until I got an idea. Do the subject areas written on the post-it notes mean anything? Do they form some kind of pattern, revealing not only my taste in books, but also—and perhaps more importantly—my intellectual development over time? Curious, I start slapping post-it notes up on the wall behind my worktable, each post-it note retrieved from the top of a book stack. *What's the pattern?* I ask myself as I rearrange the post-it notes into clusters. After half an hour, the clusters of post-it notes start to form into a kind of genealogy chart and I start to see a pattern. Yes, I definitely see a pattern—and it all starts with creativity.

That's the post-it note at the top of my wall chart, as if every other post-it note descends from it in some way. And when I think about it, they do. Although I was interested in creativity for personal reasons (I was your classic "creative"—or goofy—left-handed person), my sustained interest in creativity was somewhat more academic. Not only did my doctoral dissertation involve testing elementary school-aged students in various domains of creativity using the ever-popular Torrance Tests of Creative Thinking, but also during the summer months I co-directed a residential gifted and talented program that brought middle grade students to Montana State University from all corners of the state.

Moreover, the first two professional articles I published involved explorations of play and creativity. In the first article, I interviewed a "rough-and-tumble" play therapist for his views on the connection between creativity and human touch (Ashley Montagu was an early influence of mine). In the second article, I explored the relationship between a child's manipulation of physical objects and an adult's manipulation of abstract concepts, titling the article "From Play Dough to Plato: On the Nature of Creativity."

I say this because the first books I purchased for my office library were on the topic of creativity, books like Arthur Koestler's *The Act of Creation*, Howard Gardner's *Art, Mind & Brain*, Edward de Bono's *Lateral Thinking*, and Mihaly Csikszentmihalyi's *Flow: The Psychology of Optimal Experience*. I purchased them because I had just discovered the used bookstore.

Chicago's a big place—a lot bigger than Bozeman, Montana—with used bookstores in almost every neighborhood (this was before big-box bookstores forced the closure of many independent bookstores). Bozeman in the 1980s, on the other hand, had one independent bookstore, a small chain bookstore in the mall, and several Christian bookstores on the edge of town. That was it. And that's why my heart pounded every time I discovered another bookstore—new or used—during the first few years we lived in Chicago.

At first, I bought impulsively, just for the joy of bringing home a book to put on my bookshelf (no floor-to-ceiling bookshelves yet, those would come later). Over time, however, my book-buying activity changed in two major ways: I bought less—budgets exist for a reason—and I began to focus more on specific interests. Although human creativity heads the list, acting as the trunk of my tree of knowledge, the branches that slowly emerged over months and years of book buying reveal other interests: the art of writing systems, the development of the Western alphabet, the medieval manuscript, Gutenberg and the printing press, folk literature (especially legends, fables, and folktales), the art and history of storytelling, and the psychological dimensions of story.

At first blush these might seem disconnected, but to me there's a discernible thread that weaves its way through all of them—story, its origins, evolution, and transmission. Admittedly, the list paints only a partial picture of my interests (since they reflect only a third or more of the books on my bookshelves). To understand the full picture, I'll have to share more of the books that I've collected over time, but that means more ladder climbing, more shelf cleaning, and more book dusting. In other words, it means more work; so I think I'll do something else—I think I'll open my mail.

As I reach for it, the headline from the neighborhood newspaper catches my attention: "Uptown's *Shake, Rattle & Read* Is Giving Away All Its Records and Books." The article that follows records the demise of yet another independent bookstore in the Chicago area. The Uptown record-book-and-ephemera store officially closed its doors last Saturday, but for the next few days the remaining inventory will be marked down in a sale of epic proportions. Basically, for two days this week every single item in the store will be free. That's right—*free*. Bring your own box and you can haul out as much stuff as you'd like. What doesn't get removed goes in the dumpster. As soon as I read this, I head to the local appliance store to get a couple of refrigerator boxes.

13 | $11.11

IT'S AMAZING HOW MUCH mail can accumulate after only ten days away from home. A mound of it awaits me. But like everyone else I know more than half of it is junk mail—advertising and whatnot that keeps the United States Postal Service afloat. My junk mail is easy to spot: it usually comes addressed to Ms. Lisa Nikola. That's because no one can figure out my name. I mean, who—or what—*is* W. Nikola-Lisa? *A man? A woman? A postal box?* Admittedly, it's a hard name. What does it mean? Where did I get it? Why the "W" at the beginning? And, for heaven's sake, why do I have a woman's first name as part of my last name?

Even though it's a hard name, I try to have a little fun with it. When I start a school program I usually ask the younger kids what they think the "W" stands for. Their guesses are amusing, to say the least: *Winston, Wilbert, Windsor, Willy, Walter, Wendy* (I guess this child wasn't really paying attention), and, my favorite, *Writer*. Yes, *Writer*. It makes perfect sense. If you're a kid and you have an author speaking to your class and his first name is the initial "W" it makes sense that you might think that his first name is "Writer," unless you're in kindergarten and you're working on the sounds that letters make. Then you might think that the "W" might stand for "Wuh," which is exactly what one kindergartener thought (of course that was during the presidential administration of one George W. Bush).

In any case, I said that these were responses from young students. I don't ask older students what the "W" stands for. The reason: I asked them once and it didn't turn out so well. It happened at a middle school (as everyone knows *anything* can happen at a middle school). With an auditorium filled with 5th and 6th graders, I began my author program the way I do with young students: "Hey, who knows what the 'W' in my name stands for?" A boy sitting with his friends in the middle of the auditorium raised his hand.

"All right," I responded, expecting to add another name to my growing list, "tell us, what does the 'W' stand for?"

"Weiner!" he shouted, grinning at his friends.

The place fell apart. It was total chaos. Teachers stood up, trying to quiet their students. The principal came to the front of the auditorium waving his hands. It was, to say the least, a very embarrassing moment *and* the last time I ever asked older kids to guess what the "W" in my name stands for.

Now I just tell them outright: the "W" stands for William, which it does (and has for every first-born male in my family for several generations). But since I use "Nikola" (half of my last name) as my first name, I reduce William to its first initial and use W. Nikola-Lisa as my pen name, which invariably leads to the question: *Why Nikola-Lisa?*

Like most things in my life, there's a short answer and a long answer. I usually give the short answer in a large public setting, like a multi-age school assembly: *Nikola* is my given last name and *Lisa* is my wife's last name. When we married, we hyphenated them because we thought they went together so well. There's a musical quality to the name *Nikola-Lisa.*

That's the short answer.

The long answer is a little more complicated and I usually reserve it for more intimate conversations with adults. You see, *Nikola* is my given last name, but *Lisa* is my former wife's last name. That's when people start to look at me funny.

You kept your former wife's last name?

To me, it's quite natural: we had two daughters and after we split up I raised them. Since they had the last name Nikola-Lisa, I decided to keep it myself so we would have the same last name. And, anyway, my second wife looked at both of my names and said, "I don't want either one of them." In fact, she tried to get me to change my name when we married. Since I use Nikola as a first name, she thought I should change my name to Nikola Cooper (Cooper being her last name). Not only did she think that it was a great name for a writer, but she also thought that I wouldn't have to explain my name anymore.

Since I had already started my publishing career with the pen name W. Nikola-Lisa, I thought Nikola Cooper would just complicate things, so I stuck with the more melodious but enigmatic W. Nikola-Lisa.

I did use Nikola Cooper as my alias, but only once. My wife and I bought a house together about twenty years ago. In the process of getting it ready to move into, we had to deal with a lot of workers: plumbers, carpenters, roofers, electricians, and the like. Well, every time it was the same thing. I'd call someone and talk to them for a while and at some point they'd ask, "What's your name?" When I said, "W. Nikola-Lisa," they'd say, "What?" and then I'd have to spend another ten minutes trying to explain it.

One day, while I was talking to a contractor, he asked, "What's your name?" and without thinking I replied, "Nick Cooper." And that was it: no follow up. Nothing. He got it immediately (who wouldn't: it's kind of like saying your name is John Smith). For the next few weeks I went by the name Nick Cooper ("Hi, Nick Cooper here, have any nails?" "Hi, Nick Cooper here, have any paint?" "Hi, Nick Cooper here…"). It worked like a charm.

After the house stuff died down I went back to using W. Nikola-Lisa. Then, one day the phone rang. I answered it. A woman on the other end asked, "Is Nick Cooper there?" I hesitated, then said, "Well, yes, I'm Nick Cooper." She replied, "Nick, you haven't paid your hospital bill." It turns out that the woman worked for a hospital and was trying to track down a former patient by the name of Nick Cooper who had neglected to pay his hospital bill.

"Well, I'm not really Nick Cooper," I said, backtracking, "I mean, I only used it a couple of times."

I'm sure she thought I was a little wacky, but I managed to convince her that I wasn't the Nick Cooper she was looking for.

I'M THINKING ABOUT THIS as I quickly sort through the mail, tossing those addressed to Ms. Lisa Nikola into the recycling bin. After the quick mail sort, my focus shifts to the small pile of mail that's left. One envelope catches my eye. It's from a publisher, a publisher that I've published several books with in the past. Using an old-knife-turned-letter-opener, I rip the top of the envelope open and pull out the enclosed letter. It's a royalty statement.

I unfold it excitedly, and get right to the chase—the last line indicating how much money I've made this royalty period (for the record, traditional publishing usually pays semi-annually, whereas non-traditional publishing, especially if it's a digital product, usually pays monthly). This statement is from a traditional publisher, so the figure I'm looking for is for six months' worth of book sales. But wait. What's this? You've got to be kidding. It's a royalty statement for—trying not to laugh (or cry)—eleven dollars and eleven cents.

Eleven dollars and eleven cents!

I try to see the symbolism behind this paltry amount. Now, I'm not superstitious or anything, but $11.11 is an odd arrangement of numerals, kind of like my oldest daughter's birth date—Friday, November 13th (which, for some reason, reminds me of the movie *The Shining*). But I don't think that I've actually earned eleven dollars and eleven cents. You see, over the years I've developed a conspiracy theory that goes something like this: there's a room full of accountants at each publishing house that takes great pleasure in sending out fake royalty statements, just to goad authors, to take them down a notch, to make them appreciate the publisher's efforts to publish their work and keep them alive.

The more I think about my royalty statement, however, the less agitated I become. After all, it's for two books published in the 1990s. I'm lucky there's a twinkle left in them at all. I published the books when you could still make sense of the publishing world (which means I gave all of my rights to the publisher, including my first-born child), and that's why royalties are still dribbling in. But I shouldn't complain; after all, they did fairly well—at least one of them did.

The one that did well is a children's picture book about life on a medieval manor titled *Till Year's Good End*. I wrote a dual text: one to read aloud to young students; the other for older students who want more detailed information to read to themselves. I learned this from Hans Christian Andersen's "The Bog King's Daughter," where the narrator tells the reader that while young storks are quite satisfied with *muddle-duddle, cribble-crabble*, the older storks want something with a bit more meaning. The idea for the book came from reading about the medieval "Labors of the Months." If there is one theme that describes the Middle Ages, it is survival: peasants worked every day, tending to their landlords' crops and animals first, then, if time permitted, to their own small plot or "croft." The book resonated with teachers because thematic units on the European Middle Ages are a big deal in school.

The other book was a nativity story that featured a black holy family. It didn't start out that way: it started out as a fairly traditional nativity story featuring Mary, Joseph, and baby Jesus. But I got stuck halfway through the piece and couldn't move forward. Nothing was gelling, so I put it aside and started to work on some other writing. Then, one day, I ran across Bruce McMillan's *Mary Had a Little Lamb*, a picture book version of the popular children's song. The book stunned me: McMillan, a photographer, presented the text in its original version, but not the characters. Although the lamb was a soft, downy white, Mary was black.

The contrast between the *white* lamb and the *black* Mary shook me to the core. As a white male born in the 1950s, the Mary in "Mary Had a Little Lamb" was always white, no question about it—*always*. McMillan's presentation effectively turned this world upside down. But not just this world; he also turned that *other* world upside down, too—the world of Mary, Joseph, and baby Jesus. Instantly, I started to envision an entirely different nativity story, one in which the principal characters were black (which isn't that hard to imagine given the fact that the holy family was of Middle Eastern origin, and possibly, according to some historians, of North African descent). The resultant book, with illustrations by Cynthia Saint James, was gorgeous, but it had limited success (two other nativity books came out the same year, each one featuring Jesus as a person of color).

But that was then, and this is now; and *now* both books are print-on-demand paperbacks in the Simon & Schuster backlist. Did I have any say in the matter? Of course not: that's how contracts worked in the pre-digital age. Rights don't necessarily revert to the author unless formally asked for in writing or until the book is effectively out-of-print for at least two royalty cycles. But convert a traditionally published book to a print-on-demand paperback and—*voila*—the book *never* goes out of print (and the rights never revert to the author).

And that's why I just received $11.11 in the mail from Simon & Schuster. It's also why I slowly made the transition from traditional publishing to non-traditional or independent publishing.

14 | Buyer Beware

THERE'S OTHER MAIL, OF course, and it's been stacking up on my desk and in my email inbox for several weeks; no, make that months. The first stack I tackle is the trade magazine and catalog pile. It's the usual: catalogs from Daedalus Books, the SCWBI monthly bulletin, several back issues of *Horn Book*, newsletters from several state reading and library associations, and the last six issues of the *IBPA Independent*. It's the last pile that catches my attention.

The Independent Book Publishers Association is by far the most active and comprehensive professional organization addressing the needs of the Indie author and publisher. Since I've been a member, for a little more than two years, I've seen its tent grow in size, offering services for both self-published authors and small independent publishers. As I mention in another writing, the term "Indie" has been adopted by a whole host of entities: local independent bookstores, small regional presses, academic university presses, and the independent or self-published author. In this kind of environment the IBPA has tried to stay fluid. In her "Director's Desk" editorial for the February 2016 issue of the *IBPA Independent*, titled "Choose Change," Executive Director Angela

Bole quotes a line from Japanese scholar Kakuzo Okakura: "The art of life is a constant readjustment to our surroundings."

If there is one area of the economy that is in constant flux, it is the publishing industry—and it has been for more than a decade. Recognizing this, the IBPA has tried to offer its members the tools they need to succeed in this ever-changing, dynamic world. A brief survey of the themes the *IBPA Independent* addresses quickly indicates the constant reskilling that authors and independent publishers need to do in order to succeed. Here are a few of the topics the magazine has covered in the last six months:

The ABCs of Acquisitions
Real Lessons on Promoting Fiction
Do Librarians Prefer Print?
Marketing Savvy
Making Sense of MARC Records
A Crash Course on Royalty Audits
Three Surefire Ways to Fail at E-book Cover Design
Which Review Outlets Should You Target?
Marketing with a New Mindset
Virtual Book Tour Essentials
Innovation Through Collaborative Partnerships
Legal Quandaries
Getting the Royalty Treatment
Using Radio to Get the Word Out

The first thing you notice is that the topics are all over the place, not in an erratic, disconnected manner, but in a way that shows you how much an independent author and/or publisher must know in order to navigate the self-publishing world. The topics also reflect the fact that it's a two-sided coin: on one side, the skills necessary to create and produce a book; on the other, the skills necessary to market and sell a book. Most traditional publishers have specialized departments to navigate one or more of these areas; the Indie author has to do it all.

The worlds of traditional and non-traditional publishing come with their own pros and cons. I know this because I've been on both sides of the fence. What's refreshing now, in this amazingly dynamic environment, is the transparency that continues to emerge. Fueled by the rise of social media, the pervasive nature of the Internet, and the begrudging acceptance of the do-it-yourself, self-publishing world, independent authors have incredible access to all aspects of the publishing business. Twenty years ago this just was not the case. You'd be lucky to pry loose any tidbit of information about your newly released book from your editor. And forget about your backlist. No one is going to spend an ounce of time looking into that on your behalf. Oh, and questions about your latest royalty statement? Good luck. That's not to say that this doesn't happen in the world of self-publishing. There are unsavory characters in the self-publishing world just waiting to trap an unsuspecting author into a straightjacket contract. Though the industry has changed, it is still a *Buyer Beware* market—on both sides of the coin.

Enough said, let's return to the list of topics covered in the last six months of the *IBPA Independent* and focus on the one about targeting review outlets. I picked this topic for a reason: I just received a note from James Cox, editor-in-chief of *Midwest Book Review*, informing me that *Shark Man* was not chosen for a review. It's too bad too: *Shark Man* could really use a boost right now. According to MBR's editor, *Shark Man* "failed to achieve a review assignment." On the good side of things, the editor stated that it wasn't a reflection of the quality of the writing, because it easily passed the initial screening process. In the end, however, it came down to "too many books, not enough reviewers." If there is a silver lining it's that the letter ended with a list of—and appropriate hyperlinks to—their free book review resource database where I will find a variety of resources: freelance book reviewers, book review magazines and publications, book review web sites, and book review blogs. I can't resist; I click on the hyperlink provided and find an amazing amount of resources, and a list of at least 40 book review outlets. It's a freaking goldmine.

But it's also back to square one, which in the do-it-yourself world means "me." I will be spending the next several weeks—possibly months—working my way through the list without any guarantee of success. But DIY seems to be the name of the game in the independent or self-published author's world.

Instead of clicking on any of the links, I return to the *IBPA Independent's* article on review markets. The article, by Kristina Radke, NetGalley's international account director, starts with a truism: "You know that book reviews matter. They are one of the linchpins that retail sites use to create algorithms that can boost a book's visibility and help to generate word-of-mouth buzz out in the wider world." In other words, it's not enough anymore to buy up thousands of copies of your own book in order to increase its rank on *The New York Times Book Review* bestseller list. That can go a long way, but it's just not enough anymore. Now, according to Radke, you have to be mindful of "effective frequency," that is, how often your book gets in front of the reading public.

The key to effective frequency is the book review—the more the merrier. Like anything, there's more to it than meets the eye. It's not just about getting eyeballs on your book; it's about creating "buzz" And what is buzz? It's nothing more than excitement, and excitement is what creates movement, and movement is what gets your book reviewed, and reviews are how a large part of the reading public discovers your book. But as Radke warns: be strategic, clarify your goals, identify your audience, and budget realistically—then do your homework. Radke then outlines four types of book review markets: (1) the consumer review (e.g., *Amazon, Goodreads, Readers Place*); (2) the blogger review (e.g., *Literary Musings, Ashley's Bookshelf, The Bewitched Reader)*; (3) the trade or industry review (e.g., *Publishers Weekly, Kirkus Reviews, Booklist*); and (4) the public media review (e.g., *NPR, The Wall Street Journal, New York Times Book Review*).

Although there is some overlap in these review markets, each market has its own audience. So, before you thrash around in each one, go back to what Radke says: be strategic, clarify your goals, identify your audience, and budget realistically. And recognize that this is only one way to divide up the pie. For instance, I took a more geographic approach with *Shark Man*, recognizing the difference between state, regional, and national markets. Since *Shark Man* is a surfing adventure for the middle grade reader set in Florida, I targeted Florida readers before looking elsewhere. That's why I attended the Florida Library Association's annual conference in Daytona Beach, advertised in the Florida Reading Association's conference program, sent postcards to every surf shop in the state, and flooded middle schools with flyers announcing the book's release and my Florida background.

I did this because it is necessary. With the amount of books being published each year, you don't stand a chance if you don't advertise. My method is to try to get a foothold in one market and then work from there. I did this with an earlier book, *The Men Who Made the Yankees*, when I began my marketing campaign by sending postcards to every baseball museum in the U.S., as well as to every independent bookstore within a hundred-mile radius of Yankee Stadium. And that's not all I did: I made a square postcard (the size of a drink coaster) and sent a dozen or more to every bar and tavern within a mile radius of Yankee Stadium with the message: *Have a few drinks on me!*

I'm taking a different approach for the book you're reading right now. I'm releasing the book in four parts, similar to how Stephen King released the four novellas that make up *The Green Mile*. Each part, which loosely corresponds to one of the four seasons of the year, will be released as a Beta version e-book (which simply means that I will make subsequent revisions, synthesizing the feedback that readers give me). Once all four parts have been separately released and I have revised and re-uploaded each version, I'll combine them into one volume, both in e-book and paperback editions. Not only does the slow, staggered release of each part allow me to make subsequent revisions, but it also allows me to market the book through social media over a protracted period of time.

Not only is it a DIY world for the self-published author, it's also a TOB world—a Think-Out-of-the-Box world.

15 | Sherwood in the Twilight

IT'S SINKING. I KNOW it's sinking.

What's sinking?

The house, that's what. My wife and I have known for a long time that our house sits atop old Lake Michigan sand dunes. We found that out when we moved in 20 years ago and had to take up the basement floor, which was made of tongue-and-groove fir, a beautiful thing to behold—except for the fact that it wasn't level. So we pulled it up and replaced it with a concrete slab.

How could you?

We had to, but "we" didn't do it. We hired a strapping young man from Romania to pull it up and replace it. First, he removed the wooden floor. (That's when we realized that the house was sitting on Lake Michigan sand dunes; there wasn't a stitch of dirt or clay beneath it, just pure sand.) Next, he dug out a foot or more of sand to lower the floor. (My wife already had eyes on the basement for her studio and needed more ceiling height for her sculptures.) Then, he hauled in wheelbarrow after wheelbarrow of wet cement to cover the sand. (It must have been hard work because he stopped every hour or so to throw down a couple of shots of vodka with our next-door neighbor, also of Eastern European origin.)

Now add shelf after shelf of books in one concentrated area of the house—the southwest corner, my office—and no wonder I think the house is sinking. To assuage my feelings, I make regular inspections of the corners of the room to see if there has been any widening of the cracks that started to appear several years after we moved into the house. Oh, yes, it is definitely sinking. But there's not much I can do about it right now, and anyway we've been in the house over two decades and it's still afloat, so I think I'll turn my attention to something more important—sorting through the remaining piles of books on my office floor.

Several stacks catch my attention, each one reflecting an abiding interest in some facet of the European Middle Ages. That interest, as I've already mentioned, began when my high school girlfriend gave me a copy of Hesse's *Narcissus and Goldmund.* It continued throughout college as I read—for part of my major—tracts on the medieval church, monastic life, and other Church-related material. One of those tracts, William Manchester's *A World Only Lit by Fire: The Medieval Mind and the Renaissance,* still sits on my bookshelf (next to another favorite of mine: Barbara Tuchman's *A Distant Mirror: The Calamitous 14th Century*). Both the Manchester and Tuchman books are narrative histories of the utmost order, capturing in great detail the daily grind—and complexity—of medieval life, both religious and secular.

Over the years I bought more books: on medieval art and architecture, medieval court life, monasticism and the medieval church, the art of the illuminated manuscript, ancient and medieval British history (with a special section on the Norman invasion of England in 1066), and medieval British legends and folk heroes. Whereas most students of English folklore develop a fascination with King Arthur and the Knights of the Roundtable, I developed a penchant for England's lower-class folk hero—Robin Hood. There was something about this quick-witted, swashbuckling fellow that captivated me (aside from his wardrobe: green tunic over forest-green tights). More than likely I was introduced to him as an adolescent when, stuck at home on a rainy Saturday afternoon, I turned on the TV and watched *The Adventures of Robin Hood.* Although it wasn't a life-changing experience, nonetheless I quickly fell under the spell of Robin Hood (and the young dashing Errol Flynn who played him).

Remember what my principal said when I was interviewed for the second grade position: "I don't care what you do as long as parents don't complain." That statement really resonated with me, ultimately unhinging me from the typical constraints of the elementary classroom curriculum. Free to experiment, I developed several literature-based, thematic units: one of them, which I used to end the school year, revolved around the legend of Robin Hood and the history of 12th-century England.

Wait. Stop. This is second grade, isn't it? Why on earth would second graders be interested in 12th-century England? Robin Hood? Maybe. But 12th-century England? Isn't that stretching it a bit?

It would be if I had let my students pick the end-of-year theme. More than likely, they would have chosen something less consequential like a history of the Berenstain Bears or Clifford the Dog (after all, they're *only* second graders). No, I'm not underestimating my students' aesthetic choices or even their decision-making abilities; it's just that I have a strong belief that the role of the teacher in the primary classroom is to unleash *passion*—both the students' and the teacher's. I've always believed that if teachers aren't interested in the curriculum, why on earth should their students be? So the first passion I ignite is my own, and Robin Hood in 12th-century England ignited that passion. For the half dozen years I taught second grade at Irving Elementary School in

Bozeman, Montana, I ended each year with a six- to eight-week thematic unit on Robin Hood, one of England's most enduring—and to many, endearing—personalities (along with Queen Elizabeth I and Henry VIII).

How did I start the unit? By reading, of course. And I had a few choices, at least that were available to me at the time: Howard Pyle's *The Merry Adventures of Robin Hood* (Scribner's 1946 edition of the original 1883 version); Henry Gilbert's *Robin Hood & the Men of the Greenwood* (Bracken Books 1984 release of the 1912 original), and Paul Creswick's *Robin Hood* (Scribner's 1984 classic that includes N. C. Wyeth's paintings created for publisher David McKay's 1917 edition). Of course, there are other versions, many of them not worth the paper they're printed on. These three (along with Robin McKinley's quirky *The Outlaws of Sherwood* that appeared in 1988 and led a feminist re-examination of the legend) stood out as the best and most appropriate to read to young children.

I chose Paul Creswick's tale mainly because of Wyeth's luminous illustrations, but also because the writing is accessible and the chapters brief. Our after-lunch ritual was always the same: I'd dim the lights and draw students close to me at the front of the room to read a chapter or two. Sometimes, when the material was difficult to understand, I'd pull out a hand puppet that I had made (a cross between a fairytale princess and Maid Marian) and retell some of the more obtuse parts, taking plenty of time to answer student questions. I'd also have students retell parts of the story—to test their understanding—or have them do some improvisational acting. Once the group was hooked, when all they wanted to do was listen to and talk about Robin Hood and his exploits, then I started to introduce the historical context behind those exploits: *Who were the Normans? Where did they come from? Why did Robin Hood live in the forest? Where was Nottingham? Who was Prince John?*

Yes, they were hooked. Once I realized this I turned the classroom upside down—literally. With the help of the school custodian, I carried all of the student desks into the basement and replaced them with trees made out of cardboard and construction paper. I did this over one weekend, so when the students came back to school the following Monday, they were met with the semblance of a forest, which we continued to shape and mold until we felt as if "we"—not just Robin Hood and his outlaw friends—were living in a forest. But it wasn't just the physical environment that we transformed; we changed the entire curriculum. No more reading. No more math. No more spelling. No more social studies. No more science. No more, that is, as separate subject matter. Now everything issued from our laser-sharp focus on Robin Hood and life in 12th-century England.

We lived and breathed Robin Hood from the moment school began in the morning, beginning each day by reciting Alfred Noyes' early 20th-century poem "Sherwood." We began by memorizing a couple of lines at a time until we could recite the entire 52-line poem by heart (impressing more than a few sets of parents). Reading, reciting, acting, storytelling—these were just some of the ways in which we brought the legend of Robin Hood to life. We also used our hands: we made replica motte-and-bailey castles (the precursor to the European stone castle) and crude siege weapons (that actually worked); we turned scenes from Creswick's book into dioramas (that we then enacted using homemade shadow, string, and hand puppets). We created "research notebooks" in which we summarized—and illustrated—our accumulated knowledge. In short, we used every modality—or, in today's jargon, "intelligence"—available to us to bring the story of Robin Hood and life in medieval England to life.

I say "we" because I read and worked and studied right along with my students. Although I was the conductor and they, for the most part, the orchestra, I learned about life in medieval England right alongside of them. I had to, not only to better plan the evolving unit, but also to keep up with my students' questions. All of this meant that I went to every library in the area to find reference materials to help me. I also began visiting in earnest Bozeman's new and used bookstores, slowly building the foundation for a personal library.

Today, that library is filled with all sorts of books related to medieval English history (or will be as soon as I get them off my office floor), which are grouped by theme:

Castle construction, siege warfare, and court life
English cathedrals and monasteries
The art of the medieval illuminated manuscript
Everyday life of medieval travelers
Atlases and timelines of British history
The Kings and Queens of Britain
The Norman Conquest
English folk and fairy tales
The legend of Robin Hood

During the five or six years that I taught the Robin Hood unit, not only did I ignite my students' curiosity, but I also fired up my own imagination. I began to dream about writing stories for young readers based on what I learned about England during the medieval period. I've already alluded to one of them—*Till Year's Good End*—which is based on the concept of the medieval "Labors of the Months." Although the other piece of writing that I published for young readers about life in the Middle Ages came much later, I'm convinced that the seed for *Magic in the Margins*, a tale about medieval bookmaking, was planted while I explored the life and times of Robin Hood with my second grade students at Irving Elementary School.

16 | Medieval Cats

I KNEW IT WOULD come to this—lifting some of the heaviest books in my collection. They're heavy because they're large. They're large because they're illustrated. They're illustrated because they're about some of the most beautiful handmade items on earth—medieval illuminated manuscripts. And right now I have to move them from the floor of my office to an empty bookshelf about five feet above my head. The process is slow and laborious since I have to haul them up a six-foot ladder, often one at a time. Yes, they're that large and that heavy.

I start with the heaviest: J. O. Westwood's *The Art of Illuminated Manuscripts: Illustrated Sacred Texts*, which takes a survey approach to illuminated manuscripts taken from Biblical texts created between the 4th and 16th centuries. It's a heavy book, made even heavier by the subject matter and presentation. Raymond Cazelles and Johannes Rathofer's slightly larger *Illuminations of the Heaven and Earth: The Glories of the Tres Riches Heures Du Duc De Berry* is a much more pleasing and readable book, as it focuses narrowly on one object—a Book of Hours created in the 15th century for Jean de Berry, a royal French bibliophile and noted collector. Since each one of these hardcover books weighs in at over three pounds,

I wisely haul each one up the ladder by itself, laying them flat on the shelf as I do all oversized books.

The next book in the pile catches my attention not only because of its size and heft, but also because it is by far the most definitive book ever written on the illuminated manuscript. It's author, Christopher de Hamel, is a recognized expert in the field, having been head of the Western Manuscripts department at Sotheby's in London since the mid-1970s and, currently, Fellow and Librarian of Corpus Christi College, Cambridge. De Hamel's *A History of Illuminated Manuscripts* published in 1994 by Phaidon also takes a survey approach, but unlike Westwood who looks exclusively at biblical texts, de Hamel looks at the kinds of books made at different times for different people: books for missionaries, books for emperors, books for monks, students, aristocrats, collectors, and the like. Richly illustrated and thoughtfully researched, *A History of Illuminated Manuscripts* is a must-have for any book collector interested in the history of the book, illuminated or not.

Once these three books go up on the shelf the rest is easier because the remaining books are thinner and lighter, and include Barbara Shailor's *The Medieval Book*, Jonathan Alexander's *Medieval Illuminators and Their Methods of Work*, Marc Drogin's *Medieval Calligraphy: Its History and Technique*, Patricia Seligman's *The Illuminated Alphabet*, Michael Brown's *Understanding Illuminated Manuscripts: A Guide to Technical Terms*, Krystyna Weinstein's *The Art of Medieval Manuscripts*, and two other de Hamel books—*The British Library Guide to Manuscript Illumination: History and Techniques* and *Medieval Craftsmen: Scribes and Illuminators.*

But none of these books grab my attention as much as Elizabeth Wilson's *Bibles and Bestiaries: A Guide to Illuminated Manuscripts.* Produced in collaboration with the Pierpont Morgan Library in New York, *Bibles and Bestiaries* contains the source of inspiration for *Magic in the Margins*. Toward the beginning of the book, Wilson includes an illustration from an edition of St. Augustine's *City of God*, written around 1140 CE. The illustration depicts Hildebertus, a monk working in a scriptorium, shooing a mouse away from a nearby piece of cheese. Pictured below Hildebertus is a young apprentice, who continues to paint border designs on a scrap of parchment oblivious to Hildebertus' annoyance. Although Hildebertus dominates the composition, I couldn't help but wonder about his young apprentice. Why did he live in a monastery? How did he come to work in the scriptorium? What was his education or training like? Would he ever become an accomplished scribe himself? Like so many stories I've written, this one welled up from the questions I posed.

At first, I thought about writing a how-to manual, exploring the various stages of bookmaking during the early medieval period when books were made by hand primarily in monastic scriptoria. This thought didn't last long because it had already been done by Bruce Robertson in *Marguerite Makes a Book*, a fictional story set in the Middle Ages that explores the stages of bookmaking in great detail. Next, I thought about using my research notes to write an alphabet book based on processes and materials involved in the illuminated manuscript, but Jonathan Hunt beat me to it in his gorgeous, large-format picture book *Illuminations*. But I didn't give up. I just kept reading, thinking, taking notes, and then it hit me—there are two sets of illustrations in most medieval manuscripts: the prescribed text-bound illustrations (prescribed because everything is symbolic; color, shape, and composition mean something, so they have to be followed, i.e., copied); and then there are the loosely drawn, whimsical, often irreverent illustrations in the margins. To me, that's where the true creativity and genius of a medieval illuminated manuscript resides. With that in mind I circled back to

Hildebertus' apprentice and began to think once more about his training, not the mechanics of how he learned to draw and paint, but how he learned to use his imagination in the artistic process. In doing so, I had inadvertently circled back to my primary interest, expressed in the top category of my tree of knowledge—creativity.

AS I FINISH THIS piece of writing I turn and notice that I only have a small pile of books on my office floor that still needs to get hauled up to its place on my bookshelves. The books in this pile are all children's books, ranging from picture books for young readers to novels for older readers. Despite the intended audience, they are all wonderfully written and illustrated. For the primary reader, there's Donald Carrick's *Harald and the Great Stag*, Joe Lasker's *Merry Ever After*, Aliki's *Medieval Feast*, and, one of my favorites, *Anno's Medieval World*, written and illustrated by the Japanese artist Mitsumasa Anno. For the intermediate reader, there's Barbara Cohen's *Geoffrey Chaucer's Canterbury Tales*, Nancy Ekholm Burkert's *Valentine & Orson*, and Paolo Guarnieri's *A Boy Named Giotto*. And for the older reader, there's E. L. Konigsburg's *A Proud Taste for Scarlet and Miniver*, Frances Temple's *The Ramsay Scallop*, and Karen Cushman's *Catherine, Called Birdy*. And then there's the weird and wacky *Medieval Cats*.

That's right, *Medieval Cats*. No, it's not a reference to a jazz band from the Middle Ages—far from it. It's a re-envisioning of some of the most famous paintings of the medieval era, only with cats—that's real, life-like felines—standing in for their human counterparts. There's Peter II in prayer—a sleek feline dressed in royal garb. There's King David playing the harp (straight out of *The*

Hours of Bonaparte Ghislieri). There's St. Luke, an orange tabby, with a blue shawl wrapped over his green frock, studying a relic. Then there's Charlemagne in regal dress, perched upon his throne, clasping a sword in one hand and the Imperial Orb of the Holy Roman Empire in the other.

It's an ingenious piece of handiwork created by painter and art aficionado Susan Herbert (one of several books she's published featuring the feline figure: *The Cat's History of Western Art*, *A Cat's Victorian Journal*, and *Impressionist Cats*). I'm reminded entirely of Chris Van Allsburg's *The Mysteries of Harris Burdick*. It's the same set-up: someone finds something out of the ordinary, something mysterious, some time passes, and then the finder of the something decides to present it to the world. Here's Herbert's set-up:

> The sensational discovery in 1991 of a cache of delicate paintings beneath a fragmentary pillar of the disused, indeed demolished, Abbey of St Wilderic in the deserted outskirts of the Alsatian village of Tierk-les-Bains set the world of medieval scholarship on its ear. The excavation took place originally because of a group of real estate speculators wished to break ground for a giant shopping development, and the laborers who discovered these precious paintings, kept safe in a strange package of straw, took time off from their work to have a good laugh at these funny pictures of cats, of all things—cats in costume, cats as people, cats even as angels!

Ultimately, the foreman of the construction crew takes the strange package of paintings home, stashes it away, and then opens it up one day, only to admire—and subsequently publish—the strange, fanciful paintings held within. As fanciful as this book might seem, as creatively on-the-edge it might appear, a close inspection of many medieval manuscripts reveals the same high degree of ingenuity. *Where?* In the margins, of course. You see, I've always known it: there's *Magic in the Margins* in most medieval books. You just have to know where to look.

17 | Fool's Cap

I'M STARTING A NEW project. I'm not talking about this one, the one I'm currently working on. I starting a new project for young readers and I need to get some information about trim sizes. So I pick up the phone and call Ingram, one of the print-on-demand companies that I deal with on a regular basis. Even though I have half a dozen books with them, I still don't understand everything on their file creation guide sheet. So I call them. I'd like to say "they" (meaning a person) answered, but, no; first I had to navigate a minefield of automated operators until finally, and only after some very loud and unpleasant music, I come face-to-face—well, really, ear-to-ear—with a real-live operator.

Operator: "Hello, may I help you?"
Me: "I'm looking at your trim size guide sheet and there are a few terms that I don't understand."
Operator: "Yes?"
Me: "For instance, what does "pinched crown" mean?
Operator: " That's a glued flat spine that, at least theoretically, lies flat when opened."
Me: *"Theoretically?"*
Operator: "Well, yes, you can count on it, I'd say 90% of the time."

Me: "Ninety percent of the time? What about the other 10%?"
Operator: "If you're thinking about trim sizes, you really should visit our price calculator. It can help you make all of your trim size decisions?"
Me: "But right now I'm not sure what size…"
Operator: "The price calculator can help you."
Me: "Right."

We hang up. Well, at least I do. It seems that this millennial has never picked up a book—a physical book, that is. If he had, he'd know how important the look and feel of a book is. How on earth can an electronic price calculator help someone make a decision about the look and feel of a book? The only way is if the book in question is an e-book read on an e-reader.

IT MAY SEEM THAT I have books on my mind most of the time. And, I guess, you'd be right to think that. Recently, I made a pilgrimage to my doctor's office for my annual physical exam. I was due, actually somewhat overdue, for the annual ritual. Although I'd like to report the results of the visit to you, I don't have them yet. Nor are they important. What is important is the conversation that I had with my primary care physician, not about my health status or even about the state of Western medicine, which is something we often talk about. During this visit, we talked about books.

I'm curious about people. I stop and talk with anyone who piques my interest: total strangers often. (It drives my wife crazy: she's always telling me, *TMI! TMI!)* I'm interested in what motivates people, what drives them. And what I've found over the years is what motivates a person often has nothing to do with his or her job. Take my neurologist for example: he's fantastic, very empathetic, extremely intelligent, and it's obvious that he loves what he does. However, in probing a little more, I found out that he also likes to write. Not only has he completed one novel and is working on another, but he just finished a screenplay, which he wrote in German (and was recently performed by the classmates in his German class). Whenever I see him, which is twice a year, he asks me about my writing and I ask him about his.

With my primary care physician it's the same, only after we talk about my writing, the conversation turns to his interest in playing the piano. And we're not talking popular show tunes that he plays for his cat at home. No, he's a serious classical pianist who is completing a Master's Degree in Performance Piano at a local university. When he begins to talk about music, he lights up—literally—his eyes widen and his face flashes a brilliant smile. "If I wasn't a physician, I'd probably be a professional musician," he once confided.

It reminds me of the time my wife and I went to a financial advisor to get our financial house in order. We met with the local representative of a national investment firm. It was a painful meeting, with the advisor plodding over our finances and his company's investment strategies, painful until I noticed some handmade ceramic vases populating the shelves behind him. "Excuse me," I interrupted at a low point in the conversation, "are those your vases?" He paused, glanced at the vases behind him, and then lit the room up for the next fifteen minutes telling us about his passion for throwing pots. I remember telling my wife as we left his office that I would never give our money over to someone who was more passionate about his pottery than our pennies (though I certainly respect his passion).

Over time, I've come to realize that many people live dual lives: one preoccupied with the necessity of making a living, the other energized by a deep passion for the arts (or some other veiled interest). It's only the lucky few who are able to integrate these two sides of themselves into their primary profession. Most people, like my neurologist, my primary care physician, and the young, but-not-hired financial advisor, live out—or, more accurately, live with—the split between their work-a-day world and their after-hour interests.

Now, as my primary care physician was hooking me up to an EKG machine (okay, so it wasn't the usual annual physical exam), he casually asked me, "So, what are you working on?" When I told him about my current project, writing a book about books, he instantly launched in to tell me about his book collection, in particular his interest in the work of Émile Zola: "Some of the first books that I ever collected came from my aunt. After my cousin moved to Europe, my aunt offered me some of the books that he left behind. That's how I discovered Zola."

Aside from his love of Zola's work, especially books in Zola's *Les Rougon-Macquart* series, a couple of things struck me about my doctor's declaration. First of all, in each of the books he had received from his aunt, his cousin had written the year and place in which he had acquired the volume: "Yes, and to this day I remember where and when I acquired books that I purchased. Several years ago I picked up three Zola volumes at a small bookstore in Quebec City published in the same Penguin Classics format, and for only three dollars apiece."

After this proclamation, my doctor began talking about book purchases in the digital age: "I mean what associations can you possibly have with the purchase of an e-book?" he asks. I smile knowingly. "Can you possibly remember where and when you bought it, and, more importantly, where you were developmentally?"

Interesting questions. Important questions. I'm reminded of the story about French writer and filmmaker Jean Cocteau.

Cocteau, a man with a singular artistic vision, recounts the time when he returned to the village of his youth. He recalled every street, every building, and every surface that he had trailed his fingers along as he strolled through the village as a young boy on his way to school. They were faint memories, barely discernible, until he bent down and touched the textured surfaces of the walls and buildings he had run his finger along at a height closer to that which he'd done as a child, at which point his childhood memories returned in full prismatic color:

> Just as the needle picks up the melody from the record, I obtained the melody of the past with my hand. I found everything: my cape, the leather of my satchel, the names of my friends and of my teachers, certain expressions I had used, the sound of my grandfather's voice, the smell of his beard, the smell of my sister's dresses and of my mother's gown.

How can we possibly have such rich associations with the e-book purchases that we make? If we cannot remember where and when we bought a book (without a tangible reminder of that purchase—the physical book itself—we are bound to forget those details), how can we possibly remember where we were developmentally at the time of the purchase? *And why is this important?* Because, as much as a book's content is responsible for the impact it has upon the heart, mind, and soul of a reader, the rich associations a reader has with a book are equally important and impacting.

Take Hermann Hesse's *Narcissus and Goldmund*, for example. Just picking up the volume elicits an excess of memories—of my high school girlfriend, my years surfing on the Florida beaches, the inner struggle between the intellectual and artistic sides of myself.

Sometimes, when the air temperature is just right in Chicago, where I've lived for the past thirty years, I'm transported back to my young adult years spent in Florida—now some fifty years ago. Memory is body-bound; it is locked into the senses, as well as released by them. How can an e-reader transport us back in time? How can the mere act of picking up a sleek mechanical device unleash a flood of memories in us of an earlier time, a time of questioning, a time of developmental crisis? I don't think it can. And because it can't, I think we suffer a loss, and not just a loss of memory: we suffer an equal loss of being.

RECALLING COCTEAU'S REVERIE CALMS me down, but I'm still nonplussed by the phone conversation I had with the ill-informed operator. More than that, I'm burning with curiosity: along with "pinched crown," what do these other terms mean—Demy 8vo, Royal 8vo, Crown 4vo? These were some of the other terms that I didn't understand on the file creation guide sheet, and that we never got to discuss (remember: the price calculator knows all; please consult). So I fire up my computer, go online, and start to search, finding most of the answers to my questions, and then some. The "and then some" is a reference to foolscap.

Foolscap? Now there's a name. And it is: named after its distinctive watermark, Foolscap is the name of an oversized paper (generally 8 ½ by 13 ½) commonly used in Europe and the British Commonwealth before the adoption of the international standard A4 paper. Today, however, the term refers more to the common legal pad. Perhaps I should send the operator one as a gift, along with a real "fool's cap."

18 | Tip of the Iceberg

IT'S A BALANCING ACT: producing work and promoting it. And now that the busiest months of the year are upon me—mid-March through early June—every school and public library wants a little of my time, so balancing adequate writing time with life on the road is often a trick. It's also a pleasure.

One of the great pleasures of my life is participating in the Near South Planning Board's Author-in-the-Schools Program. Wow, that's a mouthful, but it's easily boiled down to this: I get to visit third graders in a variety of schools on Chicago's south side. The visits are all prearranged and paid for. That's part of the pleasure—having the administrative and financial aspect of a school visit handled by someone else. The other part, of course, is visiting the schools.

I'm a born storyteller, and it doesn't hurt that I'm pretty musical and have a decent speaking and singing voice. So it's easy to imagine that school visits are a place where I thrive. As my wife says, "Just give him a stage, and he'll perform—anywhere, anytime, and for anyone." And, she's right. It's second nature to me: I'm a storyteller first, a musician second, and a writer third. Always have been; always will be. I guess that's why I get a lot of positive feedback, from Welcome-to-Our-School banners to Thank-You-Very-Much cards. Those are the more formal ways teachers and students tell me that they appreciate what I do. The unofficial feedback is just as rewarding, usually delivered on the spot, impromptu, by students of all ages:

Will you read my story?
Don't leave.
May I go home with you?
When will you be back?
I love you.

Then there are the silent tributes, like the girl who reached out and held my hand as her teacher took a class photo. Now, any teacher or administrator in his right mind would not hold hands with one of his students in public, but I could just tell that this girl needed it. Maybe she didn't have a male role model in her life, or maybe she did but who either ignored her or, worse yet, abused her. I don't know. All I know is that for one long moment we held hands, quietly, secretly, in the back row surrounded by her classmates, while her teacher raised her smartphone and said, "Say *cheese*," which I'm sure we did.

AS I LOOK AT my schedule, I see that I'm booked, maybe even overbooked, for the next couple of months: a handful of Author-in-the-Schools programs, a similar handful of school and library programs scattered throughout the Chicago suburbs, a weeklong excursion to Appleton, WI, for the Fox Cities Book Festival, and a panel presentation on non-traditional publishing for the SCBWI's Midwest Conference in Naperville, Illinois. And this just takes me through the beginning of May. I'm already exhausted and I haven't even gone out the door.

Another reason I haven't gone out the door is because every spare minute I have is spent addressing postcards. Remember the *Shark Man* promotion timeline? Well, I'm still sending out postcards to every surf shop in Florida. I've already sent out a bunch to schools and libraries in the Daytona Beach area (not one, but two rounds before the FLA conference in early March). Now, I'm canvassing surf shops. After all, that's where the action is, or at least—theoretically—the most age-appropriate readers who might be interested in my book. Along with the printed information on the postcard—a description of the book, ISBN and price information, and my contact info—I add a handwritten note, something like: "Hey, surf's up, and so is *Shark Man*, a Florida surfing adventure. Please post. Thanks." I imagine a tall, bleach-blond nineteen-year-old clerk behind the counter looking at the postcard, flipping it over, back again, and then tossing it in the trash. That's why I usually send a second postcard several weeks later. And that's why, for the last few weeks, it's been nothing but scribble an address on a postcard, add a handwritten note on the back, then slap on the required postage. I do it because I'm a non-traditionally published author who writes, publishes, promotes, distributes, and hawks his wares wherever he can in order to pay the bills.

And that means my books have to make money.

Money! Yes, money. All right, I know you've wanted to ask me this question for a long time: "Just how much money *do* you make?" (Or, as the occasional fifth grader puts it: "Do you drive a Mercedes?") First of all, when it comes to money, you have to think of income streams. In this day and age, in particular, you don't just get a royalty check from your publisher every six months and that's it. There are several income streams that I try to cultivate: stipends from school and public library presentations; direct book sales (from schools, libraries, literacy conferences, and book fairs); royalties from my traditionally published books (which are self-generating at this point); and online sales from my self-published titles. When you put all of these income streams together, things start to add up. We're not talking gazillions of dollars, but we are talking a healthy supplemental income, enough at least to keep my publishing efforts in the black.

Of course, I really haven't answered your question, have I? You know how it is, ask a friend how much he's saved for retirement and he just stares at you, or worse, tells you it's none of your business. So, following that protocol, I don't think I'll say much more, except to leave you with this story. About ten years ago, I had the opportunity to talk with Philip Lee, a founding partner of Lee & Low Books, the company that published *Bein' With You This Way*. The book had just celebrated its 10th anniversary and was still selling through the roof. In my enthusiasm, I babbled on about how good the book was to me; how it had put my daughters through college, *blah, blah, blah*. Philip listened patiently as I prattled on and on. After I finished, Philip smiled and said, rather bluntly, "Put my daughter through college, too." So, yes, books can generate income—and not only for the author.

I WOKE UP THIS morning thinking about *Shark Man*. I mean, it's just not getting off the ground. It's not selling. You would think that every teenager in Florida would jump at the chance to read a book about surfing on the Florida beaches, especially a book with such a catchy name—*Shark Man*—and a really cool cover photo of a bleach-blond kid on a surfboard trying to outrun a school of sharks. It's been on the market for over six months and I've yet to make an online sale. I have made some direct sales, but that's to be expected (not only do I push the book hard at events, but the cover alone rings up sales). Otherwise, it's not selling. So, I run down to my office, dig out my *Shark Man* promotional timeline, and review what I've done so far:

1. Release *Shark Man* chapters on WordPress blog.
2. Release *Shark Man* chapters on Wattpad.
3. Post blog updates on FaceBook.
4. Create links on website to WordPress and Wattpad.
5. Complete CreateSpace paperback edition.
6. Order 25 copies of *Shark Man* for GoodReads giveaway.
7. Use PhotoShop to develop a standard mailing postcard.
8. Mail postcards to…

As I review these steps, something hits me: not what I have or haven't done to promote *Shark Man*, but the fact that every digital company on earth seems to use a compound word (unhyphenated no less) for its online handle. Just look at this list…

WordPress
Wattpad
Facebook
CreateSpace
GoodReads
PhotoShop

And this is just the tip of the iceberg…

BlueDot
Firefox
Bloglines

Filmloop
Netvibes
Salesforce
Tagworld
TechMeme
YouTube
Pageflakes
Webshots
Rapleaf
Songbird
SoundCloud

Here are the best and the brightest minds of the industry putting their heads together and what do we get: one algorithm for generating business names for the entire tech world. *How brilliant is that!* Maybe I should have titled my book *SharkMan*—to hell with the conventions of punctuation and grammar. It only goes to prove that finding a truly unique vision in the world is difficult. Trying to stand out above and beyond everyone else is not easy, especially in a world so tightly woven together by social media, which only reinforces an ever-tightening collective mindset.

Uniqueness? A thing of the past. A late 19th-century phenomenon. I could go on and on about stuff like this, as only my wife knows, but unfortunately I can't. I don't have the time. I have to get back to my marketing campaign. Let's see, where was I?

8. Mail postcards to Florida surf shops.
9. Sign up for Florida Reading Association's annual conference.
10. Run a quarter-page ad in the FLA conference program.
11. Order 50 paperback and 25 hardcover books for FLA conference.

12. Submit *Shark Man* to the SCBWI's Spark Award.
13. Submit *Shark Man* to the IBPA's Ben Franklin Award.
14. Send second round of postcards to Florida surf shops.
15. Send postcards to schools and libraries in the Daytona Beach area.
16. Promote *Shark Man* in Ingram's Children's Advance circular.
17. Take out ad in the IBPA's library and bookstore catalog.
18. Resend postcards to schools and libraries in the Daytona Beach area.
19. Run ads in regional and national surfing magazines.
20. Record sample chapters of *Shark Man* on SoundCloud.
21. Send out postcards to all middle schools in Florida.
22. Send sales sheet to book distributors in the southeast.
23. Go back to the top of the list and start all over again.

19 | Oops

IT'S A BEAUTIFUL DAY in April, chilly but clear. Clumps of snowdrops and crocus flowers poke through thin layers of winter mulch. A circle of daffodils joins them. Nearby, last year's stand of false indigo and Joe-Pye weed sit idle, waiting for the heat of summer. Only the hardy kiwi vine stretched across the front fence and several spirea bushes in the tree lawn show any interest in putting forth a spray of greenery. I take all of this in sitting on the top step of the front porch, sipping hot tea. As I do, I run down my checklist one last time:

Overnight bag
Storytelling suitcase
Presentation materials
Box of books for book sale
Audio equipment
Water bottle
Lunch

After breakfast, I load the car and take off. My destination is the grand old city of Appleton, Wisconsin.

One of the beauties of being a published author is engaging with readers. And that's what I'll be doing for the next couple of days at the Fox Cities Book Festival held each year in the lovely city of Appleton, Wisconsin. I've been to the festival before, several times. When I'm invited, usually it's the highlight of my year.

One reason is getting there.

When I was younger and had a lot more balls in the air to juggle, I'd race from one event to the next, not taking much time to enjoy the in-between times. Now that I'm older, and maybe a bit wiser, I take more time traveling to events. To get to Appleton, I could jump on the interstate and head north, through Milwaukee, then along the west side of Lake Winnebago, arriving at my destination less than four hours later. A half-day's drive at best.

But I don't do that. I break it into a two-day trip, stopping overnight at the surfing capital of the Midwest—Sheboygan, Wisconsin. It's a great place to stop, but not for its waves. Rather, for what the city has to offer: a quaint little motel on the river, a "locals" coffeehouse nearby, an incredible art museum sponsored by the Kohler Foundation, and *Trattoria Stefano*, one of the best Italian restaurants in the area. If there's time, I'll head to the Kohler-Andrae State Park south of Sheboygan and stroll along the boardwalk that weaves its way through ancient Lake Michigan sand dunes. Although it's the midpoint of my journey, Sheboygan feels like an endpoint, and a very satisfying one at that.

The next day I throw my things into the car, ready for the second leg of my journey: a slow meander through back roads east of Lake Winnebago until I reach Appleton. This is a pretty little piece of Wisconsin that—other than the gigantic wind farm near the lake—is a throwback to the German Catholics who settled the area in the early part of the 19th century. You can tell this as you travel northwest out of Sheboygan not only from the small Catholic churches dotting the surrounding farmland, but also from town names—St. Anna, St. Joe, St. Peter, St. Cloud, Mount Calvary, and Jericho. By the late 19th century, there were so many German Catholic immigrant families in the area it was affectionately called "Holyland." Today, I decide to take Rt. 32, the more direct route, through Howards Grove, Kiel, New Holstein, and Chilton, before swinging west on Rt. 114 to Stockbridge and Sherwood. Above Sherwood, I catch Rt. 10, which takes me into the heart of downtown Appleton.

Interstate 41, the 441 by-pass, and Rt. 10 draw an almost perfect square around Appleton. The square is bisected, however, by the Lower Fox River, which runs from the north end of Lake Winnebago, just below the southwest corner Appleton, northeast to the city of Green Bay, where it empties into Lake Michigan. To get out of Lake Winnebago, the Lower Fox River first squeezes past Doty Island, between Neenah and Menasha, before it heads due north. At Stroebe Island, the river turns slowly to the northeast, preparing for its forty-mile run to Green Bay. But before it does, the Lower Fox River makes an "S" turn near downtown Appleton, at the foot of Lawrence University, where pulp and paper mills used to dot the riverfront from the mid-19th century on.

I arrive at my hotel, one of several in the downtown area. There's also a small convention center and a museum dedicated to Harry Houdini, who grew up in Appleton. (The other famous native son, of course, is Senator Joseph McCarthy, architect and chief prosecutor of the 1950s "Red Scare.") Other than that, downtown Appleton is like many small Midwestern towns—a sleepy, provincial outpost with quiet tree-lined neighborhoods spreading out on either side of College Avenue, the central north-south dividing line.

But I'm not here to admire Appleton, or even to provide a detailed history of the city. I'm here for the Fox Cities Book

Festival. When I ask about the plural form of Fox Cities, I'm told that it refers to several cities along the Fox River that collectively consider themselves a regional whole. The chain of cities includes Neenah, Menasha, Appleton, Little Chute, Kimberly, Combined Locks, and Kaukauna. It's an important bit of knowledge because the Fox Cities Book Festival doesn't take place only in Appleton, but in all of the cities in the chain. But I've been contracted by the main branch of the Appleton Library and an elementary school on the east side of the city.

IT'S NOT THE FIRST time I've been to Appleton. Several years ago I participated in the book festival, doing presentations at three schools and the public library. I remember the trip fondly, but most of all for a potentially embarrassing moment.

A librarian at one of the elementary schools arranged my visit. From our email exchanges I could tell he truly loved children and books. The week before the festival he sent me an email, requesting that I bring the Golden Archer Award that I had received for *Shake Dem Halloween Bones*. The librarian wanted his students to actually see the award medal. The Golden Archer Award is the students' choice award for the State of Wisconsin, which *Shake Dem Halloween Bones* won in 2001.

"No problem," I replied. "Of course I'll bring it along." But I only remembered to throw it into my book bag at the last moment.

When I arrived at the school later that week, the librarian was really excited, especially because I was going to show his students the Golden Archer Award. Of course, I was equally happy to share the award with them as I had not shared the award with anyone yet. When it came time to bring the award out, I made a big fuss over it: *What an honor… I'm so thankful… You don't know how much it means….* And then I reached into my book bag and picked up the award. But as I lifted it out of the bag, I froze. In my haste to pack my bag I grabbed the wrong award. Instead of the Golden Archer Award, I grabbed the Christopher Award, which I had won in 2007 for *How We Are Smart*, a collective biography that takes a multicultural look at Howard Gardner's theory of multiple intelligences.

Now, hold that thought, because if you remember I said earlier that I remember this visit for a "potentially" embarrassing moment. Here's why: I did throw the wrong award—the Christopher Award—into my book bag, but fortunately I caught the mistake right before I left home. So, I decided to milk the "mistake" for all that it was worth. When it came time to show the librarian and his students the Golden Archer Award, I fumbled around with my book bag, stuttering and stammering the entire time. And then I fessed up…

"I think I brought the wrong award," I said sheepishly.

"What?" exclaimed the librarian.

Everyone was dead silent, waiting for my response.

"Well, I *almost* brought the wrong award," I said, explaining how I had initially thrown the Christopher Award into my book bag, but caught the mistake at the last moment.

Heaving a palpable sigh of relief when I finally raised the Golden Archer Award (and the Christopher Award as a bonus), the librarian beamed and then led the students in a rousing round of applause.

THIS YEAR EVERYTHING WENT off without a hitch. No problem whatsoever. I had a great time at a local elementary school, and I had an even better time at the main branch of the public library that drew an unusually large crowd for my presentation. I even had dinner with the librarian who had arranged my previous visit, and, once again, we had a big laugh over my earlier embarrassing—but only momentary—faux pas.

And now the winner of the 2001 Golden Archer Award. The envelope please—or, in this case, the medal…

Oops!

20 | Authorpreneur

THE UPSIDE OF MY yearlong office-cleaning project is that half of my office is finally organized. Things are starting to make sense. It looks orderly and I can find things. The downside is that the other half of my office is a mess, a total wreck, and I can't seem to find the things I really need to find, like my notes for the upcoming SCBWI's Wild Wild Midwest Conference, held in lovely—but extremely congested—Naperville, Illinois.

I got snookered on this one. A couple of months ago, I got a call from the coordinators of the Illinois SCBWI chapter, asking me if I'd like to participate on a panel on independent publishing during the Midwest conference scheduled in early May. I've done things for the local chapter before so I know there's no money in it. I try to think of it as another form of marketing, of getting my name out there, and hopefully making some more contacts that might lead to a school visit or two. Nonetheless, I innocently asked, "Is there a stipend?" "Oh, no," the voice at the other end of the line replied, "but we'll give you $50 off the conference registration fee." *Fifty bucks*, I thought. *Well at least it's something.* "Sure," I said, "happy to participate."

I hung up and didn't think about it again, until I received an email from the conference organizers reminding me to register for the upcoming conference. So I went online, filled out the registration form, then hit "Calculate Fees." That's when I nearly went through the roof. The registration fee was a whopping $295. That is, if you signed up and paid by February 1st, but it was already the middle of March and the fee was now $310. Let's see, $310 minus the $50 discount is $260 plus tax. Add to this the fact that my session is bright and early Sunday morning and that Naperville is no small drive from my house, so I'm looking at a mind-boggling $350 ($260 for the conference fee and $90 for one night in luxurious Naperville). And all so I could share the stage with two other people for forty-five minutes in order to talk about being an independently published author. And I already know what people will ask: "Excuse me, but how much money do you make?"

NOT MUCH AT THESE PRICES!

But it's too late. The die's cast. I've made a commitment. And besides I can always tent-camp in a nearby suburb the night before. So I hit "Pay Now," fill out the required credit card information, hit "Submit," and wait for my application to process. It doesn't take long, and I'm in. Now I can start preparing for the panel. I prepare by keeping a notebook with me and anytime I get an idea about independent publishing I jot the idea down, however lame. My ideas easily fall into several broad categories.

What do we call you? First of all, let's clear up some terminology. When I wrote and published my first book I called myself a "self-published" author. By the time I published my third book, I was using the term "non-traditional" author. Now, with six books under my belt, I consider myself an "independent author/publisher." It's a lot of change in a short period of time, but then change has been the name of the game in the publishing industry for over a decade. Basically, everything is up for grabs as the industry comes to terms with the flattening of its vertical structure, thanks to the DIY self-publishing revolution made possible both by the availability and lower cost of creating, producing, distributing, and marketing a book.

The universal availability of these industry tools has caused an upheaval of seismic proportion. Think of it as two continental plates crashing against each other causing the current state of disruption. It's the classic battle between two titanic forces: between a 20th-century elitist literary model and an upstart 21st-century entrepreneurial model (or, in modern—or is that post-modern—slang: an "authorpreneurial" model).

This is not theoretical. The clash is often played out in extremely personal ways. Case in point: the wife of my former college roommate refuses to acknowledge any of my self-published books, looking down her nose at me for breaking ranks with traditional publishing. With a BA from an ivy-league college and an MFA from one of the top writing programs in the country, she scoffs at my self-publishing endeavors, seeing them as beneath her stature. Her "stature," reflected in her online resume, discloses that over the last forty years she has published a handful of short stories (more if you count a couple that were reprinted) in several literary magazines. Aside from a couple of award nominations and a handful of good reviews, that's it. Stuck in a 20th-century elitist literary model that pays deference to agents and editors and the entire edifice of traditional publishing, she can't self-publish her work; doing so would be an admission of failure (failure to reach her career goals, which, of course, include being a traditionally-published, award-winning author).

What does Beatrix Potter have to do with it? In my college roommate's wife's world there is a firm barrier between traditional publishing and self-publishing, between the classical elitist literary model of the modern era and the emerging entrepreneurial model of the post-modern era. Of course, when the new self-publishing model began to gain traction in the early 2000s there was a deep divide between the two. Why not? Self-publishing has been around for some time (Beatrix Potter self-published her first Peter Rabbit books, until Fredrick Warne signed her up—but only after having rejected her work initially). Over the last decade or so the barrier between traditional and nontraditional publishing has become more and more porous.

How do we know this? In the early days of the self-publishing revolution, editors refused to consider self-published authors, major review bodies barred their work from their domain as well, and self-publishing "services" existed exclusively outside the realm of traditional publishing. Not so today. Editors from large publishing houses (or their minions) actively troll the Internet, looking for top-selling self-published authors; review agencies not only accept self-published work, but offer fee-based review services as well; and, when it comes to self-publishing services, you will find even the most established agencies offering them—for a fee, of course.

Case in point: *Kirkus Reviews*. If you've been in the publishing industry for any time at all, you know that *Kirkus Reviews* is the gold standard for book reviews. Authors salivate over the possibility that *Kirkus* will review their book. Of course, a review by *Kirkus* doesn't always mean a positive review; but you know that it will be unbiased, insightful, and extremely well written. The only problem is that it's not easy to get *Kirkus* to review your book (after all, there are tens of thousands of books published each year). And if you're a self-published author—*forget it!*

Well, that was then, and this is now. Now *Kirkus Reviews* has a new offering—*Kirkus Indie*. If publishing today is all about getting discovered, then *Kirkus Indie* is for you, offering "professional, unbiased book reviews for self-publishers from one of the most prestigious magazines in publishing." It's funny, but when I think of *Kirkus Reviews*, I've always thought professional, unbiased, industry leader, *and* stodgy, meaning stuck in a 20th-century elitist literary model. But you can't say that about *Kirkus* anymore. Nope, they've adapted to the times, to the digital revolution that's given legs—and prominence—to the self-publishing world. It's all there, reflected in the menu bar at the top of the *Kirkus* home page: *Book Reviews, Bestsellers, Authors, Kirkus TV, Blogs, Contests, Kirkus Prize, Pro Connect,* and *Services for Authors*. Click on the last button and the drop-down menu offers fee-based services to help you edit your book, to review your book, and, once finished, to promote your book. In short, the once firm barrier between traditional or legacy publishing and self-publishing is more than just porous; it's pretty much a thing of the past.

Who is Mark Dawson? When I think of the types of individuals that might choose to self-publish, I quickly think of four different types. The first group of people is made up of "digital natives." These are 18- to 28-year-olds who grew up swimming in the world of social media. Completely at home on the Internet, used to publishing their ideas in a nanosecond, this group of people has no interest in traditional publishing as they have grown up completely in the 21st-century authorpreneurial model. Leave them alone and let them swim; they have no interest in or need for the traditional publishing world. And, besides, it's so doggone slow.

The second group of people is made up of 28- to 42-year-olds. This group is older, wiser, and still working hard to get a foothold in the traditional publishing world (because, in their mind, that's where the money and prestige is). Although tech-savvy, they're not digital natives. They have to work hard to maintain their computer skills and online presence. They've been writing—seriously—for a decade or two, but haven't gotten as far as they would like. And they're starting to get tired of knocking on doors, doors that seem harder to open with each passing year. So they start to consider self-publishing, not as a career change, but as a way to build a publishing record. Their mentality is: If I could just build a track record (and a following, which they've heard is just as important), maybe editors would start to pay attention to me. So they pick a project and self-publish it. If they're lucky, they get noticed and their career upticks. If not, *well*...

The third group of people is made up of 42- to 58-year-olds. This group can be divided between "mid-career authors," writers who have a solid publishing record, but have been overlooked by the big publishing houses, and "marquee authors," top-tier writers at the top of their game. Although different in their publishing successes and career trajectory, members of each group want the same thing: more control of their writing and more of the take. Here are two cases in point.

The first one: lawyer-turned-novelist Mark Dawson. According to *The Telegraph*, UK-based Mark Dawson is "the literary sensation you've never heard of." Although you may not have heard of him, his growing fan base has. Like many young professionals, Dawson dreamed of being a novelist, writing on his commute to work and during his lunch break, while working for a London-based law firm. Secretly, he dreamt of being a successful novelist. And he was, sort of: while working as a lawyer, he published three novels with traditional publishing houses, including Macmillan. But his career never took off; his novels came and went, leaving him with little to brag about and even less income. Around 2013, on the advice of a friend, he decided to self-publish a novel through

Amazon's Kindle Direct Publishing e-book program. In only three short years, Dawson made the transition from working for others to working for himself. With almost two dozen novels to his credit, Dawson sells worldwide, raking in a six-figure annual salary.

The second case involves contemporary romance and women's fiction writer Barbara Freethy. Freethy fits into that second category: top-tier authors with a solid publishing record. Not only is she a two-time winner of the Romance Writers of America's RITA Award (*Daniel's Gift*, 1996; *The Way Back Home*, 2012), but she's also had 18 books make the *New York Times Book Review* best-seller list. So why would Freethy want to self-publish? The reason: to gain control of her out-of-print backlist, making it available to her large and still-growing readership. It was a good decision: not only has Freethy sold more than five million books, but she was recently named Amazon's KDP Bestselling Author of All Time.

Okay, I get it, but really how many self-published authors actually make money?

According to Claude Forthomme, author of Nougat's Blog, only 40 self-published authors made money in 2015 (if you define "making money" as selling more than one million e-book copies in the last five years, which Forthomme does). That means, using Forthomme's definition, tens of thousands of authors didn't make money. And, yet, fully one-third of the 100 best-selling Kindle e-books were self-published titles. In the end, however, as the old adage goes: writing is a poor man's profession.

And that brings us to the last group of people made up of 58- to 99-year-olds (or something like that). This group of people is made up of grandparents, retirees, and more than a few burnt-out authors. Yes, this is the group of people who just want to make a book, to say, "Hey, I did it," or they want to leave behind a legacy, a trace of their life on earth. It's also made up of a number of authors who don't want to play the game anymore: they just want to make books (even though they may still harbor visions of grandeur). The latter group puts most of its energy into making a book, worrying less about it once it's published. They write for the pleasure of writing.

I think of the narrator in Jim Harrison's autobiographical novella *The Land of Unlikeness*. After spending forty years or more as an art professor, critic, and high-end art appraiser, Harrison's narrator returns home—ostensibly to care for his elderly mother—to rekindle his early love of painting. In the process of rediscovering his early passion, he soon realizes that he is no longer interested in becoming a painter (a social designation that carries considerable baggage); he just wants to paint. For many, in this latter category, they just want to write. At this point in my life, with most of my writing career behind me, I find myself identifying strongly with Harrison's protagonist: that is, I'm more interested in writing than in being a writer. And that's the message I want to bring to Naperville, along with some of the nuts-and-bolts of how to navigate the self-publishing world.

21 | Exercise Rule #39

I'M PSYCHED. I'M JACKED. I'm ready for the SCBWI Wild Wild Midwest Conference and I'm ready for the independent publishing panel (I'm just not ready to go to the evening masquerade party dressed as a cowboy). I have a ton of notes, a stack of books, and a gazillion handouts. I just haven't decided to tent-camp or not.

I arrive at the hotel convention center early. The parking lot is packed. I mean packed. I find a spot in an adjacent lot a block or two away from the hotel. It's a hike, but as I walk to the hotel I remember reading an article several years ago about how to exercise naturally. Exercise Rule #39: *Park as far away from your destination as possible; the walk will do you good.* So I'm walking, I'm not too happy, but I'm walking, and I do feel a little better by the time I get to the front door of the hotel.

The thing is I don't have to be here today as the panel discussion is tomorrow morning, but I've decided to attend Saturday to see how many people have signed up for the conference, and maybe to sit in on a session or two. I notice three things upon entering the hotel lobby. First of all, there are stacks of vintage luggage everywhere: in the windows, by the front door, in the lobby, by the reservation counter. Either they had a run on vintage luggage somewhere nearby or the hotel's interior decorator has a penchant for vintage. In any case, I'm tempted to snatch one and take it home. My wife loves old, I mean vintage luggage (we keep all of our winter clothes in them during the summer months). As much as I'm tempted to lift a piece of luggage, I don't and continue through the hotel lobby.

The second thing I notice is a lot of women. They're walking in the hallways, gathered around the registration table, sitting in small clusters in the lobby waiting area, and lined up waiting to get their morning coffee. I guess it makes sense; after all, this is a conference on writing books for children. Who better to write those books than women: mothers, wives, teachers, and caretakers, it's that maternal instinct. I'm sure men write children's books too, and looking around, I see a handful of them. But they don't seem as relaxed as the women milling around. Perhaps the younger ones do, the primary school teachers and stay-at-home dads. But the older ones, the retirees and grandfathers, they look more than uncomfortable; they look downright distressed.

And that leads me to the third observation: the conference coordinators—women, of course—have turned the first two men's restrooms I come across into temporary women's restrooms. It's totally understandable. And, besides, if you think the line of women waiting to get coffee is long, wait till they all need to use the restroom at the same time. Since I need to use a men's restroom after two cups of coffee and an hour's drive to the suburbs, I press on, finding a men's room at the end of a long, dark corridor.

Now, I'm ready to engage. I'm ready to sit in on a session. I scour the schedule for an appropriate session. I see a lot of SCBWI-sponsored sessions, most of them presented by a PAL author (a.k.a. "Published and Listed" authors). I settle on a session that explores the use of rhyme and rhythm in creative nonfiction for young readers. A very dynamic woman from the SCBWI's Wisconsin chapter—an SCBWI PAL member, I'm sure—guides us through some of her books. Her books are delightful and her use of language engaging. She reminds me of some of the authors who inspired me when I began to write: Mem Fox, Margaret Mahy, Nancy Willard, Reeve Lindbergh, and, one of my earliest influences, M. B. Goffstein. The session presenter is superb and I leave more than satisfied; I leave inspired.

The next session I attend is less than satisfying. I chose it more by the process of elimination than anything else. It's about how to repair your online reputation, which I thought was a catchy title for how to use digital media to advance your career. Unfortunately, it's a WYSIWYG, a rather dull look at what to do if someone doesn't like you and posts bad things about you all over the Internet. Now, I'm thinking audience: a lot of young and unpublished authors. Why on earth would they want to know how to repair their online reputation when, more than likely, they don't have one to start with? But it all comes together toward the end of the session when the presenter says that he is on the program because a friend of his wife is one of the conference organizers. In and of itself, the statement is not too off-putting. But when he says that his degree in marketing more than compensates for his lack of experience with authors and that he'd be happy—for a fee, of course—to help us market our next book, I stand up and leave (and I don't think the marketing-guru-turned-children's-book-enthusiast even noticed).

By noon I've had it, so I make the long trek back to my car (reminding myself with every step that the exercise is good for me). I drive home, debrief the day's outing with my wife over dinner, and go to bed (glad that I decided not to tent-camp). The next day I'm up at dawn. I wouldn't have to get up so early except for the fact that my session was rescheduled to accommodate another presenter's travel plans. So I'm up with the birds and off to the suburbs at first light. It's a beautiful drive, a beautiful morning, and I even get a parking spot close to the front door of the hotel (so much for Exercise Rule #39). I arrive a good 40 minutes or so before the panel discussion is slated to begin, so I head to the Starbucks in the hotel lobby, but even at this early hour the coffee line snakes out the door, so I sit down at a nearby table and review my notes.

THERE ARE TWO KINDS of people in the world: those who arrive ahead of time and those who don't. I'm definitely in the first camp. I like to get to the airport two hours before my plane leaves. My wife likes to stroll up to the gate just as the plane is about to take off. I'm ready for company an hour before they arrive. My wife is still getting dressed when the doorbell rings. So, naturally, I get to the session room ahead of most people. There's only one person there, leafing through the conference program. Soon afterwards the session moderator arrives, along with several other attendees. I walk around, talking with people, asking them why they've decided to attend this session. Not only does the idle chatter relax me, but also I learn a little bit about who's in the room. With a couple of minutes to go, the other two panel members arrive. The moderator introduces us, and off we go.

There are two other types of people in the world: those who think with clarity and those who don't. I'm definitely in the latter group. Things happen, but only later do I realize what happened. I'm the kind of guy who thinks of things to say hours after I should have said them. So, when the other two panel members start putting out their books and promotional materials, I should have taken their cue and put mine out. But I don't. I put everything under my seat. I mean, who knows when I might need them, when I might want to hold a book up and say this and that about it. So, under the seat it all goes, and for me that usually means "out of sight, out of mind." And that's exactly what happens: I forget to hold up any of my books or accompanying materials.

There are two other types of people in the world: those who talk and those who don't. I fall into both groups. In most social settings, I'm usually a very social, even gregarious person; I have no problem taking center stage. I'm a natural storyteller; and jokes: they regularly roll off the tongue. My wife says I should have been a late-night TV host or the ringmaster of a traveling circus. But, then, there are times when I clam up and can't utter a single word. That's usually when I'm in the company of strangers and someone else has already taken center stage.

That's precisely what happens during the panel presentation. It's a free-for-all (the moderator obviously hasn't read *Robert's Rules of Order* or any other manual for panel moderation). For most of the 45-minute session the two other panel members engage in a verbal tennis match about their self-publishing experience that leaves me mute at the end of the table, mute, that is, until the conversation turns to how you distribute your self-published book. When the person next to me—a former local TV personality—replies, "I can't tell you. It's a secret," I explode: "What do you mean you can't tell us? Isn't that why we're here, to share our experiences, to help others understand the self-publishing world (namely, the audience members who've paid good money to be here)?"

Either I blanked out or the session ended abruptly, I don't remember which: I just remember I left the session fuming. It would have been a good time to observe Exercise Rule #39. The long walk to my car would have done me good and the ride home would have been a lot calmer.

I KNEW IT WOULD arrive—my SCBWI membership renewal reminder. It's been on my desk for several weeks. I just can't seem to open it. Two years ago I faced the same thing when I was mad about the SCBWI's PAL policy. But after I won the Spark Award, I bit the bullet and paid my dues. But this year, I don't know. I just don't know. I'm going to have to think about it some more before I pull the trigger.

22 | UpublishU

I'VE BEEN TO A lot of conferences in my time, most of them sponsored by a professional organization that is known primarily by its acronym: ChLA, IBBY, ALA, NCTE, IRA, to name a few. As my writing career shadowed my academic career, I looked for conferences that addressed literacy, reading instruction, and children's books, primarily focused on the primary and upper elementary grade levels. It's the old "two birds with one stone" approach: the conferences stimulated both my academic interests while they satisfied—even inspired—my creative writing endeavors.

But first, let's get our bearings and dissect the alphabet soup of acronyms that represent several professional organizations:

ChLA. The Children's Literature Association is perhaps the premiere meeting place for children's literature academic types, who gather once a year to enjoy—perhaps a little over stated here—listening to each other read professional papers, often about things most consumers of children's literature—and even some academics—find difficult to understand. True to their mission, the ChLA is an association of "scholars, critics, professors, students, librarians, teachers, and institutions dedicated to the academic study of literature for children."

IBBY. Although similar to the Children's Literature Association, the International Board for Books for Young People is much more international in scope. ChLA is international to the extent that it emphasizes the English-speaking world of children's books and their creators, which means American, Canadian, British, and Australian authors and illustrators. My only gripe with IBBY is that the acronym should really read IBBYP (but IBBY is so catchy, and in the world of children's literature "catchy" is everything).

ALA. Although I joined the American Library Association for only a smidgeon of time, I have attended many of their regional and national conferences, especially when they are held in Chicago, the organization's home base. If you want to hobnob with the second line of gatekeepers of children's books (the first line of gatekeepers is, of course, editors who buy authors' manuscripts in the first place), then the ALA is for you. Among the many services the ALA renders, its sponsorship of the two most prestigious children's books' awards in the business—the Caldecott Award for illustration and the Newbery Award for writing—is perhaps the most well-known and coveted.

NCTE. If you teach English at the junior high, high school, or college level, you probably belong to the National Council of Teachers of English. I didn't fully understand this when I joined in the mid-1980s. I saw "children's books" and thought: "This is the place for me." And it was for a time until I realized that a better place for me was the International Reading Association. I stuck it out several years more than I should have only because the NCTE sponsors the absolute best Saturday Night Sock Hop on the planet (that is, the planet populated by erudite, button-downed English teachers who, by the way, love to gin it up and dance).

IRA. You would think that if you dropped "IRA" into an Internet search engine you would get the International Reading Association, but you don't: you get an awful lot of advertisements from investment companies wanting to invest your hard-earned dollars in their individual retirement account (a.k.a. IRA). Maybe that's why the IRA recently changed its name to the ILA or International Literacy Association. In any case, of all the professional organizations that address reading instruction, literacy, and the use of children's books in the classroom, the ILA is by far the most well-known and generally best organized. I joined not only because of their national presence, but also because the Illinois chapter of the ILA is one of the most proactive state affiliates integrating children's literature and its creators into its annual state conference program.

Now that we have our bearings I'd like to announce that today, twenty-five years after the publication of my first book, I no longer belong to any of them. I belong to the SCBWI and the IBPA—the former only thinly (the membership renewal form still sits on my desk unopened); the latter as a full-fledged, participating member. The SCBWI you know: in an earlier writing I told you about the feud I had with them over their PAL membership policy. Although I still think the SCBWI is head-and-shoulders above any other professional organization dealing with all things children's literature, I don't think it's for me. After a membership of thirty-three years, I believe my affiliation with the SCBWI is coming to an end (and probably will soon if I don't respond to the latest membership renewal reminder).

I'm much more interested in the IBPA, which is to an independently published author what the SCBWI is to a traditionally published children's book author. The IBPA offers more resources and services to the independently published author than any other extant professional organization. And I try to take advantage of all its offerings: I get its newsletter, listen to its podcasts, attend its online seminars, bookmark its diverse resources, submit my books to its annual book awards, and attend its annual national conference. And, most recently, I signed up for (read that: purchased) shelf space at the IBPA booth at BookExpo America (BEA) in order to display—prominently, I hope—my latest book, *Shark Man*.

Shark Man at BEA—now I'm really psyched. Psyched because with my IBPA membership and recently purchased shelf space I can attend the convention for free. *Free*—now that's something, especially because the convention is in Chicago this year at spacious McCormick Place, which means I can ride my bicycle. That's no small feat, mind you. It's quite a ways: eight miles one way through the heart of Chicago, and through some pretty rough neighborhoods. At least they were rough, but thanks to the work of Mayor Richard M. Daley the entire south loop area has been cleaned up ("white-washed," if you will).

Advertised as "the largest publishing event in North America," BEA is an independently published author's dream come true: rows and rows of publishers, large and small, traditional and non-traditional; acres of recently published books on display; tons of start-up companies that service the self-publishing world; podiums teeming with informed and energized speakers; and an exhibition area the size of Chicago's O'Hare airport. It's incredibly immense, overwhelming; but I'm going. I want to learn all about cutting-edge technologies in the world of producing, distributing, promoting, and selling my independently published books. So, I'm pouring over BEA's workshop and speaker schedule and I'm jacked. Here's a taste:

The New Digital Audio Landscape
The Future of Retailing in a Just-in-time Marketplace
Self-Publishing and Print-on-Demand
FaceBook 201: Advanced Book Marketing to Drive Sales
Pay to Play for Publishers and Authors
How to Use Cover Design to Build Author Recognition
Understanding the Business Side of Self-Publishing

Essentials for Self-Publishing Authors: The Seven Must-Haves
Psst! The Library Is the Self-Published Author's Secret Weapon
Top 10 Trends Shaping the Future of Publishing

Before I sit in on any sessions, however, I mosey into the exhibition area. To get my bearings I stop at the information booth directly in front of me. Two young Asian women smile at me as I approach. I smile back. They say hello. I return their greetings and start in with my questions, the first being: "Can you tell me where I might find the UpublishU stage?" Yes, that's right, *UpublishU*. If BEA, indeed the entire publishing industry, needed a sound bite to define the future direction of publishing, *UpublishU* is it. I don't think there is a better slogan in the post-millennial, DIY publishing world than YOU PUBLISH YOU.

But back to the two very nice Asian women, who are now giggling after I inquire about the location of the UpublishU stage. It turns out that their booth is the information booth for several Chinese publishers directly behind them, not the information booth for BEA. They know nothing about UpublishU (and why should they: Chinese publishers are more interested in WE PUBLISH YOU, whether or not you've actually asked them to).

I move on and inadvertently stumble upon the IBPA booth where I feverishly start to look for *Shark Man*. That's right, I dipped into my marketing budge and paid to have a copy face-out on the IBPA booth shelves.

Let's see, it's got to be here. Not there. Not there. Yes, here it is—far right, bottom shelf. Hmmm.

I quickly put on my this-is-my-book-and-it-should-be-front-and-center hat, check to see if anyone is looking, snatch *Shark Man* off the bottom shelf, and reposition it front-and-center on the top shelf. I'm sure I'm not the first author—self-published or otherwise—to do this.

There, that's better, I sigh, before sauntering off.

I crane my neck to the left and right, trying to read the signs hovering over nearby booths. I have a one o'clock appointment at Ingram and it's twelve fifty-two, so I need to hurry. There it is, three aisles over: a very large blue-and-white sign sporting the Ingram logo. I arrive at the "booth" (really a field of booths strung together) and ask where I should go for my appointment. I'm directed to a small table and told that "Seth" will join me in a moment. I sit down and, as I review the questions that I jotted down for the Ingram rep, a well-groomed young man sits down opposite me.

Seth: "Hi, my name is Seth. What can I do for you?"

Me [pulling out books from my backpack]: "I have a question about the print quality of some of my Ingram titles."

Seth: "Anything in particular?"

Me [placing two copies of *Shark Man* on the table]: "Well, yes, look at the difference between the quality of printing between these two books. [I open each book to the same page and point to the header] Do you see how uneven the header is in the Ingram book?"

Seth: "Hmm, yes, there does seem to be an issue here."

Me: "Maybe you can tell me…"

Seth [interrupting me mid-sentence, turns to someone walking by]: "John, I need your help. This looks like an issue for pre-media."

John [taking the empty chair and extending his hand to me]: "Hello, my name is John…"

It turns out that John is the director of pre-media for Ingram. He just happened to be walking by our table when I posed my concern about print quality to Seth. I was impressed that Seth quickly recognized that he needed help answering my question and flagged John so quickly. John joined us at the table, looked at the two copies of *Shark Man*, and said that more than likely this was an anomaly, and that I should call Ingram's customer service and order two free proof copies. Then he scribbled his name and extension on a piece of paper, stood up, and said, "If you have any problems, give me a call." Now that's the kind of service I want from a service provider.

23 | Game-changer

I LEFT MCCORMICK PLACE floating on cloud nine. The entire atmosphere of BEA was exhilarating. I filled an entire spiral notebook with ideas, contacts, and resources. I felt inspired, re-energized, and once again ready to dive into the self-publishing world—until I returned home and to the tedium that awaited me.

Like any artistic adventure, the tedium of making things far outweighs the glitz of their success (if, indeed, there is any success). And, so, returning home I put aside my notebook of ideas and took up the mundane task of repricing some of my books. It wasn't something that I wanted to do, but several months after their publication I realized that I had overpriced them relative to books similar in content, length, and format. It's all a mystery to me. I swear I spent several hours (okay, minutes) analyzing the prices of comparable books. I was certain that the price I slapped on the back cover was in the ballpark. (At large established publishing houses they have multiple committees that do this work: I guess redundancy has its place.) But, then again, it is just me: it's me writing the book; it's me editing the book; it's me designing the book; it's me producing the book; it's me promoting the book; it's me selling the book. And why not, as my wife is constantly reminding me, "It's *always* about you." So, why shouldn't

I make these decisions? I mean, after all, it *is* only me. But there's a built-in narrow-mindedness (read that: narcissism) in such a point of view. But publishers—traditional and non-traditional—have budgets to consider; so I make choices about what I can afford to farm out and what I can't. If I have to hire someone to determine the price of my books then I know I'm in trouble, so I do it myself. And that's why I'm sitting here in a snit trying to adjust the price of several books since it appears that I originally overpriced them. Of course, I could be patient and just wait: as everyone knows, most retailers discount—or return—their inventory over time. Unfortunately, I'm not the patient type, so I spend most of the afternoon and the next day creating a grid to help me compare and then calculate a new price for each one of my books. I'd love to spend more time on this wonderfully tedious job, but it's time to move on to Aer.io.

I learned about Aer.io at BEA, quite by accident, just kind of stumbled into it. After my half hour appointment with Seth (you remember Seth: he and John, Ingram's director of pre-media, helped me with a quality issue), I sat in on a session just down the aisle from my appointment. It was about a new and revolutionary digital product, Aer.io. The name itself caught my attention, so I sat down in one of the handful of folding chairs and listened to the presenter (who, it turns out, works for Ingram, which, coincidentally, publishes and distributes my self-published work).

What is Aer.io? It's probably one of the greatest game-changers in the publishing industry since the rise of digital self-publishing a decade or two ago. What Aer.io allows you to do is to create a website to sell your self-published books along with any other book in the Ingram catalog. Of course, Aer.io wouldn't survive if it only serviced self-published authors. According to Ingram, Aer.io is "a service that allows publishers, retailers and authors to sell and fulfill print and digital books directly to readers via their websites, blogs, and social networks." That's a nice statement, but somewhat generic. So, let's look under the hood a tad longer.

San Francisco-based Invention Arts designed Aer.io (originally called Aerbook) several years ago to support the development of a diverse and decentralized publishing marketplace. The goal was to make a multifaceted marketing and commerce service that had the power to make any Internet-based point of presence into a dynamic point of sale. Using Aer.io, a host of entities—authors, publishers, self-publishers, retailers, media companies, and even individuals—could easily "curate" a product line that could be made available on any website or social media outlet. Talk about the leveling of the traditional hierarchical publishing world, Aer.io just might be the sledgehammer that flattens it completely (well, not completely, but at least more than it is now).

The introduction of Aer.io really begs the question of where we are in the self-publishing revolution. As I see it, we've gone through at least three distinct phases:

When the major pieces of the self-publishing world fell into place (production, promotion, and distribution), both unpublished and traditionally published authors decided to jump on board. Overnight, we became non-traditional, self-published authors (who, by the way, make up the majority of published authors today).

However, in doing so, we quickly realized that we could not just be an independent author; we also had to act and think like a publisher. We needed to—indeed, were forced to—understand and operate a variety of industry mechanisms, including designing a book from the ground up, filing for copyright, securing ISBN and LCCN numbers, creating a barcode, writing front, back, and flap matter, and creating, managing and updating a marketing/

distribution website (not to mention a variety of other social media platforms).

Enter Aer.io, and again, almost overnight, we've morphed into something else: now, along with being an independent, self-published author/publisher, we are also independent booksellers, selling our books and the books of others. Oh, yes, this is a game-changer. Now, all published authors (and bloggers, and online booksellers, and boutique retailers, and flower shop owners, and shoe repairmen) not only can sell their own books, but they can also sell the books of other authors *and* make a profit doing so.

That's the radical game-changing element. In the business world we call Aer.io a disruptive technology. So, listen up all you independent, brick-and-mortar *and* online booksellers: you have competition and it's not Amazon (although it's still the bane of your existence). It's everyone with an online presence. That's right, you don't even have to be a self-published author: you only have to have an online presence and you can start selling books from the Ingram catalog. So, let's say you sell gummy bears online; I mean, that's your specialty. You've cornered the market on gummy bears—every shape, color, and flavor. Well, don't just sell the little chewy critters; sell books *about* gummy bears, and chewing gum, and stuffed animals (and whatever else you'd like), and double your income overnight.

Yes, Ae.io is a game-changer!

Recognizing this, I signed up for an Aer.io account as soon as I could. The first thing I did was to put up two of my baseball books: *The Men Who Made the Yankees* and *Dear Frank: Babe Ruth, the Red Sox, and the Great War*. Then I combed through the 10 million books, Blu-Rays, music CDs, audiobooks, graphic novels, and novelty gifts (this is no exaggeration; it's right there on Ingram's website), to find a dozen books to go with each title. And *voila!* I had an Aer.io bookstore embedded in my Gyroscope Books website ready for business. That was three months ago: so far, no sales—so much for disruptive technologies.

But I'm no quitter (neither is Ingram or Aer.io). I've been around long enough to know that you have to stay flexible. You have to do a variety of things to get your business off the ground (maybe that's why I was drawn to Aer.io in the first place: it has that "off the ground" kind of feel to it). So, I put my head down and soldiered on, on to the next item on my task list: adding purchasing links to IndieBound.

IndieBound, for all you diehard independent bookstore supporters, is for people who absolutely refuse to buy a book from anyone other than their neighborhood brick-and-mortar bookstore (an extension of the current "buy local" trend, I suppose). So, now you can—through IndieBound, which will gladly direct you to your local bookstore.

IndieBound. It's a catchy name. Go to its website and you'll find links to all things "Indie": *Indie First, Indie Bestsellers*, and *Indie Next List.*

Indie? Indie? Indie? Isn't that what I am—an independent or Indie author? So, how is the term "Indie" used on this website? Let's take a look at one of the Indie links and find out. I click on the *Indie Bestseller* list and then on the first link in the dropdown menu—hardcover fiction. Here are several titles from that list:

Colson Whitehead's *The Underground Railroad* (Doubleday)
Carl Haissen's *Razor Girl* (Knopf)
Jonathan Safran Foer's *Here I Am* (Farrar, Straus and Giroux)
Emily Cline's *The Girls* (Random House)
Amor Towles' *A Gentleman in Moscow* (Viking)

Two things jump out at me. First of all, we're not talking independent or self-published authors. With names like Carl Haissen and Emily Cline, we're definitely not talking self-published authors; we're talking marquee authors. The second thing that strikes me is the list of publishers: Doubleday, Knopf, Farrar, Straus and Giroux, Random House, and Viking. These are not the monikers of independent self-published authors; they're not even the names of small independent or university presses. These are the biggest names in the business—the business of traditional publishing, that is. To double-check my findings, I go back to IndieBound's home page and click on *Indie Next List*. Guess what I find? Ann Pachett's new novel *Commonwealth*, published by Harper.

This confirms it. For the folks at IndieBound, the term "Indie" refers to the world of locally owned "independent" bookstores and not self-published "Indie" authors. It's all there on their website under FAQs: "A product of ongoing collaborations between the independent bookstore members of the American Booksellers Association, IndieBound is all about independent bookstores and the power of 'local first' shopping."

But the term "Indie" refers to other entities as well; just ask Robert Gray, industry critic and blogger, who raises all sorts of questions about the nature of books, authors, and publishing, especially what it means to be an independent publisher. According to Gray, an independent publisher can be a self-publisher, an author/publisher, a do-it-yourself publisher, or a traditional publisher. An independent publisher can be brand new or in business for decades and can have one title or 10,000 titles. An independent publisher can work from home or from a high-rise office building and can have anywhere from one to 500 employees.

Yes, an independent author/publisher (for that's what he is really talking about) can be anyone or anything. And that thought leads Gray to observe that maybe we've come to a point where we should relook at the terminology we apply to authors, publishers, booksellers, and the like. I agree with Gray's conclusion, but who has the time? I have to stay focused on writing, editing, producing, marketing, and selling my independently published titles. I really don't have time to fuss around with the meaning of words.

THE OTHER DAY I was standing in line to get my morning cup of Joe at a local coffeehouse when I overheard a conversation between the barista and the first person in line. They were parsing the various meanings of the word "pretentious." They must have spent five minutes arguing back and forth about its various meanings and usage. I couldn't help myself. I interrupted their heated conversation (heated because it seemed they were more interested in each other than in the finer points of word usage). "Excuse me," I said, somewhat exasperated, "but you must *not* be writers." "What?" they turned toward me in unison. "Yes, a writer is more interested in the sound of words rather than their meanings." At this they scoffed and turned back to their conversation.

But the more I think about it, the more it makes sense. When I write I'm not thinking about the meaning of words and their proper usage (I don't have to, or, at least, I shouldn't have to; if I did, I shouldn't be writing at all). So, what do I do when I write? I sing, of course. Yes, I sing—to myself, to my wife, to our cat, but primarily to my readers. Maybe that's why I love to write, because I've always loved to sing.

24 | Palimpsest

IT'S A FEW WEEKS after BEA and I'm reviewing my notes. One of the things that I heard repeatedly from speakers is how important it is to update your website on a regular basis. Sure, of course. Everyone knows this. But the reason is more than just to make your site current. It turns out that every change you make boosts—or hinders—client searches for your site. Okay, well, not every change. Small content changes don't impact your SEO—your Site Engine Optimization.

Site Engine Optimization. Everyone knows this. Actually, I only learned of it when I Googled "How do changes to your website impact client searches?" (Funny how brand names quickly become verbs, e.g., "I think I'll Xerox this piece of paper later today.") Anyway, no need to worry about changing website content, or links to external websites, or internal keyword usage, at least so say the people at TopRank Marketing Blog. According to them ("them" being Lee Odden), you only need to worry when you change the following: domain name, content management systems, overall website design, and/or your website host. That's when you really need to pay attention (and probably hire an SEO expert). But I'm not doing that: I'm just making a few content changes, so I have nothing to worry about (I think).

Right now, I'm working on my "What's New?" page. After adding a note about the several books I repriced and inserting a description and link to my new Aer.io bookstore, I decided to change something else. I moved a note about the reformatting of *Dear Frank: Babe Ruth, the Red Sox, and the Great War* to the book's product page. Earlier this year I worked with a graphic designer to overhaul the look of the book. Since it's written in an epistolary fashion I thought that each entry should actually look like a letter. So, I did just that: not only did the graphic designer reformat each entry to look like a letter, but he also chose a handwriting script invented in the early 20th century that goes perfectly with the setting of *Dear Frank*, a work of historical fiction set in Boston in 1918 when Babe Ruth pitched for the Red Sox. Along with a note about these changes, I also posted an example from the interior of the book to give the reader an idea of the new interior look.

AS I PONDER OTHER changes to my website, my eye catches a pile of mail sitting on my desk. I take a moment and breeze through it, looking for anything of importance. A few of the letters immediately catch my attention: they're addressed to Gyroscope Books with a return address from one of several Eastern European countries—namely Poland, Slovakia, and the Czech Republic. Curious, I rip them open and find inside a form letter congratulating me on my successful trademark registration and inviting me—for a nominal amount, anywhere between $1,500 and $2,350—to register my trademark name in their international trademark registry.

Welcome to the world of global commerce.

I shred them and reach for another pile of mail. The first letter I encounter is from a Chicago law firm. Now that piques my interest because it's the same law firm that's handling my trademark application case pro bono. I open the letter to find several documents enclosed, the first being a letter from my contact at the law firm.

> Dear Mr. Nikola-Lisa: Here is your official certificate of registration for your trademark, Gyroscope Books. As you will see, there are additional required documents you must file in order to maintain your trademark. These documents are described on the reverse side of your certificate. These documents...*yawn*...must be filed at certain times...*yawn*... also described on the...*yawn*...certificate. Though the scope of our attorney-client agreement does not...*yawn*... *yawn*...*yawn*...

It is, of course, a bit of legalese, interesting to the extent that it confirms what I've been waiting for: the successful resolution of the trademark application process. I'm elated (and will deal with the ancillary paperwork later). More than that, I'm relieved.

I began the trademark application process several months ago with a brief email to the Chicago-based Lawyers for the Creative Arts. The group's aim is to help artists navigate the legal world of creative production. They sent my request out on the airwaves, hoping a junior partner at a law firm would take up my case pro bono. Several weeks later I received an email from Bryan Munster, who works for a large Chicago law firm. After several email exchanges, Bryan agreed to help me file all of the necessary paperwork for my trademark application. We did and then it became a waiting game as the application worked its way through the various stages of the process, the last being a month-long wait to see if anyone contested my chosen trademark—Gyroscope Books.

Gyroscope Books? Yes, I thought you might be wondering how I came up with that name. Well, it wasn't easy. First of all, I made a list of all the possible trademark names that I thought adequately captured my self-publishing interests. The final name that I adopted would ultimately become my brand, visible on my website and email address, as well as various and sundry social media accounts. In a nutshell, it would be *me* (or my publishing interests) boiled down to a "swish" or some other recognizable logo or brand name.

The list I generated was quite long and it took me nearly an entire week to vet each name. Some, which I thought very original, turned out—surprisingly—to be the name of an already established brand. Take *Square Fish*, for example. Now that's original. Who on earth would think of that name? Not only that, but I liked it. It was fresh, original, and a bit mysterious. Yes, that said it all; that most certainly was me—fresh, original, and mysterious. And I would have used it, except for the fact that the first item my Google search turned up was Square Fish Books, "a children's book imprint representing the best of Farrar, Straus and Giroux, Henry Holt, and Roaring Brook backlists, but reformatted, repackaged, and reissued with a mass market children's and teen audience in mind."

Unbelievable. Not only was Square Fish a registered trademark, but it was also the name of a major publisher's imprint. Definitely not me, unless I wanted to shell out several grand for the right to use it, which I doubt the publisher would grant. But how did I come up with it in the first place? More than likely, I came upon the name of the imprint at a national literacy conference, or stumbled upon it in some professional trade journal. In any case, I came upon it, filed it in the back of my mind, and then forgot about it—until I needed a unique trademark name. Then I dug into my subconscious, pulled out Square Fish, and, not recognizing it, deemed it mine, uniquely mine. But it wasn't mine, just as Carl Sandburg's first line of his poem "Fog" wasn't mine.

Sandburg? Fog? What are you talking about?

Before I explain the Sandburg reference, let me say a few words about plagiarism. In school we learn that plagiarism occurs when a writer knowingly uses someone else's writing and calls it his or her own. Most people understand this kind of plagiarism and know that's it's wrong. But there's another type of plagiarism, one less talked about. Mark Twain, the great American storyteller and humorist, called it "unconscious plagiarism." That's when a writer unknowingly uses the forms, structures, intonations, and phrasings of another writer in the creation of a piece of writing and calls it his or her own. However, Twain's position toward plagiarism is ambivalent at best. In one breath he states: "Nothing is ours but our language, our phrasing. If a man takes that from me (knowingly, purposely) he is a thief." Then, in the very next breath, he utters: "If he takes it unconsciously—snaking it out of some old secluded corner of his memory, and mistaking it for a new birth instead of a mummy—he is no thief, and no man has a case against him." Obviously, Twain stole a few lines from others as well—unwittingly, of course. In my case, it was an unconscious act, inexcusable and indefensible. Sadly, it took an editor at a major publishing house to point this out.

I'm sorry, but I'm really not following you here.

Okay, let's rewind the tape. It's the mid-1980s. I'm a greenhorn, a novice, and I've written a picture book text (somewhat in the vein of Jane Yolen's *Owl Moon*) that I'm really excited about. *Night Is Coming* captures the mood of sunset coming to a farm. It's a peaceful, idyllic piece, and I'm convinced that it will make a great bedtime story. At least I think it will. I also think it's ready to send to an editor. So I do, with these opening lines:

Night is coming.
Crawling in on little cat feet.
Edging over hill.
Creeping through forest.
Stealing its way in.

Now, thirty or more years later, I laugh when I read these lines. Of course they never got published, *because they already were*—in Carl Sandburg's poem "Fog." Without realizing it, I had borrowed—a generous term—the central image of Sandburg's famous poem. I probably read the poem when I was in eighth grade, came across it here or there over the years, and—like Square Fish—forgot about it, until I was searching for an appropriate image to open my picture book story.

It's a clear case of Twain's unconscious plagiarism. But a good editor can get an author to realize his or her sources, and to go beyond them when necessary. That's what my editor did (after she scolded me for not being more prescient). She kept prodding me, pushing me, questioning me: *What are you trying to say? Who is the narrator? Where are your images coming from?*

Her constant prodding finally unlocked the door to my childhood. As it opened, memories of growing up in Texas flooded my mind. And it was those memories ultimately, not Sandburg's poem or any other literary source, that formed the basis for my revised—and subsequently published—text:

Night is coming,
and out of the rustle
of Grandpa's wheat,
you can hear the whippoorwill's
hollow song arising.

Out in the fields you can smell wild clover
mixing with the scent of freshly mown hay.

And if you stay very still
and squint way up high,
beneath the straying clouds
you'll catch the glimmer
of a red-tailed hawk
endlessly circling.

It's one thing to appropriate the work of other writers unconsciously; it's another to use other writers' work as a springboard for new ideas. Authors do this all the time—so do I. For instance, *No Babies Asleep* is based on the popular song "99 Bottles of Beer on the Wall." *Summer Sun Risin'* mimics the syntax of Eve Merriam's rhythmic story *Train Leaves the Station*. And, as I mentioned earlier, *To Hear the Angels Sing* is best sung to the tune "Mary Had a Little Lamb" (unless your song repertoire is limited and you think it's "This Is the Way We Wash Our Clothes").

Medieval literature has an appropriate term that we can apply here—*palimpsest.* A palimpsest is a manuscript that has been written over a partly erased older manuscript in such a way that the original words can still be read (especially if the medium is parchment and the ink has soaked into it).

We are all palimpsests of sorts: all of us carry around layers of writing, a multitude of voices, many of which are not our own. The task of a writer is to break through these culturally embedded recordings in order to find his or her own unique voice. Ultimately, that's what makes writing satisfying, what moves us: in short, *what incites us to sing!*

Part III

Today I've been thinking about what Roger Kahn calls "the boys of summer." Yes, I'm thinking about major league baseball. I'm thinking about it because we're in the doldrums, the dog days of summer. It's August and it's hot. And our attention is elsewhere—on a much-needed vacation, the Summer Olympics in Rio, the bruising sparring match between Democrats and Republicans (well, at least some of us are still paying attention to that).

25 | Midsummer Night's Dream

I'M FREEZING. GOD, AM I freezing and it's the beginning of May. It's the beginning of May and I'm setting up for the Chicago Waldorf School's annual May Celebration and Book Fair. It's the first time that I've participated in this event. I thought since it's local that it would be a good thing to do. And, besides, I'm into Rudolf Steiner—or was.

When I started teaching at the World Family School, the alternative school that was tucked away in the attic of a house on a backstreet in Bozeman, Montana, I was reading all things Steiner. I like to think that I brought Rudolf Steiner to Montana. None of my friends had ever heard of him. And the woman who ran the school, she'd never heard of him either—and she'd married an Austrian and had traveled all over Europe. But Steiner is definitely not part of the mainstream. Why he's even more radical than the pipe-smoking Scottish educator A. S. Neill, who founded the ultra-progressive school Summerhill in the 1930s. Where Neill is laissez-faire to the extreme, Steiner is strict and regimented, but not in a militaristic manner. No, Steiner is strict because of his adherence to the spiritual vision that informed him throughout his life. In this sense, then, the two are quite alike: both dogmatic to the nth degree about their views of children and education.

Although I respond to Neill's non-coercive educational theory, it is Steiner's unique, even cultish, views on child development and education that attract me. I bought every book that he wrote on the subject. I bought them as much for the content as I did for their physical presence. The covers were always the same: an exotic text, often handwritten, floating on top of a solid background color. Take *The Education of the Child in the Light of Anthroposophy*. Floating on a background of solid midnight blue is a rather delicate pink script that announces the title of the book and its author. Or, take *The Child's Changing Consciousness as the Basis of Pedagogical Practice*, where maroon and pale blue fonts alternately float upon a sea of deep pink. There is something always very dramatic about the physical presence of a Steiner book. You know you're holding something special—even otherworldly.

Even though I use the word "otherworldly" to describe Steiner's ideas about life and the spiritual world around us, I wouldn't necessarily use it to describe his educational ideas. The word "commonsense" comes more to mind. Here are three of his deepest-held beliefs:

Educate the whole child. Above everything else, Steiner believed in the education of the whole child, which the Waldorf School's motto—*Head, Hands, and Heart*—connotes. To educate the whole child, you have to look at each child as an individual in a non-competitive, open (but not laissez-faire) environment. To Steiner, this meant no classification of students into intellectual levels, no class lists, no examinations, no honors or advanced classes, no report cards, and no compulsory homework.

Respect the developmental process. In order to educate the whole child, one has to respect the child and the child's developmental process, which means that the Waldorf School curriculum responds to the child, not vice versa. Unlike the Swiss psychologist Jean Piaget, who used discrete tools to measure a child's development, Steiner believed that the best way to understand a child's development is through observation over a long period of time and this is why one teacher takes a group of students successively through the first eight years of school. The teacher becomes more than an observer however; she becomes an important authority figure—a surrogate parent if you will.

Nurture the imagination. In Waldorf education the imagination is everything, and what better way to nurture the imagination than through story. Folk and fairy tales, myths, fables and legends—all of these forms of story are integrated throughout the Waldorf curriculum. Each story form has a lesson or teaching embedded in it, though not necessarily a moral. Often they are paired: whereas folk tales teach us about the life of peasants, fairy tales teach us about the life of the aristocracy; while fables teach us about human foibles, legends teach us about extraordinary feats of heroism. The Waldorf curriculum is always about balance, for that is the only way to teach the whole child.

And that's what I'm doing right now—*balancing*—because I'm teetering on my tiptoes trying to help the vendor next to me set up his clothes rack (for the third time) after the wind blew it down. He's from Nigeria and has only been in Chicago a few months. You can tell because he's definitely not ready for a blustery day in early May that Chicago can readily produce. I thought I was cold, when I look at him I notice that he's wearing a pair of summer slacks, a short-sleeve shirt, and a pair of leather sandals. Definitely not the kind of apparel you'd want to wear on a chilly day in May.

We finally get his clothes rack set up. I even encourage him to put on a few extra pieces of apparel from the rack. As he does, people begin to arrive for the fair. Since the fair is held in Rogers Park on Chicago's north side, I expect to see a very diverse population. But the people streaming into the fair look more like Ken

Kesey's Merry Pranksters than families from Rogers Park. There's lots of tie-dye t-shirts, braided hair adorned with tufts of dandelion flowers, loose-fitting leather sandals, and hand-woven woolen hats. It's an eclectic bunch, mostly young, I'd say high school age or younger, with the occasional parent escort. And they're all here to celebrate May Day with a May Pole dance. I mean, who besides the Soviets celebrates May Day?

Folks at the Waldorf School do and I'm glad they do because even though it's a biting 45 degrees out and I haven't sold a single book, boys and girls, moms and dads, and even a few teachers are prancing around a large May Pole in a scene reminiscent of Shakespeare's *A Midsummer Night's Dream.*

26 | Brilliant

I SPENT THE MORNING measuring the trim size of 40–50 books. Why? As an independent author that uses print-on-demand publishers, it's best if I conform to their "standard" trim sizes. Of course, "best," like beauty, is in the eye of the beholder. For print-on-demand, or POD, publishers, "best" really comes down to this: *Please use our standard trim sizes because it's easier for us to print your book* (because standard trim sizes are already programmed into their printers).

So for the better half of the morning I pull books off of my bookshelves and measure each one's trim size, comparing it to the publisher's trim size sheet, which is available on its website. This isn't the first time I've done this, but hopefully it will be the last. Not because I'm giving up being a self-published, independent author and going traditional; no, not at all. It's because not only have I written the trim size on the cover of each book, but I've also created a separate place on my bookshelves for them.

And what have I learned from this exercise? First of all, I learned that "trim size" is a term derived from offset printing when one of the last phases of book production involved "trimming" the edges of the book after the galley was folded and bound together. I also learned that calculating the trim size of a paperback is fairly easy, because it's WYSIWYG. Just measure the width and height of the cover (which should be flush with the leaves inside) and just like that you've got the trim size stated as width by height. For hardcovers—case laminate and cloth bound—it's a tad more involved: since the cover overhangs the leaves, you first have to open the cover and measure the page width and height to get the correct trim size, wedging your ruler deep into the spine to get to the page edge. It's usually not a big difference, but it is a difference nonetheless.

But what I really learned from this exercise is that "standard" is not so standard after all. Of the 40–50 books I measured, less than 20% fell into the "standard" category. In fact, it was quite frustrating trying to find a sample from my bookshelves for each of the standard trim sizes on the publisher's trim size sheet. The reason for this is that most of my books pre-date the print-on-demand revolution, which means that they reflect the older, more traditional world of offset printing. In that world, trim size could vary greatly, or, in just as many cases, ever so slightly. In other words, irregularity is the norm (everyone wants to stand out on the bookrack; a unique trim size is one way to do that), but not in the print-on-demand world. In this world standardization is the norm.

In the print-on-demand world, turn-around time is everything, and what best facilitates this goal—standard trim sizes. It's ironic that in the world of digital publishing choices are actually less than in the offset world of four-color printing. And it's not just turn-around time that dictates this; it's also volume. A POD publisher keeps its printers humming with new orders every day. That is, after all, the nature of print-on-demand: print it when it's ordered (and get it out the door in 24 hours or less).

But wait, we're not through. Standard trim sizes are dictated at the other end of the spectrum: by the bookseller. I learned this from

Joel Friedlander's post on *The Book Designer*. Friedlander admits that although there are very few rules concerning book sizes, there are a number of conventions that Indie writers should be aware of when it comes to marketing and selling books. He then parses out the various recommended trim sizes for the following books: mass market books, trade paperbacks, manuals and workbooks, novels, collections of short stories and essays, general nonfiction, and, rounding up the list, art and photography books.

It's all kind of mind-boggling, and really quite easy to get lost in the world of book production. Why am I thinking about all of this? Because I'm contemplating reformatting *Dragonfly: A Childhood Memoir*, one of the first books that I self-published. I published it after the market crash in 2008. No one was buying anything. Editors were turning well-established authors away. The publishing industry had ground to a halt. So, I thought: *What the heck? I'll do it myself.* And I did, publishing *Dragonfly* in 2010. But I was a greenhorn and made a few mistakes. The first mistake that I made was to buy the publisher's design package. Although the cover came out great, the interior was far less satisfying (awkward font style, inappropriate paragraph indentations, unappealing line spacing—and these were only a few of my complaints). So I rang up Tom, a friend of mine who's a very competent and creative graphic artist and scheduled an appointment with him.

I met Tom at his office on a warm day in early June. We sat around the office table, which was strewn with a variety of projects, including samples from Tom's growing collection of pre-WWII paper-engineering models. Tom pushed a few of the projects out of the way to make room for me. I reached into my backpack and took out a proof copy of the paperback edition of *Dragonfly*. Tom picked it up, leafed through it, grimaced, and asked, "Who did the interior design?" I shifted slightly in my seat, smiled faintly, then let loose with all of my complaints. Tom listened quietly, nodding his head in agreement here and there. When I finished, Tom leafed through the book one more time, looked up, and said, "Let me take a stab at it."

He did and soon I had a new edition of *Dragonfly*, which is a world better than the original edition. So why am I resizing the book? The reason has nothing to do with the cover design or Tom's new interior layout. It has to do with distribution. When I first started to self-publish, I thought I'd do a paperback and an author-only hardcover with CreateSpace and an e-book with Kindle Direct Publishing. Since CreateSpace and KDP are Amazon subsidiaries, I thought I had all the bases covered: I'd sell the e-book and paperback version online through Amazon's worldwide distribution system, and use the hardcover for direct sales at book signing events. I immediately encountered two stumbling blocks. First of all, publish with Amazon and that's the *only* place your books will appear, leaving non-Amazon buyers in the lurch (not to mention incurring the ire of independent bookstore owners). Secondly, after a couple of years of publishing author-only hardcovers, CreateSpace unexpectedly stopped: *Sorry authors, we're just not doing that anymore.* If those were the only roadblocks I encountered, I might have left everything alone. But there was one more thing nagging me: I made an editorial boo-boo. I mean, a big mistake. I used a song lyric without gaining permission to do so.

I didn't do it deliberately, nor was it a simple oversight. I did it because I cut my teeth in the professional world of higher education, which is governed by a fairly generous "fair-use policy." Discuss a song lyric or piece of poetry in your classroom, no problem. Publish an academic article using a song lyric or a line or two of poetry, still no problem (as long as you cite it in your references). But in the proprietary world of trade publishing—traditional and independent—that's a big no-no. A violation punishable by... Well, I don't think I'll go to jail, but it could cost me a pretty penny or two. Anyway, I used the first stanza and chorus of Johnny Cash's "Ring of Fire" in an early chapter of *Dragonfly*. Shocking, I know. Once I understood the ramifications of this, I decided to delete it from the paperback and e-book editions (it was a lot easier than trying to secure permission to use it; and anyway, time was of the essence). But I didn't delete the stanza from the hardcover edition, because there were none—CreateSpace had stopped publishing them—which left me with the question: *Do I just give up on the hardcover edition or do I go with another company?*

Enter Ingram.

The distribution question had nagged me from the start. In the back of my mind I kept wondering if publishing with Amazon was enough. *What about all those non-Amazon buyers?* It was a question that just wouldn't go away. So, early on, I decided to publish with Ingram as well. Publishing a paperback edition with CreateSpace and Ingram meant that both the Amazon and non-Amazon markets were covered. But that's the retail market. What about the institutional market—schools and libraries? For this market I'd need a hardcover edition, either case laminate or hardcover cloth. Schools and libraries want a book that will last; they want hardcover. So I started to publish paperback and hardcover editions of my books with Ingram, hoping this would satisfy my distribution needs.

And that's why, motivated by my editorial misstep, I'm in the middle of creating a hardcover edition of *Dragonfly* for Ingram. In order to create the hardcover edition I have to pick a standard trim size from Ingram's *File Creation Guide* since the original paperback trim size wasn't a standard size (why should it be; it wasn't an issue at CreateSpace). All of this explains why I spent the morning measuring the trim size of 40–50 books. You see, in order to pick a trim size for a book, I have to hold a surrogate—a physical book—in my hands. I have to turn it over, flip through its pages, study the spine, smell it, generally inspect it from one end to the other—all this in order to pick the perfect trim size. Of course, "perfect" in this case means picking a trim size that is listed in Ingram's "Trim Size Matrix," which you'll find at the end of their *File Creation Guide*.

SERENDIPITY STRIKES AT THE oddest times. Several months have gone by since I wrote the above reflection. I'm online tooling around, looking for articles to help me flesh out my *Dog Eared* marketing plan, and I happen to stumble upon a couple of articles about why you should use *both* CreateSpace and IngramSpark (a subsidiary of Ingram) for your self-publishing platform. The first article, by novelist Karen Myers, details how authors should use both of these publishing platforms, especially for their print or physical books. After outlining the various services that each publishing platform offers, Myers concludes that CreateSpace is perfect for the Amazon buyer, but not for the non-Amazon buyer (that's because your CreateSpace book will only show up on Amazon). That's why you need Ingram, for all of your non-Amazon book buyers. But there's more. When a bookstore orders your book, and it's only published through CreateSpace, it will show up in the Ingram database as "Publisher=CreateSpace" (even if the author obtained a unique ISBN number). Since many bookstore owners despise Amazon, this can be a problem as they might elect not to order your book. To avoid this, turn off your CreateSpace "expanded distribution" option, and then, after waiting several weeks to allow Amazon to pull the plug on its expanded distributors, produce the book through Ingram as well. Now when a bookstore orders your book from Ingram—along with Baker & Taylor, one of the largest book distributors in the world—they will see "Publisher=YourPublisherName" in the database (and not associate your book with CreateSpace, an Amazon affiliate).

The other article I found was an updated account of Amy Collins' post on *New Shelves*, her incredibly well-organized website that offers self-published authors information about the changing landscape of the DIY publishing world. The article, titled "Why You Need IngramSpark and CreateSpace–Updated," reinforces everything that Myers highlights in her post, and ends with this synopsis:

1. Use CreateSpace for Amazon. It does a great job and takes less money for each sale.
2. Use IngramSpark in addition so that your book can be ordered by the bookstores and libraries from the large wholesalers with which they prefer doing business.
3. Use your own (Bowker-provided) ISBN so that you have the benefits of your publishing company's brand on all databases.
4. Don't cheap out. IngramSpark and CreateSpace are two different tools for two different markets. If you don't want to be in the retail store and library market, then you don't need IngramSpark. But if stores and libraries are your goal, then spend the money to provide the books to them in the manner that gives them the best chance of saying "yes."

Good advice from both authors. I'd even say *brilliant*—because I figured it out all on my own (even though it did take a few years to do so).

27 | The Quintessential Quail

I DON'T KNOW WHY, but I woke up this morning thinking about a book. Not just any book, but Tolkein's *The Hobbit*. I have a copy in my office and I'm pretty sure I know just where it is. Right. Well, I do know that it's in my children's folk and fairytale collection, which includes some fantasy as well (the English are so good at that). *Let's see, where is it? Over there? No. There? No. No. Ah, there it is.*

I probably should fetch the kitchen ladder, but I'm not. I'm going to do what I usually do. I hop up on the seat of my office chair, step up onto the edge of my computer desk, stand on my tiptoes, and reach for a hardcover book in a dark green slipcase—J.R.R. Tolkien's *The Hobbit*. I bought a copy when my daughters were young, intending to read it to them when they were old enough to digest Tolkien's magical story. And I'm sure I did, along with Kenneth Grahame's *The Wind in the Willows*, Lewis Carroll's *Alice's Adventures in Wonderland*, E. B. White's *Charlotte's Web*, and every other classic of children's literature. Right now, however, I'm only interested in *The Hobbit*. I'm interested in it because I didn't buy just any edition; I bought a collector's edition published to celebrate the 50th anniversary of the book's release. Naturally, it's a beautiful book: lush green hardcover boards, gold embossed lettering, deckled paper edged with green marbling, hand-drawn maps, and illustrations by Tolkien himself, and all of it sliding neatly into a decorative hardcover slipcase. Yes, it's definitely a collector's item, even though it's not a first edition. I'm sure I'll pass it on to my daughter and her husband to read to their children—just not yet. I think I'll reread it before I do.

As I balance on the corner of my computer desk, thumbing through *The Hobbit*, I look up for a moment and realize that I still have to tackle the bookshelves from which I just plucked Tolkien's book. The bookshelves line the west wall of my office. Yes, I'm slowly making my way around my office bookshelves.

East wall? *Check.*

South wall? *Check.*

West wall? *In progress.*

In progress, yes, but the progress is mind-numbingly slow. This wall of books, however, should be a delight to handle as it contains most of my books related to children's literature. There are books on literary criticism, historical perspectives of children's literature, the production of children's books, especially picture books for young readers, essays and anthologies, several full-blown biographies important figures (i.e., Margaret Wise Brown, Maurice Sendak, Eric Carle, etc.), and an eclectic collection of books on myths, legends, folk and fairy tales, and fables. There are also several themed collections, namely alphabet books, children's poetry, and nursery rhymes. And they all have to be hauled down, culled through, dusted off, and then re-shelved. After re-shelving *The Hobbit*, I dive into the bookshelf that contains alphabet books, children's poetry, and nursery rhymes, and two other special collections: one on Little Red Riding Hood; the other on Noah's Ark.

To see me through the mindless task of pulling books down, cleaning the empty shelf, and then the books themselves, I put on a little music. Lately, I've been stuck on early Neil Young. So I boot up iTunes, search my playlists, and select *After the Gold Rush*, Young's third studio album. Since my wife's out for the afternoon, I crank up the volume and start hauling books down from their respective perch. As I said, it's a mindless job, a total no-brainer, so I start to sing along with Neil Young at the top of my lungs: *Down by the river. I shot my…*

But I hardly get the line out when my eye falls upon David Pelletier's *The Graphic Alphabet*. It's a gorgeous book. I remember buying it because it was not your usual alphabet book for kids. I take it down from its perch, lean against the edge of the desk, and start to thumb through the book. Pelletier is a graphic designer who lives and works in New York City. Children's books are not his bread and butter—commercial accounts are. But Pelletier has had a longstanding fascination with letterforms, especially in the relationship between image and meaning. In *The Graphic Alphabet*, Pelletier created images guided by a central concept: "the illustration of the letterform had to retain the natural shape of the letter as well as represent the meaning of the word." Guided by this principle, Pelletier has created a very engaging book. Here are a few of his images.

Avalanche. An oversized "A" floats on top of a solid black background. As it does, the thick backside of the letterform appears to be crumbling, giving the appearance of an avalanche rumbling down a mountainside.

Iceberg. Here, Pelletier tilts the letter "I" on its side, covering the bottom half with a sea of blue, while floating the angled top half of the letter and its "dot" in front of a pitch-black sky, creating the illusion of a full moon hovering above an iceberg on a cold arctic night.

Vampire. To imply the fangs of a vampire, Pelletier cuts two v-shaped wedges of white "teeth" into the top of a solid black block. That's it, nothing more. It's a stunningly simple and effective design.

Pelletier's book leads me to Paul Thurlby's alphabet book, eponymously titled *Paul Thurlby's Alphabet*. Whereas Pelletier's images are spare, even stark, Thurlby's are redolent with color, shape, and, just as often, implied movement. Let's compare Thurlby's letterform "B" with Pelletier's treatment of it. Although each artist chooses the same word—"bounce"—to illustrate, they execute their ideas in very different ways. In Pelletier's world, the letter 'B' is depicted as a series of midnight blue dots that bounce along on top of a solid background, "spelling out" the letter "B" as they do. In Thurlby's world, the letter "B" is somewhat static—it's a large blocky beige letter sitting on top of a vibrant red background. Movement is implied both by the word "bounce" written at the bottom of the page in a jaunty, animated manner and the multi-colored "balls" that make up the two circles or bulges in the letter "B" above it.

Let's compare one more letterform—the letter "X"—and its associated word. Both artists use the word "x-ray," which is not unusual in an alphabet book. Along with "xylophone," it's one of the more frequently used words you'll find. In Thurlby's world, a boy whose body forms a large "X" is depicted holding an x-ray over his midsection, which allows us to see into his abdomen (where we find it cluttered with letters of the alphabet, giving him an apparent bout of indigestion). Along with the predominant colors of red, black, and yellow, there are a lot of swirly lines implying movement, which is Thurlby's signature graphic element.

In Pelletier's world, the viewer is met with a solid block of blackness that contains the barely perceptible drawing of an x-rayed hand. Looking closer, we see that two of the fingers of the hand are crossed to form the letter "X." It's as subtle as it is engaging. Whereas Thurlby almost hits you over the head with streaking lines, bouncing dots, and bold patches of color, Pelletier gives you the minimum, just enough to get his point across.

Generally, alphabet books fall into three categories: books that teach young children letter recognition and simple vocabulary; books that use the serial nature of the alphabet as a springboard for an author's imagination; and books that showcase an illustrator's graphic talents. You'll find Pelletier and Thurlby's alphabet books in that latter pile. It's also the pile of books in which you'll find one of my all-time favorite alphabet books—Leonard Baskin's *Hosie's Alphabet*. To execute this book, Baskin, an accomplished printmaker, graphic artist, and illustrator, enlisted the help of his three children—Hosea, Tobias, and Lisa. While the three siblings offered up the text, Leonard, their talented father, crafted the images. Here's what *The University of Chicago Guide to Children's Books* had to say about the book: "Not since Milton Glaser's illustrations for Conrad Aiken's *Cats and Bats and Things with Wings* has there been such a display of virtuosity in a picture book. Leonard Baskin's range of techniques is as impressive as his pictures are dazzling."

Although Baskin's images are incredibly compelling (my favorites are his illustrations for "crow," "iguana," and "whale"), let's not forget about the text. It is as masterfully crafted as Leonard's imagery. Some examples:

The armadillo, belted & amazonian
The imperious eagle, spangled and splendid
A ghastly garrulous gargoyle
A quasi kiwi
The quintessential quail
The cadaver-haunted vulture

I imagine many a discussion at dinnertime over the wording of more than a few of these choice phrases. No matter their origin, or who had final say over them, the writing is as brilliant as the accompanying illustrations. Kudos to Leonard. Kudos to Hosea, Tobias, and Lisa.

ONCE AGAIN, I LET time slip away from me. Once again, I didn't get too far in my office-cleaning project, just one stretch of books and that's it. But not to worry: I'll get back to it tomorrow, or the next day, or the next. Right now, I have to get ready to go out; at least that's what my wife just reminded me of as she rushed past my office. No, it's not our anniversary, or my birthday (that's next week). It's the annual Harold Washington Literary Award Dinner. The gala is held the Thursday evening before the start of Chicago's Printers Row Lit Fest, by far the Midwest's largest and most prestigious book festival.

28 | Chattering Away

ONE OF THE PERKS of participating in the Near South Planning Board's Author-in-the-Schools program is that I get two complimentary tickets to the annual Harold Washington Literary Awards Dinner. I always go, and I always take my wife, who enjoys the event as much as I do. After all, it's not that often that we get to hobnob with Chicago's movers and shakers at The Union League Club of Chicago.

But we don't go for the company, or even the sumptuous dinner. We go to hear the recipient of the Harold Washington Literary Award speak. And we're not talking about little known, up-and-coming writers. We're talking about the best of the best, the crème-de-la-crème. Writers like Toni Morrison, Robert Pinsky, Margaret Atwood, Dave Eggers, Barbara Ehrenreich, and Sara Paretsky.

I remember when Ms. Paretsky won the award. The year was 2012. My wife and I attended that year along with our niece who had an interest in writing and had just finished her first year at Kenyon College. I remember the 2012 awards dinner for another reason: it was the year that the Near South Planning Board's Award Committee acknowledged former Chicago Mayor Richard M. Daley for his support of the arts during his twenty-two years in office. It's ironic that Mayor Daley received the Union League Club's acknowledgement at the annual Harold Washington Literary Award dinner. After all, it was Harold Washington who defeated Daley in the 1983 Democratic primary.

I met Mayor Daley once. Briefly. It was 1990. My wife and I had moved from Montana to Chicago several years earlier. Coming from the hinterlands, we were bug-eyed at everything around us; it was a far cry from rural Montana. (*You mean they actually drive the new cars you see advertised in magazines?*) And, yes, we wanted to take in as much as we could. So, in March of 1990, we went downtown to take in the annual St. Patrick's Day Parade. A big mistake. First of all, it was crowded, very crowded, near claustrophobic crowded. Secondly, I wasn't dressed for it: green just isn't one of the colors in my closet. And green was definitely the preferred, if not mandatory, color: there were green hats, green shirts, green pants, green shoes, green socks, even some hairy green chests and shiny green heads. And if that wasn't enough, the Chicago River was also green.

That's where I met Mayor Daley, on Michigan Avenue, near the bridge that spans the north branch of the Chicago River. I stepped around a barricade and inadvertently plowed into a small, stocky man—Mayor Richard M. Daley. He didn't smile; but he didn't frown either. An aide quickly stepped between the two of us, and in a flash he was gone.

When I saw him at the Harold Washington Literary Award dinner standing in a small art-filled room off to the side with one of his aides, I thought this was my chance, to remind him of our meeting, and to say some encouraging words to him (he had just lost his wife, Maggie, a true supporter of the arts). So I grabbed my niece's arm and said, "Let's go meet the Mayor." And we did, we walked right up to Mayor Daley. I introduced myself, and then my niece. It was cordial, and, like the barricade encounter, very brief. When we returned to my wife, who was not interested in meeting Mayor Daley, I told her of our encounter. She smiled.

Wife: "I see you talked to Mayor Daley."
Me: "Yes, you know he's a bit shorter than I thought."
Wife: "Oh, really. And what did you think of Sara Paretsky?"
Me: "Sara Paretsky?"
Wife: "Yes, who did you think was standing next to Mayor Daley?"
Me: "Wasn't…that…one of his aides?"
Wife: "No. *That* was Sara Paretsky, the person being honored tonight."
Me: "Yes, of course, Sara Paretsky."

I wish I had talked to Sara Paretsky because I love her work. My wife and I often listen to her books when we drive to my wife's parents' home in Cleveland. We like the crime books set in Chicago that feature V. I. Warshawski, Paretsky's fictional private investigator. It takes about six or seven hours to listen to an entire book, which is perfect for our drive to Cleveland. Sometimes, when the book is longer than our drive, we'll pull up at my in-laws' house and sit in the car until we finish the book (which is usually no more than half an hour or so). Sometimes, while we're listening, I'll gaze into the rear-view mirror and see my wife's parents peeping through the kitchen curtains, wondering why we're still in the car.

Tonight, we're not listening to Sara Paretsky. We're listening to Marilynne Robinson, the 2016 Harold Washington Literary Award recipient, known primarily for her trilogy set in Iowa. The saga is comprised of *Gilead*, which received the Pulitzer Prize; *Home*, awarded the Orange Prize; and *Lila*, winner of the National Book

Critics Circle Award. She delivers a searing talk, not about the state of reading or writing in America, but a polemical speech decrying the current state of politics (we are, after all, halfway through the 2016 presidential election cycle, and you know who's on everyone's mind).

Ms. Robinson is intelligent, witty, articulate, and extremely political—and well deserving of the 2016 Harold Washington Literary Award. We return home satisfied, especially because on the train ride home we are entertained by a legion of college students from Brazil who chatter away a mile a minute in their native Portuguese, while one of them slips off to flirt with two girls sitting next to us.

"My, he's handsome," whispers my wife.

I just smile and pull at my graying beard.

29 | A Sniggglement of String

IT'S PRELIMINARY—THE HAROLD WASHINGTON Literary Award Dinner. The real attraction is Printers Row Lit Fest in sunny downtown Chicago (well, at least that's what every vendor is hoping for). Imagine three city blocks filled with book vendors, performance spaces, author-signing tents, and gobs and gobs of people.

For the past fifteen years I've been appearing on the festival's Kid Lit Stage as a book author and storyteller. But it's taxing work, definitely for the young at heart. I've never enjoyed the open warfare of an unsupervised children's audience. Give me a school auditorium filled with 250 kids patrolled by a garrison of stern-faced teachers any day over an unsupervised audience of 20–30 kids. So, last year I called it quits. No more telling stories into the wind—and sometimes rain—hoping that a few kids hear me. Now my Printers Row Lit Fest appearances are contained to a few well-orchestrated events.

First of all, I attend the fair as a member of the Near South Planning Board's Author-in-the-Schools program, which means that I can sign up to sell books during a two-hour slot on either Saturday or Sunday of the festival at the NSPB's booth. And, every other year, I'm invited to speak about writing to students and their families associated with the NSPB's school programs.

Another way that I attend the festival is as a guest of the Chicago Writers Association. "Guest" is a funny word: what it really means is that I signed up before other authors who also wanted to attend the festival. The invitation means that I can sell books during a four-hour slot at the CWA's booth along with other authors who write for the adult market. The authors in this crowd are different from NSPB's children's book authors. They're more serious and usually better at playing the publishing game.

You also get to meet some very interesting people. For instance, my tablemate this year was Dave Berner. Never heard of him? Me neither (sorry, Dave). But that voice. There was something about that voice that fascinated me. I know I've heard that voice before. It's so lush, so deep, and so melodic. Why, he could be on the…

Radio! That's it. I've heard Dave Berner on the radio. And why shouldn't I? He's been a fixture on Chicago radio for years, as a radio reporter and, more recently, news anchor for CBS radio. And he's also an award-winning author (at least that's what his promotional materials say). He's written quite a few books too, including *Accidental Lessons*, *Any Road Will Take You There*, and *Night Radio*, his latest release. Oh, my gosh, wait until I tell my wife that I sat next to Dave Berner at Printers Row Book Fest.

Whom? she'll ask.

Dave Berner, I'll repeat.

Never heard of him. She'll shrug.

Dave Berner? Never heard of him?

Nope. Sorry.

Aghh! What do you know?

Anyway, I think I'm going to enjoy rubbing elbows with adult authors occasionally. They're…they're…so interesting. And so is the entire weekend of book-related activities. Here are a few things that I look forward to. First of all, I love strolling through the crowd—more elbowing my way through than strolling—looking at bookshelf after bookshelf of new and used books. As a rule, I tend to go for used books. More than that, I go for the rare or antiquarian bookseller, hoping that I might find a book that I not only like, but also one that I can afford. And, I usually do.

Last year I picked up a 1991 reissue of Alistair Reid's 1958 edition of *Ounce Dice Trice* for a nifty $25. It's a slim hardcover volume containing samples of Reid's unique style of wordplay. Drawing on years of note taking, Reid cobbles together a patchwork of word groups. For instance, here's a list of "rude" words: *rapscallion, flippertigibbet, fussbudget, coystril, taystril, joskin, bumpkin, cloaf, clodhopper, slammerkin.* And "squishy" words: *squiff, squidge, squamouos, squinny, squelch, squash, squeegee, squit, squab.* There are other lists as well. Lists of collective nouns: *a scribbitch of papers, a tumbletell of church bells, a snigglement of string, a gundulum of garbage cans.* Word definitions for these oddities: *frangipani, puggree, paxwax, tirrivee, gongozzler, thrumbled.* And brief descriptions of commonplace sounds. For instance, did you know that *mrraaowl* is what cats really say, and that *ploo* is the sound of a shoelace breaking, and that *croomb* is what pigeons murmur to themselves? It's a marvelous book. I imagine Lewis Carroll carrying it around in his back pocket (that is, if it had been published during his time and was pocket size).

As exciting as scrounging around an antiquarian bookseller's bookshelves is, the real reason I go to Printers Row Lit Fest (and, please, don't tell my wife) is to chow down on a hamburger at Hackney's, a landmark pub that's been in the neighborhood for years. Now, I'm not a big burger kind of guy. Hardly touch the stuff. The last one I had was at the Daytona Beach Tap Room while playing trivia with a couple of bikers from South Dakota.

But Hackney's is a must, a definite go-to. And I always get the same thing—the Kobe Burger. Just listen to this mouth-watering description: *domestically-raised Kobe beef burger served with Wisconsin blue cheese, smoked bacon, grilled onions, and roasted tomatoes; served on our homemade brioche bun.* Yes, I always order the same thing and I always arrive at the same time—11:00 a.m. I learned this the hard way after a few aborted attempts of trying to find a seat during the noon hour. *Impossible!* The book festival's just too crowded during the lunch hour to find a seat. It seems everyone—including me—has only one thing in mind: to eat lunch at Hackney's. So I arrive an hour before noon and usually have the place to myself. I pick a small table outside where I can sip on an ice-cold beer, eat a leisurely lunch, and people-watch.

Ah, the life of an author…or sailor…or truck driver…or politician, anyone who enjoys an occasional mouth-watering hamburger.

30 | This Is Going to Cost Me

WE MADE IT TO Penland. And why shouldn't we? My wife's been coming to Penland School of Crafts set in the mountains of western North Carolina for almost four decades, first as a student and now as an instructor. I tag along—her chauffer and personal valet. When we meet other people, usually over lunch or dinner, invariably they ask, "What do you do while your wife is teaching? Are you taking a class?" When I answer in the negative, saying that I'm more of a voyeur than an active participant, they look at me quizzically and the conversation usually turns to something—or someone—else.

My wife usually saves me, however, jumping in to tell them that I'm a writer. Then all of a sudden the light bulb goes on: "Oh, a writer, well you're probably here to write, aren't you?" "Yep," I reply, stoically. And I am. I carry my world in my head (and on my back in a backpack filled with books and a computer). I used to say a lot more about being a writer, when I was younger and more enthralled with the social designation. Being a writer—or, more precisely, a published author—carried a lot more cachet than it does now. Now, in today's do-it-yourself world of digital publishing, anyone can be an author, which takes a lot of the luster off the label. So I tend to think a lot more about the process of writing than I do about being a writer.

And that's what I'm doing right now at DT's Blue Ridge Java Coffee Shop & Café in downtown Spruce Pine, North Carolina. That's because my wife and I limped into Penland a couple of days ago in our aging Subaru and need a mechanic to get us home. And since I'm the designated chauffer, valet, and all around go-to guy, I get the job of taking our car to Lamar's Auto Shop for a look-see. At ten thirty in the morning, Lamar tells me, in his lilting North Carolina mountain dialect, "It'll be a few hours. I'll call you once I get under the hood."

So here I am at DT's with a couple of hours to kill. But isn't that what writers do? We kill time. We kill it by keeping ourselves busy with our own ideas (precisely why I don't sign up for a class at Penland: I *am* my own class). Avi, a prolific middle grade and young adult author, said it best through his principal character, Mangus, in *Murder at Midnight*: "Fabrizio, a book must first be written. To do so, the writer exchanges days for words, months for paragraphs, and years for chapters–time turned into books." Yes, I suppose Avi is right: writers don't kill time; they exchange it for books. And that's why I'm at DT's. It's about a six-block walk from Lamar's Auto Shop, not far, except that it's straight down a steep hill. I would have thought twice about the descent except workmen tinkering with a train engine on the tracks below distract me. The world of objects has always eluded me. Unlike my wife, whose world is all objects (band saws, drill presses, screwdrivers, and socket wrenches), my world is all sound (bird calls, door slams, tire screeches, and police sirens).

At DT's I find a solitary table, boot up my computer, and start to bang away at the day's journal entry, all the while thinking of the workmen on the train tracks and the mechanics at Lamar's Auto Shop: men who dive into the world of objects, understand how something works, and, by God, fix things when they need fixing. I can fix things, but in my own way (which means they usually need re-fixing shortly afterwards). I also think of the conversation I had at breakfast with a young woman, a photography student at Penland, who admitted, once I told her I was a writer, that she couldn't write; that she struggled with the simplest writing task. To me, writing is like a water spigot that won't quite close, words constantly pouring out.

But enough ruminating: it's time to get down to business. Usually I have a specific task I want to complete, and I do: along with completing my daily journal entry, I want to read another chapter in David Sedaris' *Me Talk Pretty One Day*. I brought two books to read at Penland: Sedaris' *Me Talk Pretty One Day* and Sherman Alexie's *The Absolutely True Diary of a Part-Time Indian*. I picked these for a reason. For most of my life, my writing has been divided into two lines: writing for children and writing for adults. My children's writing consists primarily of rhyming, picture-book texts that have a song-like quality and a humorous twist. My adult writing is the dry academic type, for trade or professional journals. For the most part, the two have kept to themselves. Only once did they converge.

In the early 1990s, several years after receiving tenure, I served as the chair of our department (shoot me the next time I raise my hand for that job). We had a complicated department, with programs spread across three states and one foreign country—and an even more complicated and often infuriating faculty. Believe it or not, the high point of my tenure as department chair was moderating a contentious faculty discussion on the natural position of the toilet seat: *Is it up or down?* (Ask me about it later; I definitely have a point of view on it now.) I survived the experience, but probably because—like my predecessors—I quit after two years. During these two exasperating years, I wrote nothing, nada, zilch, zippo, except a quirky essay for a children's literature journal. I say quirky because I was able to bring those two separate strands of my writing together into one holistic piece. For the first time in my life, the free-spirited, rhyming, song-like children's voice mingled with the arid voice of academic writing. The piece was as playful as it was informative, as spirited as it was intelligent. The key was to play with the article's form as much as it was its content. And it must have worked because I got a call from a leading feminist children's literature critic from Canada who congratulated me on my article and offered to buy me lunch if I ever made it to Toronto.

Well, I never made it to Toronto, and I never had lunch with Canada's leading feminist children's literature critic, and I never wrote another piece like it while working as a full-time tenured professor. But after I retired I began to envision braiding these two separate strands of writing together in a more intentional way. And that's why I brought the Sedaris and Alexie books to Penland, because each of these authors maintains that exquisite balance between light-heartedness and sobriety, between humor and pathos.

Tom, one of my university colleagues (who survived the department chair thing longer than any of us), knew it all along, way before I knew it, because when I picked up the Sedaris book, considering it for the Penland trip, I found a handwritten note stuffed between two pages of the front matter:

> Nikola, I got this book for you because I thought you might like Sedaris' humor, but also because I thought you could top it—and write a humorous book yourself about your own experiences. Happy birthday, Tom.

Prescient? Yes. But I can't think about that now—my butt hurts. It's almost one thirty and I've been sitting at DT's Blue Ridge Java Coffee Shop and Café for the last three hours. I've eaten my way through an onion-cheddar scone, two dill pickles, a bag of potato chips, a cup of tomato soup, and half of a soggy tuna fish sandwich. Besides that, the place is packed and outside it's raining cats and dogs. And I still haven't heard back from Lamar. Even if I did and he said, "Come and get it," I couldn't, at least not without getting soaked to the bone in the torrent outside. So, I sit and wait: my head hurts, my eyes are bloodshot, my nerves are frayed, and my fingers are slowly seizing up from this morning's typing. There's only one thing I can do, and that's read, read another chapter of David Sedaris' book. I do and it's so funny that I start to sob and cry, which makes the guy at the table next to me, who's been talking into his phone for the last two hours, uncomfortable and he moves away.

As soon as he leaves my phone rings. It's Lamar. He's brief and to the point. It's not what I thought. Nothing's rubbing against the tire. No. It's worse. It's the power steering. A leak. More than that, Lamar can't fix it. He recommends the Subaru dealer across town. We hang up. *Oh, no,* I say to myself as I collect my things and prepare to make the long slow trudge up the hill to Lamar's garage. *Not a car dealership*. At the top of the hill I pick my way through a dozen car carcasses littering the front lot of Lamar's garage. It's funny, I don't remember seeing all these cars before. But then I wasn't thinking about Lamar's cars, only mine.

Lamar is unkempt and gruff-looking, but quiet in his demeanor. He doesn't charge me a thing. Says it's best if I get the leak fixed before driving back to Chicago. We shake hands. I half want to slip him a twenty for his kindness, but I don't for fear of offending him. I drive across town to the local Subaru dealership. I brace myself. I've long given up servicing my cars at a dealership: just a hunch that they don't always have the customer's best interests in mind.

A cheery-eyed saleswoman rushes out to greet me. I immediately stake my ground: "Parts and Service, please." She turns and escorts me to Parts and Service, pointing out the new cars in the showroom as she does. We walk through a set of double doors, where she leaves me in the capable hands of the Parts and Service manager. He's the spittin' image of my stereotype of a Parts and Service manager—a smooth-talking man with an oval face and slicked-back silver hair. *Uh-oh*, I gulp, *this is going to cost me*. We walk outside to look at my car. I tell him about Lamar's assessment, a possible leak in the power steering unit. "Lamar?" he muses. You'd think for a town of no more than two thousand people (and only a couple of auto shops) that he would have heard of Lamar. But the name slips over him like water over a duck's back. He pops the hood open, shows me the power steering fluid reservoir, and says, "Yep, looks like a leak. By the way, your tires look a little worn; we can throw a new set on if you'd like? I gulp again. *Steady*, I tell myself. "No sir, I think they'll be fine," I reply. "When did you have your last checkup? Would you like an oil change? We can check the radiator fluid while we're at it." I swallow harder this time and answer, one syllable at a time, "If you could just fix the power steering leak that would be nice. I just have to make it back to Chicago."

After completing an interminable amount of paperwork, his assistant hands me a set of keys. "What's this?" I ask, surprised. "Why, your courtesy car," she replies. "You need one, don't you?" "Well, yes, I guess. How much will it cost?" "Cost? Why nothing. That's why we call it a courtesy car," she giggles. *Yes, this is going to cost me. Nobody gives you a courtesy car for nothing. Nobody.* I drive off in a brand new powder-blue Subaru XV Crosstrek, guiltily waving to my car as I pass it in the parking lot, at the same time muttering under my breath: *Nobody gives you a courtesy car for nothing.*

31 | How's the Coffee?

IT'S BEEN ABOUT FOUR days since we arrived at Penland and I'm a bit frustrated, not because I can't find something to do: because I'm tired of answering why I'm here. By now everyone else has his or her line down: *I'm taking the glass workshop. I'm in lower clay. You'll find me in printmaking.*

But what about me? I'm not in glass or clay or printmaking. I'm a tag-along spouse who's not signed up for anything. "You're not taking a class? What do you do all day?" I hear this at every meal. "Well, my wife is teaching a sculpture class and I'm just tagging along, *blah, blah, blah.*" After awhile it starts to get to me, so I've been making things up.

"I'm an accountant. My firm is auditing Penland. Do you like the food?"

"I'm a pilot. Had to make an emergency landing on the other side of the hill. Don't know how long I'll be here. How's the coffee?"

"I'm a patron and I've given gobs of money to this place. Might as well get a meal or two out of it. Pass the salt and pepper, please."

"I'm a government inspector. We believe arsenic has leached into the drinking water. Have you noticed anything funny lately?"

"I'm a psychiatrist. I'm doing a study on schizophrenia. Can you tell me where the metals department is?"

"Hi, I'm here to pick up my daughter. She had a mental breakdown. Can we have seconds?"

My favorite response, however, which is not that far off the mark is: "I'm taking the writing workshop. It's a very small group. This week, our instructor is David Sedaris. Next week, Sherman Alexie."

"Wow, David Sedaris is *here*? At Penland? You must be having a great time."

"Oh, yes," I say with growing confidence. "He's so funny, just like his books."

OF COURSE, I DON'T know how funny David Sedaris or Sherman Alexie is in person: I've never met either one of them. But I do know how funny their writing is. I finished Sedaris' *Me Talk Pretty One Day* earlier this week and I'm about halfway through Alexie's *The Absolutely True Story of a Part-Time Indian.* Both are hysterical. Although each book shines a light on a different subject—Sedaris' on urban gay culture; Alexie's on rural Native American culture—both writers keep you in stitches with improbable characters and unlikely situations, not to mention a mastery of voice and comic timing.

But neither of these authors—David Sedaris or Sherman Alexie—is at the top of my must-read list right now. At the top of this list is Bill Bryson. I just picked up a used copy of Bryson's memoir *The Life and Times of the Thunderbolt Kid* (thanks to the used bookstore in downtown Spruce Pine), and I can't wait to sink my teeth into it. From the few passages I've read, it looks like I'm really going to enjoy this book. And I would read more, right now, except tonight it's the Fourth of July. Penland will light up tonight. *Big time!* First of all, there's a parade featuring impromptu floats made by students at Penland (art students are *so* much fun). Next, there's an ice cream social that brings the locals (many of them ex-Penlanders) up the hill to mix and mingle with the current crop of students. Last but not least, there's a bonfire and fireworks.

Yes, fireworks, that age-old tradition of the American Fourth of July experience, and I have the best seat in the house, literally: our faculty house overlooks both the parade route and the open field where the bonfire and fireworks are all set to go. When I say parade, don't think Macy's Parade. It's not that kind of parade. The night before the big day, the students at Penland stay up all night (with the help of a few bottles of moonshine) jerry-rigging their float together. When they're not working on the group's float, they're working on their individual costume. Penlanders are an artistic group of people, not to mention extremely quirky.

As I'm writing this, a woman in a bathing suit edged with red-white-and-blue trim chases a dog past the porch, several people dressed as three-pronged forks walk by looking for the start of the parade, and two girls suddenly stop on the road in front of me trying to relight their joint. All the while streams of people file up from the valley below, pulling wagons filled with babies, blankets, and cases of bottled beer. Color du jour: red-white-and-blue, of course. There are red-white-and-blue flags, red-white-and-blue shirts, red-white-and-blue blankets, red-white-and-blue hats, but no red-white-and-blue jackets. It's just too dang hot.

While I contemplate this, the backdoor creaks open. "Hello, who's there?" I ask, walking toward the kitchen. As I turn the corner I see a stranger in the backroom. A big burly guy with a bushy beard, deep blue eyes, an impish smile, and a fire-engine red T-shirt with the word "whiskey" emblazoned on it.

Me: "Ah, hello?"
Man: "Hey, just using your refrigerator."
Me: "Uh-huh, and who are you?"
Man: "Me, I run the bookmaking and lithography studio. The name's Jay."
Me: "Jay? Hello Jay. My name's Nikola."
Man: "You don't mind if I put some beer in your refrigerator, do you?"
Me: "No, not a problem. Maybe, next time, you'll knock."
Man: "Oh, we don't do that around here much."
Me: "Yeah, I didn't think so."

We live in Chicago where it's a problem to find a stranger in your house. But I guess that's not the case here. In fact, when I think about it, we're the real strangers, given the fact that my wife and I are here for only two weeks. Jay's here all the time. And you can tell: he acts as if he owns the place.

While I'm talking with Jay the parade rounds the corner so I hurry back to the porch. I glance at my watch: seven thirty. Unlike most things in the world, the parade starts on time—seven thirty sharp. Everything starts on time at Penland: breakfast, dinner, the nightly artist talks—*everything*. So why shouldn't the parade start on time?

It does and I settle into my chair to enjoy one of the most unusual Fourth of July parades in my life. There's a dancing Chinese dragon, a woman dressed in vines and leaves, Superman strutting his stuff in a red-white-and-blue speedo, a woman blowing a trumpet, two guys carrying a giant camera, a couple pretending to ride an invisible horse, several bikinied women pulling a beefy guy sitting in a small plastic swimming pool, and, the finale, a riotous, and somewhat overly cheerful, brigade of three-pronged forks.

You know, I'm starting to like this place. Too bad we have to leave soon.

32 | Time Present, Time Past

WE'RE STILL AT PENLAND in the mountains of western North Carolina. It's just a hop, skip, and a jump over the border to Tennessee. I look at my watch—four o'clock. If you're not from the area, it's "down time" (the intense heat combined with high humidity gets to you every day about this time). I'm sitting outside, shaded by several deciduous trees spreading their branches in thick layers. But still the heat and humidity takes its toll. So I move indoors which is better, but not much better since there's no air conditioning.

I head to the lending library, drop my backpack, and start rummaging through the shelves. I'm sure nine out of ten people who come here search the shelves containing books on art processes: photography, metals, painting, lithography, clay, and the like. But no, not me: I stop at poetry. I lift a thin volume off the shelf and take it to a small table at the window, which gives me a panoramic view of the mist-shrouded mountains.

It's so damn beautiful here—*and hot.*

The volume I lift from the poetry bookshelf is T. S. Eliot's *Four Quartets*. I study the front matter, pausing at the table of contents where Eliot's four sections are named:

I. Burnt Norton
II. East Coker
III. The Dry Salvages
IV. Little Gidding

Then, I thumb through each section. Before reading a book, I like to get the lay of the land first, see how a book is organized, know what to expect. In doing so, I notice that each section has five parts, labeled with Roman numerals. I begin to wonder: Why is the book titled *Four Quartets*? I see there are four parts, each one comprising one part of the whole. But the five subdivisions throw me off. Maybe the book should be titled simply *Quartets* for the four major sections. To me, *Four Quartets* signifies that there are four parts, each part made up of four sections. And, yes, there are four parts, but each one contains *five* sections. Wouldn't it be more appropriate to title the book *Four Quintets*? Actually, this wouldn't work because technically a "Quintet" in poetry is a type of "Quintain," a poem with five lines, the cinquain and limerick being the most well-known. It would be more appropriate to title Eliot's book *Four Quintuplets*. But, then again, in the age of in vitro fertilization, this might be misleading. No matter, I sink into a nearby stuffed chair, kick my feet up, and begin to read aloud:

Time present and time past...

But that's as far as I get. The door opens. It's Cleavon, one of the few African-American students at Penland. And he wants to talk. I can tell he wants to talk because Cleavon always wants to talk. So I invite him to sit down.

Cleavon pulls up a chair. Even though it's a library, we can talk because it's not much of a library, only two small rooms filled with books and magazines and a lonely computer.

Cleavon: "Man, I really wanted to talk to you at lunch."
Me: "Yeah, I could tell."
Cleavon: "When Shane started to talk about being stopped by the police, I wanted to jump in with my story."
Me: "And what is *your* story?"
Cleavon: "Different from Shane's, that's for sure. You see, as a black man I have a very different take on the police."
Me: "Take?"
Cleavon: "Yeah, take. I acquired it from my parents. As my brothers and I got older, my parents started to lay it on thick about how to act in the presence of The Man. Something white dudes just don't have to think about."
Me: "Well, I sure can guess. I mean it's in the news every day. Just yesterday another unarmed black man was shot by a white policeman."
Cleavon [studying me]: "You see, I was riding in a car with another dude, a white dude, and we get pulled over by the police. I guess a black man and a white man riding in a car together raises a red flag. The Man pulls us over and as he does the white dude…I didn't even really know him, just riding home from work with him, that's all…takes a bag of pot from inside his jacket and stashes it under the front seat."
Me: "You didn't know he was a pothead?"
Cleavon: "Sure, everyone at work did. The strange thing is that after he stashes it, he gets out of the car, and starts stomping around, swearing, yelling at the police: *Hey, I just got this car. Man, don't mess up my car.* You know, things like that."
Me: "What did you do?"
Cleavon: "Me, I did what my parents told me to do. I rolled down my window and stuck both of my arms out the window so The Man could see I was unarmed."

Me: "Probably a smart move, considering."

Cleavon: "Except The Man came right over to me, ordered me out of the car, and then threw me up against it. While I'm being frisked, the white dude is still ranting and raving at the police, who are patiently listening to him."

Me: "Did they find anything on you?"

Cleavon: "Sure, my military ID and my student ID. When The Man saw these, he asked why I had them. I told him: *I'm an active reservist and a student.*"

Me: "What did he do?"

Cleavon: "He cuffed me and put me in the backseat of the police car. That was about the time they found the pot under the front seat. But I had nothing to do with it. I don't smoke pot. I don't even take painkillers."

Me: "What happened to the white dude?"

Cleavon: "Well, he finally settles down, especially after they find the pot. And they put him in the police car, too, *in the freaking front seat.* They didn't even cuff him. Here I am, an innocent black man, cuffed and thrown into the back seat, while Mr. White-Guy-Pothead is yammering away with The Man in the front seat *unshackled.*"

Me: "Did they throw you in jail?"

Cleavon: "No, the white dude finally confessed that it was his bag of pot and that I didn't have anything do to with it, that he was just giving me a ride home from work. So you can see why, when a white guy starts talking about his experience with The Man, I get kind of agitated, because a black man's experience is, well, different, like night and day."

Suddenly, the door to the library swings open. It's a tall blond woman who smiles, says hello, and then announces that the library is closing. She pauses, looks around, and says, "Well, you can stay a little longer if you wish. Just turn off the lights and lock the door behind you when you leave."

Cleavon and I smile at her and nod as she disappears down the hallway. After Cleavon leaves, I resettle into the stuffed chair, swing my legs up onto the table, open Eliot's *Four Quartets*, and begin to read aloud:

Time present and time past...

33 | Shadow Country

IT'S OUR LAST MORNING at Celo Inn. We picked it out of a hat. You know how it goes: you go online and search an area for a place to stay. Lots of websites to visit: Airbnb, VRBO, Home Vacation Rentals, and the like. But they don't cover everything. So you surf the web using a variety of websites, a number of search terms; you're looking, fishing, searching, and hoping.

That's how we found Celo Inn in Celo, North Carolina. We were looking for a little post-Penland R&R, a place to stash our things while we went hiking during the day. Celo Inn was perfectly positioned: halfway between Mount Mitchell and Linville Gorge, two areas we wanted to explore. The website was, well, homey. Nicely done, but very low key. About five pages with dark, hard to read, dimly lit photos. What caught my eye were the declarations on the last page: "no television," "spotty cell phone coverage," and "no credit cards accepted."

But what really sealed the deal was the fact that the website didn't list an email address. None at all. I searched several times, but nothing. I thought it was a mistake. There was a phone number, but no email, so I called and talked with Nancy, Celo Inn's proprietor and all-around hostess.

"That's right, there's no email address," she said, after we talked about the Inn's amenities (or lack thereof). "You have to call. I like talking to people direct. And, besides, I want to be known as the last person in America to enter the 21st century."

Hmm, I thought, as I hung up, *this is going to be interesting.*

And it was.

So it was a sad day when we had to leave. We slept in a little longer that morning, lingered at breakfast, took our time loading the car, stopped to talk with Randy, Nancy's husband and all-around handyman. We took one last stroll through the front yard flower and herb garden, then slipped into our car and drove away.

But we didn't drive far. We had two stops before leaving the area. The first stop was at the Subaru dealer in the next town over where we loaded up on power steering fluid (anticipating trouble from our unresolved car problem). After that we headed to the local coffee shop and loaded up on coffee and pastries. Then the three of us hit the road.

Three of you?

Yeah, the three of us—my wife and I, and Peter Matthiessen.

Peter Matthiessen?

Of course, we always listen to an audiobook when we drive across country, and this trip's selection is Peter Matthiessen's *Shadow Country*, a National Book Award winner. It's a real thriller, told in short chapters through a variety of time periods and by a variety of characters. The imagery is vivid, the language shocking, the characters more than memorable, and the murders insufferably gruesome.

It's a raw, close-up look at south Florida during its early days of development, told from the point of view of outliers, people on the fringe of society—homesteaders, fugitives, drunks, whores, rebels—all trying to hold on to a way of life that is slowly slipping out of their grasp. The central theme revolves around the destruction of Florida's Everglades in the southern part of the state. It's a classic story: discover a natural wonder with abundant natural resources and developers start arriving daily to ravage the land and its resources.

Our first day on the road is a leisurely jog through the mountains of western North Carolina, eastern Tennessee, and southern Kentucky. As we drive through Harlan County, Kentucky, we're reminded of Barbara Kopple's award-winning documentary about the area's coal mining operations. It's a sobering film that leaves you contemplating the effect that people have on the environment and on each other. The story's the same inside the car as my wife and I listen to Matthiessen's unwinding story of murder and intrigue in the Florida Everglades. The two stories—Matthiessen's and Kopple's—are not that dissimilar, two sides of the same coin really, just set in different times and different locations.

As we drive, totally drugged on Matthiessen's prose, we stop occasionally to gas up, fill our coffee mugs, and stretch our legs, each time moving farther away from poverty-stricken rural America and closer to urban middle America with its endless lineup of chain store hotels, restaurants, gas stations, and coffee shops, each one mind-numbingly similar in appearance and service. On the one night we do stop, just over the Ohio border, we park at the far end of the hotel parking lot, eat dinner alone in our motel room, and listen to classical music on our computer rather than switch on the evening cable news. Reluctant to give up our mental retreat from the world, we stop at art museums in Cincinnati and Indianapolis, relishing in the expansive vision of artists from all over the world.

But as we draw closer to Chicago, my resolve weakens. Stuck in rush-hour traffic, I reach for the radio dial, switch off Matthiessen's story (but not without some protest from my wife), and turn on the news, only to fall at a dizzying speed into the news du jour. Today's news is that of a crazed lone-wolf terrorist who's driven a UPS-sized truck seventy miles per hour through a mile or more of Bastille Day celebrants in southern France, killing eighty-four men, women, and children. No one is safe today, not even toddlers out to see fireworks for the first time. I make the last turn onto our street choking back tears. We're home, I guess, though it feels like we've never even left.

34 | Street Views

OUR TRIP TO NORTH Carolina is the first of three excursions this summer. Next, we head to Aspen, Colorado, where my wife has an Artist-in-the-Wilderness residency, which means that while she's hiking with a guide, I'll be in downtown Aspen hunched over my computer working on something until it's time to pick her up. After that, it's on to Bainbridge Island, west of Seattle, where my wife has a three-week residency—*sorry, no spouses* (I'll join her at the end of the three-week sojourn for a quick trip to Vancouver Island).

Now it might seem that we jet around the world—or at least North America—on a regular basis, but the truth of it is we're home a lot, each of us sequestered in his or her workspace. Most of the books I write I do so within a five-mile radius of our house. But how I admire writers who travel to the location they're writing about, even if they could conduct all of their research from home. The power of the Internet allows us to do the latter now: it's the world at our fingertips, so why go out? But ask Erik Larson if he could write the books he does without visiting each locale in person. How could he possibly write about the hurricane that devastated Galveston in the early 1900s, or Marconi's explorations of Newfoundland and Nova Scotia, or Chicago's 1893 Columbian Exhibition, or the sinking of the *Lusitania* off the British coast if he didn't actually go to each site?

Impossible.

I'm reminded of David Wolman. Earlier this year I read his insightful and exceedingly humorous book *A Left-hand Turn Around the World: Chasing the Mystery and Meaning of All Things Southpaw*. It's a wonderfully rich account of left-handedness in a right-handed world. The first thing I like about the book is that Wolman is left-handed. No, correction, Wolman is *passionately* left-handed (the kind of left-hander who fist-pumps other left-handed people when he greets them). The other thing I like about Wolman is that he travels to different locales around the world—a la Erik Larson—to explore various aspects of his subject matter with the absolute sensibility of a journalist. And why not: he is a journalist, who's taken a year off to write a book about a subject dear to his heart.

However, unlike Larson, Wolman readily injects the personal into his writing style. You really get a sense that Wolman loves to travel, to explore the world, and to engage with people—no matter the subject matter. In fact, I think you can safely say that the places he visits and the people he meets are as important to Wolman as the subject matter he writes about. But, above all else, it's Wolman's journalistic eye that stands out: he understands that in order to engage readers, he has to bring them as close as possible to his subject matter. To do that, Wolman opens the floodgates of his senses in order to take in—and write about—the scene before him. Two examples:

From Chapter 3:

> The clouds below look like the rippled, winding surface of a brain, and as the plane descends toward Paris I imagine I'm inside a tiny molecule, orbiting, then diving into the vast terrain of cerebral gray matter. The next morning at 5:00

> a.m., jet-lagged beyond reason and sick of watching CNN, I venture out into the January drizzle, heading north on Hemingway's beloved Boulevard Saint-Michel toward the Sorbonne and the brains made famous by Paul Broca.

From Chapter 11:

> I'm wearing the one and only golf shirt I own. It's a white polo embroidered with the red and black logo of the National Association of Left-Handed Golfers–Japan. After my visit with Nobutaka Hirokawa in Tokyo, I hopped the bullet train to Karuizawa, a small town in the foothills of the Japan Alps and home to some of the country's premier golf courses. This weekend, Karuizawa is hosting the NALG–Japan Tenth Anniversary Championships.

Anyone can write, but only the best writers can transport readers to a new reality; in the case of nonfiction, to the place they're writing about. But it's the writers who actually get up and go, who expend the time and energy to visit the physical site and people they're writing about, who create the deepest impressions on readers through their vivid, even visceral descriptions. Wolman does this repeatedly by virtue of his on-the-ground, notebook-in-hand, newspaperman approach. I admire that. And I wish I were more like him and Erik Larson, and the hundreds of other authors who do the same, but I'm not. I relate more to Dava Sobel's statement at the end of *Longitude*, the story of John Harrison's struggle to solve the longitude problem, in which she freely admits that she could have written her treatise from the comfort of her home. Of course she didn't, as her admission reveals:

> For a few months at the outset, I maintained the insane idea that I could write this book without traveling to England and seeing the timekeepers firsthand. I owe a huge vote of

> thanks to my brother Stephen Sobel, D.D.S., for propelling me to London so I could stand on the prime meridian with my children, Zoë and Isaac, root around the Old Royal Observatory, and watch clocks at various museums.

Yes, I'm much more like Dava Sobel (though I'm sure she travels a lot as well). I'm an armchair historian, content to experience the world vicariously through a variety of sources: books, magazines, radio, television, and the Internet—all of them vicarious, many of them virtual. But isn't this the nature of our increasingly digital world, where the line between actual and virtual—indeed, fact and fiction—continues to blur?

Several years ago, while I was researching a series of murders—known as the West End Murders—that occurred in Edinburgh during the early part of the 19th century, I wanted to walk from Wester Port to Surgeon's Square in order to traverse the same route that the men implicated in the so-called "anatomical murders" did when they carted their victims to a dissection lab in Edinburgh's Surgeon's Square. And I did, but without setting one foot in Scotland. I just used "street views" from Google Maps. It's a handy tool that allows you to slip out of your local environ and into a completely different one. Although "street views" can't take you back in time, it can transport you—albeit virtually—to any location on the globe.

I'm thinking about this today because I'd rather be anywhere on earth than where I am right now (not a very Buddhist point of view, mind you): back from our long road trip to the mountains of western North Carolina, I'm standing in the middle of my office looking up at nine six-and-half-foot long bookshelves that populate the west wall of my office. That's what faces me now that I'm back home: more shelf cleaning, more book dusting, more rearranging: in short, more of the same old same old.

35 | Soul's Core

THERE'S NO TWO WAYS about it: I just have to roll up my sleeves and dive in. But where do I start? Do I start with my personal notebooks, my book inventory, a shelf of family photographs, my collection of folk literature, or several shelves of children's literature studies? In most cases I'd stop and make a list. That's the best way to get your bearings (read that: procrastinate). But I know what I have to do: I have to start at the beginning and the beginning in this case is the bottom shelf.

It should be fairly easy to deal with this shelf: it holds a collection of my writing journals dating back to the early 1980s when I first started thinking about writing children's books. I was a father and an elementary school teacher, so reading to children was a regular routine in my family and work life. By the mid-1980s I had really gotten the bug to write books for children. And by bug, I mean I got serious, and when I get serious, I tend to do things: I started keeping journals. And that's what faces me as I pull up a chair and start to pull notebooks off the bottom shelf. They're arranged by size (rather than by year or topic, which, of course, would be considerably more practical). As I begin to pull each one off the shelf, I naturally open it up and leaf through it, entertaining myself with my earlier—and in many cases, unformed—thoughts and ideas. Before I pull half a dozen notebooks off the shelf, I remember that I once published an article about my notebooks. I swivel around to my desk, fire up my computer, and search for the article.

Yep, there it is, in my Documents Folder under "published articles: educational journals." It's in a folder labeled "IRCJ 2007 Writing Notebooks." Rereading it takes me back in time, to the early days of my writing career, when I was younger and struggling to find my writer's voice. It must have been a good article because I blew off the afternoon reading it.

OKAY, SO WHAT IF I only got one shelf cleaned and rearranged yesterday. That's just how it goes. And, now, it's on to the next shelf—book inventory.

What a boring task this is: take down a stack of books, clean the empty shelf, and replace the stack of books (no need to clean books as they're relatively "dustless"). I think a little music will go well with this activity. Let's see, it's Sunday morning and my wife is still asleep, how about a little Shawn Mullins? Yes, "Sunday Mornin' Comin' Down" might be just the right song to kick off the morning's task. I open iTunes, search for *Soul's Core*, Mullins' fourth album, click on "Sunday Mornin' Comin Down," and swivel around to my bookshelves.

I'd never heard of Mullins before the release of *Soul's Core*. It came out in 1998 and was a steady play on FM radio stations around the country. When I heard the album I thought that Mullins was going straight to the top; it was—and still is—an incredible album. Mullin's easy-going guitar playing, plaintive voice, and solid storytelling really spoke to me (my favorite is still "Richard Brautigan," a soulful tribute to the native West Coast novelist and poet). But then Mullins just seemed to disappear, just dropped off the edge of the earth, even though he released another half dozen albums after *Soul's Core*. But that's the way it is with artists: one day the white heat of the media spotlight shines brightly on you and then, before you know it, the spotlight moves on.

Cleaning my book inventory shelves while listening to Mullins' soulful singing slowly drags me back in time, to the 1990s, when I published two of my most popular children's books—*Bein' With You This Way* and *Shake Dem Halloween Bones*. If ever the white heat of the media spotlight shone on me, it was during this decade. But rather than illuminate my life, the spotlight distorted it. When *Bein' With You This Way* came out it received all sorts of critical acclaim and was short-listed for several children's book awards. It even appeared on a segment of CBS' *This Morning*, touted as a great multicultural read. As a result, I sold several other stories in rapid succession and for the next few years I had one or two books coming out, each one illustrated by a person of color (whether or not the story addressed the idea of diversity). It seemed that overnight I became a hot commodity: a white man who wrote multicultural books for children.

I rode that wave partially because of the success of *Bein' With You This Way* and partially because the 1990s marked the beginning of a push for more multicultural books for children. Yes, here I was: a middle-aged white man writing about diversity. I guess it made for good press because I got invited to a lot of schools, libraries, and literacy conferences during the 1990s. By the time my fourth or fifth book illustrated by a person of color came out, people started to believe that I was also a person of color. More than that, with a name like W. Nikola-Lisa, some people thought not only was I black, but I was also a woman. And that's precisely why an African-American woman standing in line at a major national conference waiting for me to sign her book screamed when she rounded the corner of the publisher's booth and saw me—a middle-aged white man—waiting to sign her book.

But I thought you were a...

Yes, she thought I was a black woman.

But I'm not. And I don't always write books about multiculturalism either, unless the muse strikes me, which it did in 2002 at the Art Institute of Chicago. I went there to attend a lecture by Howard Gardner, the founder of the theory of multiple intelligences.

The Art Institute's Rubloff Auditorium was packed. By 2002, Gardner's theory of multiple intelligences was really taking off, especially since he was starting to apply it to educational settings. So I went with my wife, who wandered off to look at art in the Art Institute's galleries. I stayed and listened intently. Gardner is quite a fascinating speaker; his secret ingredient: high intelligence offset by low-key, self-deprecating humor. As I sat there, however, listening to Gardner explain each one of his eight "intelligences," something hit me: all of his examples of intelligent people were "dead white men"—Stravinsky, Picasso, Einstein, Darwin, Freud.

Bingo! The light went on. I mean, big time. What the world needed was a book for children about multiple intelligences, but one written through a multicultural lens. The idea gave birth to *How We Are Smart,* a collective biography of twelve people of color—six men and six women—who exhibit one or more of Gardner's "intelligences." It was an instant success in the school market, especially after it received a 2007 Christopher Award. But then, just like that, the white heat of the media spotlight fell on someone else, leaving me, and a slew of other people, groveling about in the shadows. Of course, we know why: 2007 was the beginning of the Great Market Crash when the media spotlight was almost extinguished entirely.

Although a difficult decade, the last ten years have been one of rebuilding as I try to reposition myself in the marketplace as an independent author/publisher. And that's why I'm facing a generously stocked shelf of inventory, because part of the rebuilding experience has been a recognition that not only do I have to take more control of my publishing efforts, but I also have to take more control of marketing and sales. And that's precisely why I keep an up-to-date inventory in my office for each title that's still in print, so I have multiple copies of them at my fingertips (no scrounging around the upstairs crawlspace if I don't have to).

BUT ENOUGH SAID, AND enough of Shawn Mullins. It's on to the next shelf and Tom Petty and the Heartbreakers (my wife's up, so a little rock-and-roll can't hurt anything). The next bookshelf, the third shelf from the bottom, has two collections of books: the first part of the shelf contains books that support my author/storytelling programs; the second part of the shelf houses my "trim size" collection, which you already know about. In terms of the former, books that support my author/storytelling programs, I keep two types of books: books that I've published and exemplary books written by other authors. I get a lot of curious feedback about my author programs because I'm probably one of the few authors who pepper their talks with readings from other authors' work. I particularly enjoy using classic picture books as a springboard for storytelling. Take Charles Shaw's *It Looked Like Spilt Milk.* Instead of reading the book, I recite the book from memory while tossing a chiffon scarf in the air as I name the various animals and objects that a cloud—*qua* chiffon scarf—might look like. To emphasize the rhythmic aspect of *Bein' With You This Way*, I often preface it with a "reading" of Chris Raschka's *Charlie Parker played be-bop*, shaking two bean-filled gourd shakers to Raschka's syncopated rhythm. Of everything I do that is book-related, reading books and telling stories to an audience of children is by far the most gratifying—and the most natural—to me.

36 | The Doldrums

TODAY I'VE BEEN THINKING about what Roger Kahn calls "the boys of summer." Yes, I'm thinking about major league baseball. I'm thinking about it because we're in the doldrums, the dog days of summer. It's August and it's hot. And our attention is elsewhere—on a much-needed vacation, the Summer Olympics in Rio, the bruising sparring match between Democrats and Republicans (well, at least some of us are still paying attention to that). Baseball, unfortunately, seems a distant third or fourth item on our list of attention-grabbers. So why is it on my mind? I'll tell you in a minute, but first let's parse a few of these well-used phrases.

Kahn's phrase is the namesake of his 2006 best-selling book, *The Boys of Summer*, an homage to the Dodgers during the Jackie Robinson era, as well as a sentimental journey back in time when Kahn, who grew up in the shadow of Ebbets Field, covered the Dodgers for the *New York Herald Tribune*. Unlike "the doldrums" or "the dog days of August," Kahn's phrase is not specific to a particular month or season; it's a generic reference to the game of baseball that holds the majority of its games during the summer months. But August? Hot, steamy August? That's another story. That's when baseball men and women apply terms like "the doldrums" or "the dog days of August" with almost wanton abandon.

"The doldrums" is a maritime phrase that refers to those parts of the Atlantic Ocean and Pacific Ocean that have very little wind. The area is found near the equator and is caused by solar radiation from the sun hitting the ocean at an almost perpendicular angle, causing the resultant heated and expanding air mass to rise straight up before it drifts, then descends in the northern and southern latitudes. Prior to the 20th century, when most transoceanic voyages relied on strong prevailing winds to propel their large and heavy sailing vessels, the doldrums were a region to avoid if possible. Not only were the winds—or lack thereof—unpredictable, but also the rising warm and moist air often spawned terrible squalls and thunderstorms at sea. As a baseball term, "the doldrums" refers primarily to that part of the season between mid-July and the beginning of September. In other words, it refers primarily to August, when baseball seems to slip into the nation's subconscious, as other things take center stage.

"The dog days of August" refers to the same time period, but the origin of the phrase emanates from a different source. Although both terms refer to the hot, sultry heat of late summer, "the doldrums" is a nautical term, whereas "the dog days of August" has its roots in astronomy. It refers to *Orion's* dog, the star *Sirius*, which rises each morning in late summer. The association of the heliacal rising of *Sirius* with the insufferable heat of August can be traced back to ancient Egypt as well as to the writings of the early Greeks. And all of this brings me to my mid-August musings about major league baseball.

Twenty-five months ago I published my first book for the adult non-fiction market: *The Men Who Made the Yankees*. I wrote the book for several reasons. First of all, I spent most of my summers at my grandmother's beach house on Staten Island and, with my uncle as my chaperone, I spent more than one sultry summer afternoon at Yankee Stadium rooting for the Yankees. At the end of each summer I returned to Florida to rejoin my mother and two sisters. When spring rolled around not only did I play baseball with my friends, but I also spent a lot of time at Ft. Lauderdale Stadium, the spring training camp of the New York Yankees. Built in 1962 at a cost of $600,000, the 8,000-seat ballpark beckoned me every spring during the mid-1960s. Aside from my mother dating a major league baseball player or two (I thought the Pirate's third baseman; she told me later it was a Cincinnati Reds' pitcher), the biggest baseball headline during the mid-1960s was a local story involving Roger Maris and Clete Boyer, who were charged with assault stemming from their apparent involvement in a brawl outside a local cocktail lounge.

Although my mother never married a baseball player (which really disappointed me), and Roger and Clete got off with a mere slap on the wrist, I retained an interest in the Yankees throughout my adult life. But it wasn't Roger Maris or Clete Boyer or Mickey Mantle or Yogi Berra or Whitey Ford or Bobby Richardson that captured my imagination. It was another Yankee, from another era: the Caliph of Clout, the Behemoth of Bust, the Sultan of Swat; yes, it was the Great Bambino—George Herman "Babe" Ruth. Ruth held sway over me the way no other Yankee did. Not only was he head-and-shoulders above most players of his time, but also his off-the-field lifestyle defied explanation (especially in light of today's professional athlete's training regime).

My interest in Ruth led to a curiosity about the early Yankees, not Ruth's Yankees, the 1920's Murderer's Row Yankees. No, I began to wonder how the Yankees came to New York in the first place. As I mentioned earlier, most histories of the franchise start in one of three places: 1903, when they came to upper Manhattan as the Hilltop Highlanders; 1913, when the franchise officially changed its name to the New York Yankees; or 1923, opening year of Yankee Stadium and the team's first world series championship title. Having read all I could about the early Yankees, I was still not satisfied. After all, the American League opened its doors in 1901 and the Highlanders (a.k.a. the Yankees) didn't arrive on the scene until 1903. Why did it take two years for the American League to place a team in New York City, the most lucrative major league baseball market at the time? It was that question that motivated me to write *The Men Who Made the Yankees: The Odyssey of the World's Greatest Baseball Team from Baltimore to the Bronx*. As it turns out, the story was less about great Yankee managers and players, and more about the politics and money behind major league baseball at the turn of the 20th century. I guess you could say it still is.

The book came out in July of 2014. It was good timing: the All-Star Game was around the corner. Baseball was on everyone's mind. Online sales of *The Men Who Made the Yankees* took off. It didn't hurt that I had hired a publicist to help in that regard. Sales continued to climb through October, even after the World Series. And even though the Yankees weren't in the series (the bearded San Francisco Giants played the upstart Kansas City Royals), sales continued through November and December, then into January, February, and March. They continued uninterrupted until…

This month! That's right, I haven't had a single sale, not one, nothing, from mid-July to mid-August. It's the first 30-day period in which there have been no online sales. Yes, it's the doldrums, the dog days of August. Whatever happened to the boys of summer? But I'm an optimist and, paraphrasing historian and rabid Dodgers' fan Doris Kearns Goodwin, just wait until next month.

ONE THING THAT CAN'T wait any longer is my SCBWI membership renewal form. I have to make a decision. Do I re-up or not? For most of my writing career I've identified with the label "children's book author." But over the last few years I've been spreading my wings trying to write other things, mostly for an older audience. Nonetheless, I just can't seem to cut the cord: yes, I'll re-up; I'll renew my SCBWI membership (who knows, maybe next year I'll publish a blockbuster children's book and win the SCBWI's Spark Award for a second time—*sweet*).

37 | *Hey, That's My Shoe!*

TO USE A WELL-WORN phrase, I'm on the road again. But I'm not traveling to promote a new book. No, this time I'm a tag-along husband, something I quite like to do. Although my wife is a studio artist, she often needs to get away for a while, really get away, like to some unexplored, out-of-the-way natural environment.

Please close your tray tables and bring your seat forward. We'll be landing shortly.

And we do: in sunny, cool Aspen, Colorado.

Okay, I know what you're thinking: *Aspen, Colorado? That's as far away from an "unexplored, out-of-the-way natural environment" as you can get.*

Well, yes and no. Although Aspen is the playground of the wealthy (four downtown cashmere sweater stores in a row verify that), it is also a mecca for all sorts of outdoor sports enthusiasts (what we thought was a helicopter landing pad for the hospital turned out to be ground zero for the local parasail club). But we are here for none of it: no parasails, no cashmere sweaters, no skydiving, not even the latest Gucci bag.

We are here or, more properly, my wife is here to explore the surrounding wilderness area as this month's featured Artist-in-the-Wilderness fellow. It's not a bad gig: paid airfare, cabin in the woods, a rental car, and a personal hiking guide each day. No, not a bad gig at all. And that's only what my wife gets. I get five days alone in downtown Aspen hopping from one coffeehouse to the next to work on my latest book, at least when I'm not shopping for the latest in cashmere sweaters.

After a smooth landing at the Aspen-Pitkin County Airport, we are picked up by our host, given the grand tour of downtown Aspen, and then whisked away to our cabin in the woods. The next day is more of the same, ending with a taste of the Aspen Music Festival, which is in its last weekend of the season. It's a stirring performance of Carl Orff's *Carmina Burana*—and "stirring" hardly describes the performance; it's absolutely electrifying, especially the performance of the lead soprano who's in her eighth month of pregnancy. I don't learn this until my wife tells me after the concert because I'm not lucky enough to get a ticket to actually be in the music tent where the orchestra and the almost 200 choral members are performing. Our host has only one extra ticket, which goes to my wife (why not; not only is she the featured artist this month, but also it's her birthday). I remain outside, along with others who couldn't finagle a ticket.

I survey the scene and pick a spot on the side of a grassy hill. It's a little out of the way and it's shaded (during the day the Aspen sun can be brutal). A couple and their two neatly coiffured French poodles stake out the top of the hill. I spread the blanket that our host has given me from the trunk of her car a few feet from the couple, leaving sufficient room so the poodles can move around without disturbing me. A few other people settle in close by: two men, one cradling a bottle of champagne; a single woman who instantly lies down in the grass and closes her eyes; and a pair of women, each with a large dog in tow.

While we wait for the music to start, I use the time to do a little people watching, and I notice a couple of things. First of all, there are the early birds: the rail-huggers, those who get to the music tent before anyone else so they can set up their chairs right in front of the railing that separates the in-the-tent listeners from the out-of-the-tent listeners. Then there are the hammock-slingers, who find two trees to suspend their hammock from so they can enjoy the concert while gently swaying back-and-forth in the late afternoon breeze, blocking everyone else's view behind them. And then there are the umbrella-spreaders, who find a spot toward the back of the grassy area to erect their gigantic sun-blocking umbrellas.

And, of course, there are also the latecomers. These generally fall into three groups. Group #1 is comprised of the couple that arrives late to meet their friends. They enter the crowd timidly until they locate their party, at which time they make a beeline for it. Group #2 is comprised of those people who have no prearranged meeting plans. For one reason or another, they arrive late and discreetly try to find a place to sit without disturbing those around them. Group #3 is comprised of those couples—they're always couples—that arrive late and could care less if they disturb anyone. They just plow though the group, plunk down their folding chairs (which can be anything from a small folding seat to an elaborately-engineered chaise lounge), pull out their chilled bottle of wine, and start talking or rustling about without any deference whatsoever to those around them.

And then there is everyone in between.

There are the partygoers, who range from a couple sharing a bottle of wine and a few hors d'oeuvres to a blanket full of friends indulging in all sorts of food and drink.

There are the newlyweds (wed or not, they are most definitely in a new relationship), who lie down and snuggle the entire time, hands occasionally disappearing beneath an article of clothing here and there.

There are the dog-coddlers, who settle down on a blanket, dog in lap, and stay put the entire time, only occasionally shifting their precious cargo from one side to another.

There are the dog-walkers, who can't seem to settle down at all, who are up and down the entire concert, fulfilling some unknown mobility need (human or canine, I do not know).

And let us not forget the book-readers, the gum-chewers, the soda-can poppers, the bathroom-goers, the allergy-sneezers, and the insect-scratchers. It's an endless list, which I'd gladly add to but at the moment I'm a bit distracted: while the French poodles behind me have been gnawing on rawhide sticks making one God-awful racket, the dogs in front of me have been unmercifully trying to hump each other.

But I can't think of this too much because I'm much more concerned about sliding down the grassy hill and ending up at the bottom in a lump. It turns out that my seating choice—the side of a grassy hill—was not that astute. The blanket my host graciously gave me acts more like a sled than a cushion. It is all I can do to stop myself from sliding down the hill. I even try rolling up my shoes at the bottom of the blanket to act as a kind of "stop" for my feet; that only slows, but does not check my descent to the bottom of the hill.

As I'm trying to process all of the above, my wife emerges from the music tent.

"Wasn't that a wonderful concert?" She beams as she approaches.

"Oh, splendid, delightful," I squeak, trying to wrestle one of my shoes away from one of the dogs at the bottom of the hill.

38 | What's the Hurry?

THE MUSIC FESTIVAL IS only the first stop on our Aspen tour. There are several other stops of note. On Tuesday, we drive "down valley" to meet C.C., my wife's hiking guide for the day. We spend the day outside of Carbondale at the Fins, a series of rocky spikes or "fins" that jut straight out of the side of a mountain. While my wife and C.C. march up the mountainside, I sit and read a book. Hiking's never been my cup of tea, especially when it means bushwhacking up the side of a mountain. When they return and we have dropped C.C. off at her car, my wife and I head off to view a collection of Jasper Johns' prints at the Powers Museum, a high-end, ultra-modern museum tucked away in the corner of a mega-millionaire's estate. On the way home we stop at Anderson Ranch, a well-known art center in Snowmass Village, where my wife has taught several times.

On Thursday, we head down valley again (apparently, that's where the action is if you want more than a gondola ride to the top of Aspen Mountain). While my wife and her guide-for-the-day explore Seven Castles, a collection of "castle-like" rock formations east of town, I spend the afternoon at Saxy's Café. Later that afternoon we head toward Aspen but turn off on a winding road that takes us deep into a long open valley. Our destination: St. Benedict's

Monastery. The reason: Thursday evening Mass, which is open to the public. St. Benedict's Monastery—and Sunday's Open Market in Basalt—is the highlight of the trip for me. Watching the sun go down through the birch trees in the middle of a valley in rural Colorado while listening to a dozen monks chanting makes the entire trip worthwhile.

I'm thinking about this while standing on the seat of my office chair in Chicago pulling post-it notes out of a book I found misplaced on my bookshelves. Yes, I'm still at it: trying to complete my yearlong office-cleaning job. The first four shelves went like clockwork. I plowed through my journals and notebooks pretty easily. The book inventory shelf was also a snap. Not too many surprises on the next shelf: books to support my author programs and my "trim size" collection. And the next shelf—family photographs—doesn't even count.

The last four shelves, though stocked with fourfold the amount of books, shouldn't cause that much of a problem either since they contain books about children's literature exclusively: mainly critical studies, textbooks, genre studies, biographies of leading figures in the field, and several folk and fairy tale collections. Although there's a lot to process, the books are pretty well organized, mainly because I haven't thought about the academic side of children's books for a long, long time.

My first exposure to this side of the ledger came when I was a junior faculty member and was asked to teach a survey class on children's literature by a senior faculty member who was going on sabbatical leave. Fortunately, before she left, she handed me her syllabus. The syllabus was a real mind-opener: in twelve weeks the class covered three distinct literary traditions—the Bible, Greek and Roman Mythology, and European Folk and Fairy Tales. *You can't understand children's literature if you don't understand these three facets of Western civilization*, the senior faculty member said as she handed me her syllabus and a sheath of notes.

And she was right. I don't know how you can read works by Madeleine L'Engle, C. S. Lewis, Philip Pullman, Neil Gaiman, and J. K. Rowling if you don't have a solid understanding of the basic foundations of Western literature, religious and secular. As I said, her syllabus was a real mind-opener. For me, it put the study of children's literature on par with the study of any Western literary tradition. As a result, I started to collect a variety of materials to support this incredibly expansive point of view, not only to make me a better teacher and academician, but also to help me become a better writer.

And that's why I'm standing on the seat of my office chair pulling post-it notes out of a book I found misplaced on my bookshelves in my collection of children's literature reference material. You know, I do that occasionally: I grab a book or two and stuff them between the gap that two collections make when they don't bump up against each other. It's kind of like using books as bookends. The "bookends" I found this morning are an interesting lot: Robert Pirsig's *Zen and the Art of Motorcycle Maintenance*, Harold Lamb's *Genghis Khan: The Emperor of All Men*, Fred Watson's *Stargazer: The Life and Times of the Telescope*, and Carl Jung's *Memories, Dreams, Reflections*.

It's the first book—*Zen and the Art of Motorcycle Maintenance*—that grabs my attention, and not because it's filled with old post-it notes. I bought it when it first came out for several reasons. First of all, I had just gotten a divorce and I was on a quest: I was searching for the meaning of life, *my* life. You do that after significant life events, and a divorce is certainly a significant event. Secondly, Pirsig's motorcycle adventures took him through Montana, which piqued my interest as I had been living in Montana for several years. Finally, I wanted to buy a motorcycle (that also happens after a divorce: you spread your wings a little, usually somewhat foolishly) and I thought I might learn something about riding and maintaining a motorcycle. But I learned quickly—not from Pirsig's book, but from an Indian 500 that slid out from under me while I was making a U-turn on a gravel road—that I'm not cut out to ride a motorcycle.

As I stand on the seat of my chair, holding Pirsig's book and surveying my office bookshelves, a smile spreads across my face: only one more wall—the north wall—to address and I'm done with my office-cleaning project. There's some gratification in that, knowing that I'll actually finish what I set out to do. But the north wall is somewhat misleading. It doesn't have any bookshelves on it, just two desks with a file cabinet wedged between them. But the desks and the file cabinet are laden with stacks of books and papers and other writing paraphernalia. But, not to worry, it's only September, so there's plenty of time to tackle it, especially because my wife has one more artist residency planned—a three-week "no spouse" residency on Bainbridge Island. *No spouse!* That means I have almost three weeks to get started on this last, but truly onerous task before I leave to join her at the end of the residency.

Three weeks… Alone…. At home… Hey, what's the hurry? There's plenty of time to get started. Might as well kick back and read a book. And I know just the one I want to read.

Part IV

The last few days in Chicago have been glorious with clear blue skies, and not even a hint of the usual mixture of low-slung clouds and factory smog. Against the sky, trees linger in a state of suspended animation, waiting for their first brush with winter. It's as if they're in some deep yogic pose—breathe in, breathe out, slowly now, hold that pose.

39 | Dear Mr. Pirsig

I READ YOUR BOOK. I read it three times. Twice when it first came out. And now, some forty years later, as a result of finding it misplaced on my bookshelves. I think everyone should read it: once when they're young and once years later. When I first read your book I really didn't have anything to bounce it off of. I mean, I liked motorcycles, but I quickly found out that they weren't for me. I tried Buddhism while I was in college, but it didn't stick. If truth be told, which seems to be the essence of your book, I related more to your son Chris and his problems than anything else in the book.

I'm older now, by three or four decades. Now I get it. Or at least I'm better able to bounce your ideas off of my life as it's played out over the last several decades. I understand it primarily through the lens of a writer. That be-here-now attitude that you keep coming back to is essential for any writer: we must be in the moment in order to see—and write—properly. So much goes by when you're not in the moment, when your thoughts take you away from the moment. Of course, today, being in the moment is clouded by the pervasiveness of technology.

I can't tell you how many times I see young people with their heads immersed in some electronic device as the world around them spins by unnoticed. What does it mean to be in the moment in a world where everything flashes by? Perhaps "the moment" is just that: a flash, a whirl, a flicker that goes by so quickly that it's hopeless to even try to be in it. Instead, we distract ourselves: we facebook, we tweet, we snapchat the world, hoping that someone—anyone—is paying attention to us in that particular nanosecond of time.

I just left a local coffeehouse because it was jam-packed. It was totally my fault. I violated Coffeehouse Etiquette Rule #23: never go to a coffeehouse on the weekend. I left not only because I felt claustrophobic, but also because I realized that everyone around me was tweeting, snapchatting, or facebooking. I felt awkward, out of place—a stranger in a strange land—because I was one of the few people in the place holding a book. But I am committed to books, to reading and rereading them (at least, the very best ones), and occasionally to filling them with post-it notes. It's my mental territory. I own it. And I don't feel any need to share it with anyone, at least until I'm good and ready. But isn't that what writing—or any artistic process—is? To paraphrase Avi's Mangus again: writers trade time for books. You can't make that trade if you're constantly plugged into an electronic device, paying more attention to someone else's thoughts than your own. Your message is crystal clear: stop, unplug, slow down, notice, and reflect—the world will still be there when you return. Or, as you put it:

> On a cycle the frame is gone. You're completely in contact with it all. You're 'in' the scene, not just watching it anymore, and the sense of presence is overwhelming. That concrete whizzing by five inches below your foot is the real thing, the same stuff you walk on, it's right there, so blurred you can't focus on it, yet you can put your foot down and touch it

> anytime, and the whole thing, the whole experience, is never removed from immediate consciousness.

It's all about "seeing." It's all about being present. Ram Das wasn't that far off after all when he titled his book *Be Here Now*. It's a little more obtuse than your book, but—like yours—it's right on the money. As I read your book for the third (maybe fourth) time, I see myself much more clearly in it. Not only is there more to your book than I first gleaned, there's also much more to me.

Perhaps one of the most important things I learned in this reading is the difference between being a spectator and being a participant. You deftly describe the difference when you wrote about the young mechanics that butchered your motorcycle. Rather than having skin in the game, being invested in the maintenance process, they were disturbingly aloof:

> They were like spectators. You had the feeling they had just wandered in there themselves and somebody had handed them a wrench. There was no identification with the job. No saying, "I am a mechanic." At 5 p.m. or whenever their eight hours were in, you knew they would cut it off and not have another thought about their work. They were already trying not to have any thoughts about their work 'on' the job...they were...living with technology without really having anything to do with it. Or rather, they had something to do with it, but their own selves were outside of it, detached, removed. They were involved in it, but not in such a way as to care.

In my transition from traditional author to self-published author, I've had a similar experience. When you publish a picture book for young readers through traditional channels, you're the first one in and the first one out. Let me explain. The picture book process starts with the author (unless you're that rare breed—an author/illustrator). An author submits a manuscript to a publishing house and, once it's accepted (a long shot, believe me), he or she works with the editor to revise the text if it needs it. Once the text has been approved, then you—the writer—are kicked out the door and the "real" work of creating a children's picture book begins (with the editor, art director, book designer, and illustrator banging their heads together until it's finished). That leaves me—the writer—on the outside looking in. I learned that with one of my first books when, upon receiving the advance review copy, I responded to the editor's post-it note affixed to the cover. I took the question "How do you like it?" literally and replied to her in a three-page letter. Only later did I realize that the question was rhetorical, with "How do you like it?" a stand-in for "Like it or not, it's done."

Self-publishing is a whole other game. You're not a spectator looking in, hoping that the powers that be—editor, illustrator, book designer, printer, etc.—do their job and do it well. You are much more of a participant. You are much more aware that the concrete whizzing by below your feet is real. In other words, self-publishing is a game of being present, a game of paying attention, because if you don't you will not survive (or, at least, you won't recover your production costs). As a self-published author, not only do I pay more attention to my writing, I also pay more attention to books. I look more carefully at how they're set up; I take note of font choices, text layout, front and back matter, pagination—every little detail that previously I took for granted.

Your book has reinforced for me the need to be present, to take note, and then to act accordingly out of my conscious, analytic mind (your "classic" mode), but also out of my artistic, intuitive self (your "romantic" mode). That's the great learning that I've had, the summation of the last ten years of my writing life: I can do this thing—self-publishing—as long as I commit myself to it fully. And I would except for the fact that I have to move on to the north wall of my office so I can complete my yearlong office-cleaning project.

40 | What Jane Yolen Said

THE LAST WALL, THE north wall—two desks and a file cabinet. Once I tackle these, I'm finished...done...kaput. The first thing I have to tackle is the plastic shelving unit that rises ominously from my work desk. I don't know what got into me. First of all, it's plastic; I hate plastic (my wife won't even let it into the house). Second of all, it's a really poor use of space (all those papers lying flat could easily be stored in file folders in a small drawer). But there they are: six stacks of plastic shelves, eight units tall. It's a lot of plastic.

I start pulling papers, booklets, and other oddities out of the shelving units and place them in piles on my office floor. As I do, I realize there's a lot more than just paper in there. Along with old contracts, editor correspondence, promotion materials, and a file of old headshots, I pull out book catalogs, CDs, empty file folders, old magazines, two ancient slide carousels, a slim box of "love letters" from my wife after we first met (I saved hers; I don't know if she saved mine), and several packets of "proto-books."

Alter Ego: "Excuse me—*proto-books?*"
Ego: "They're my earliest attempts at being a writer, only I wasn't thinking 'writer' exclusively; I was thinking 'writer/illustrator.'"

Alter Ego: "You, an illustrator?"
Ego: "Why not? I have a pretty good eye."
Alter Ego: "Yeah, but very little eye-hand coordination."
Ego: "Thanks a lot."
Alter Ego: "But it's true."
Ego: "But I didn't know that when I first started out. I thought that I could do it all—write, illustrate, and design books for young readers."
Alter Ego: "You and everyone else."
Ego: "Ouch."
Alter Ego: "Please don't be offended. I'm just being realistic."
Ego: "At least I tried. I wrote and illustrated four or five early stories, and one—*Sky Monster*—was a runner-up for the SCBWI's Don Freeman Award for Illustration. Not bad. Not bad at all."
Alter Ego: "Not bad, but not very good either. Go ahead, tells us what Jane Yolen said about your work."
Ego: "Jane Yolen? You mean *the* Jane Yolen?"
Alter Ego: "Yes, *the* Jane Yolen who's published over 200 children's books and won just about every award out there Go ahead, tell us, what did she say?"
Ego: "Well, she was a judge the year I entered the Don Freeman Award and she said that my work was...well..."
Alter Ego: "Go ahead, what did she say?"
Ego: "She said my work was quaint in a simple, folksy kind of way."
Alter Ego: "And you took that as a compliment?"
Ego: "At the time, I took everything as a compliment."
Alter Ego: "Well, what she really meant was *quaint* as in *half-baked*, and I don't think she meant that as a compliment."
Ego: "Okay, I get it. You're right. Actually, that's why I stopped trying to illustrate my own books. It's not as easy as you think."
Alter Ego: "I'll second that."

It's tough getting any work done when you have to stop all the time to talk to yourself. Unfortunately, it happens to me all the time. When my wife is upstairs in the morning, doing yoga and listening to the news, she often calls downstairs to ask who's in the kitchen with me: *Nobody, dear, it's just me.*

Yes, it's just me, and I do talk to myself (or, as Robert Pirsig would say, I'm in the midst of an extended Chautauqua). After finding a place for the small pile of proto-books on my work desk, and grumbling to myself the entire time, I turn to another stack of items—several unfinished writing projects. Every author has them (and we're not talking story ideas tucked away in an "ideas" folder; we're talking fully fleshed-out writing projects that for one reason or another have come to a grinding halt). The one that I'm staring at is the outcome of two previous books: *The Men Who Made the Yankees* and *Dear Frank: Babe Ruth, the Red Sox, and the Great War.*

I guess you could say I have a Babe Ruth fascination, and you'd be right: I do. I started reading about Ruth when I was in high school, mainly because I was head-over-heels in love with the game of baseball. I played varsity ball for four years at a private high school in Florida (not that I was any good; it's just that we didn't have enough players to have a junior varsity squad as well). And, as I mentioned earlier, it didn't hurt that my mother dated major league baseball players in town for spring training.

Yes, I was a baseball fanatic. And I could have been a very rich baseball fanatic if (a) my mother had married one of the baseball players she dated, and (b) she hadn't thrown out my collection of autographed baseballs while I was away at college. Through the years, however, my fascination with the original Yankee slugger—George Herman "Babe" Ruth—never flagged. I thought he was a powerhouse both on and off the field. But it was his off-the-field antics that really captured my imagination, so I wrote a tongue-in-cheek sketch of him that I called *The Things He Could Have Been, or The Almost True Story of Babe Ruth.*

I came across the idea when I was doing photo research for the books I mentioned above. I stumbled across a photo-biography of Ruth that showed quite a wide array of photographs taken of him both on and off the field. What interested me were the photographs of him off the field. He was always hamming it up, play-acting a role (in one photograph he's a fireman, in another an actor, then he's a cowboy, a musician, a teacher, or, just as likely, a policeman). And he did it so seriously. If it wasn't for the glint in his eye, that little nod to the viewer that said "Hey, look at me hamming it up," you'd almost believe him. With this in mind, I wrote:

Babe Ruth?
Why, everybody knows who Babe Ruth was.
Your mama knows. Your papa knows.
Your aunts and uncles know.
Your nieces and nephews know.
Why, your whole family knows who Bath Ruth was!
But that doesn't mean they know all the things
he could have been…

That's the lead-in, the set-up, which I followed with a dozen or more verses that captured these various spoofs in a humorous, tongue-in-cheek manner:

He could have been a jazzman,
a real razz-ma-tazz man,
a foot-stompin' rag man.
Yes, he could have been…
but he wasn't!

He could have been a fireman,
a climb-the-ladder-higher man,
a death-defying rescue man.
Yes, he could have been…
but he wasn't!

He could have been a cattleman,
a bronco-bustin' saddle man,
a rough-ridin' range man.
Yes, he could have been…
but he wasn't!

And, of course, he wasn't because, well, he was the Babe:

George Herman "Babe" Ruth,
the hard-hitting homerun king
of the world champion
New York Yankees—
A giant in his time!

I'm sure you're wondering, as I am, why the project is still sitting on my desk. And it is, in several clear plastic folders containing fragments of the manuscript, news clippings and photos, books, and several rejection letters. It's the latter pile that tells the story: no one wanted it. A typical response from an editor was: "Don't you think children might want to read about what Babe Ruth *was* rather than what he wasn't?" Well, maybe, but it's a lot more fun to poke fun at him for all of the things that he wasn't but–quite possibly–could have been.

So, there it sits. No takers. But even though my interest has flagged considerably since I first got the idea, I refuse to throw it away. I'll sort through the material, condense it, and find a new home for it in my office. But it stays. I just don't have the heart to discard it. And, besides, I know I'll publish it: I just don't know how or when.

41 | Body to Body

I FINALLY FOUND IT. I finally found the key to my bank safety deposit box—and, this, after only a couple of years looking for it.

It's in my office, honey.

Yeah, and we know what that means—*you lost it!*

Okay, I did. But I found it, like I find other things.

Early in my writing career I wrote a text for a children's picture book called *Setting the Turkeys Free*. I like to call it my anti-Thanksgiving book. In every other Thanksgiving book for young readers the turkeys don't get away: they get caught and cooked and served up to Grandma and Grandpa and the rest of the family—but not in my book. Nope, all of the turkeys get away. But then they're not running away from people. They're running away from Foxy the Fox, who is really the young protagonist's dog that has turned into a fox in the young boy's imagination. I know, it's all very confusing, but believe me no turkeys get plucked, stuffed, and baked. They all escape (even the boy's dog-turned-hungry-fox morphs back into a playful little pup by the end of the story).

But what does this have to do with losing things?

Everything. You see, I wrote the first draft one night, filed it away in my computer, and then lost it. I couldn't find it no matter how hard I looked (this was before I really understood my computer's search function). One year went by, then two, then three, but no luck: I just couldn't seem to find it. Four years drifted into five, five into six. Then, after seven long years, I finally found it. It was after midnight. I was barely awake. I was looking for something in my computer (I don't even remember what) and *presto!* There it was—*Setting the Turkeys Free.* I read it, tweaked it a bit, and sent it to an editor the next day—and she bought it, just like that.

So finding my safety deposit box key delighted me, but it didn't surprise me. Things appear and disappear and reappear in my life all the time (except my wife; she seems to be a constant). Most people get a safety deposit box so they can keep their valuable items in it, like the deed to their house, the title of their car, their birth certificate, passport, or important financial papers. But not me. I wanted a safety deposit box for one reason and one reason alone: in order to stash my book contracts, copyright certificates, trademark application verification, and book awards—you know, the stuff that really matters. So I got a safety deposit box, but I never used it. It was just too much of a hassle to run to the bank every time I wanted to put something into it, or take something out. In short, I did what most people do: I went to my local office supply store and bought a small, fireproof security box, filled it with my stuff, and shoved it under my office desk.

Anyway, the short of it is I never used the safety deposit box, which explains why I'm trudging to the local branch of my bank under a canopy of blue sky to cancel it (now that I finally found the key). When I get to the bank, I enter a very large atrium and wait to speak to a teller. After a somewhat longish wait, a teller approaches. I explain to her what I need. She motions to me and says, "Follow me." I do, down into the bowels of the bank, to the lower level where the vaults are kept. We sit down in what appears to be a very high security room (cameras pointed every which way), and start the process of canceling my safety deposit box. One question leads to another, multiple forms of identification are produced, drawers are opened, and paperwork riffled through. Finally, the teller looks up from her desk and says:

Teller: "Well, we don't seem to have a record of you ever having a safety deposit box."
Me: "Does that mean I can go?"
Teller: "No, you'll have to fill out a new safety deposit box application form."
Me: "But I don't want to apply to have a box. I just want to turn in my key."
Teller: "How can you turn in your key if we have no record of you ever having a safety deposit box?"
Me: "That's a pretty good question."
Teller [pushing a stack of papers toward me]: "I'll need you to fill these out."

For the next ten minutes or so I fill out one form after another until I have a properly registered safety deposit box. Once the teller has double-checked the paperwork, she looks up at me, smiles, and says: "Now, would you like to cancel your safety deposit box?"

"Uh-huh," I reply haltingly.

"Great, I'll just need you to fill out *these* papers."

At this point in the late-night comedy show the audience would hear a loud THUD as the guest falls over backwards in a display of disbelief. But I don't. I oblige, hoping to salvage what is left of the morning, and fill out the requisite cancelation papers. When

I finish, and the teller has double-checked the forms, she picks up the phone and calls security: "I need to go into the vault and need someone present." Within in a minute or two Jason bounds down the stairs, says hello, and disappears into a back room (so much for security). Meanwhile, the teller takes an oversized key ring from a lower drawer, beckons me to follow her, and heads toward the vault door. "You'll have to verify that the box is empty," she says rather dryly. After trying four or five keys, she finally unlocks the door to the vault and enters.

I follow her down a small corridor lined floor-to-ceiling with safety deposit boxes. After a brief search, we find mine—#2327—at the very top, just beneath the water-stained ceiling. To open the box, the teller has to insert two keys—my key and a master key. I can tell from her height that the teller is going to have a difficult time doing this. After she tries once or twice, I say, "Let me try." She looks at me, suspiciously, and then says, "Okay." Although I'm tall enough to insert the keys into the locks, I'm not tall enough to turn them and pull out the box at the same time. We look around for a stool or a chair to help us. Nothing. After a minute or two, the teller calls out, "Jason, Jason." But Jason apparently isn't within earshot. My guess is that the backroom he's disappeared into is the employee lounge and he's deep into a salami sub by now.

"Look, I really need to get going. How about I lift you up?" I offer.

She stares at me, this time with a bit more suspicion in her gaze.

"Okay, I have a better idea. I'll get down on my hands and knees. You stand on my back and pull the safety deposit box out, and we're done."

She looks at me. Then she glances left and right.

"Okay, but let's do it fast."

So I get down on my hands and knees so she can climb up on my back, only I forget a minor detail: she's wearing high heels (not tall ones, mind you; but sharp enough that they dig into my back). I must have flinched, because she lost her balance. Fortunately, Jason, fresh from his salami sub, appears, quickly assesses what's happening, and lunges for the safety deposit box that's flying through the air. He catches it just as the teller crashes down on top of me. While we lie crumpled at his feet, Jason pops the safety deposit box lid open and beams, "It's empty."

I'M REMINDED OF A similarly embarrassing experience I had many years ago. I was in the market for term life insurance and had contacted a company that sent a nurse out to assess my state of health before issuing the policy. She was a middle-aged woman of robust proportions. Most of the exam consisted of a steady stream of questions: *How tall are you? How much do you weigh? Do you smoke? Have you ever smoked? Do you drink? Have you ever had any heart problems? What about cancer?*

After the barrage of questions came the physical assessment part of the exam—temperature, blood pressure, pulse, and all of that. She took out her nurse's kit and asked if there was a place that I could lie down. Since we only have a love seat and a couple of chairs separated by several small tables in our living room, I suggested upstairs in the bedroom. She looked at me the way the bank teller looked at me, with suspicion.

"Well, I could lie down on the floor," I finally offered.

"That will be fine," she replied.

So I stretched out on the large rag rug that my wife had made in art school and waited. After fussing with her nurse's kit for some time, she proceeded to kneel down next to me, only the heel on her small pumps caught in the loose threads of the rag rug and she lost her balance. The next thing I know she's on top of me—stretched out, prone, eyeball-to-eyeball flat on top of me. As I took in the strong fragrance of her perfume, all I could think of was a song I used to sing in my yoga ashram days: *Heart to heart, mind to mind, body to body, it's so divine.*

The other thing I thought about was my wife. What if she came home right at this moment? How would I explain to her the fact that a busty, heavily perfumed woman was lying on top of me on the living room floor? I'm not sure that I could have. Fortunately, I didn't have to because the nurse, mortified by the experience, rolled off of me, jumped to her feet, and flew out the front door before I could say Paramahansa Yogananda.

42 | Location, Location, Location

I'M UP EARLY TODAY. I'm up early because I want to get to Hyde Park on Chicago's south side before all of the parking spaces are taken. I'm going to Hyde Park for the 30th anniversary of the Children's Book Fair held each September in Nichols Park. Although the fair doesn't start until 11:00 a.m., I want to get a parking spot next to the park to make loading and unloading a little easier. So I'm up before the sun and out the door by eight in order to claim a spot. As it turns out, I get the last of two remaining spots (I guess other people have the same idea as I do).

Before unloading, however, I walk around the park and look for a spot to put my vendor's table. Getting into the fair means that you get a table and two chairs. In the early years of the fair, the coordinators selected each vendor's spot, taping the vendor's name to the table. When you arrived you strolled around the park until you found your table, whether or not you actually liked the spot that had been selected for you. Since there were always no-shows, you'd see vendors trading their spot for the spot of a no-show (or, more sinisterly, you'd see vendors taking another vendor's table before the other vendor arrived).

But all of this has changed (I guess there were too many complaints, not to mention logistics to deal with). Now when you arrive the first thing you do is pick a spot and then check in with the fair's coordinators, who then deliver a table and two chairs to you at the spot you've chosen. This eliminates all of the hassles mentioned above, and cuts down on the number of tables and chairs lugged around that no one uses.

Of everything you do at the fair, picking your spot *is* the most important. It's the old real estate adage: *location, location, location.* As I survey the park and the different walking paths meandering through it, I decide on a partially shaded spot at the intersection of two walking paths. "Great spot," says one of the coordinators as she walks by. I think so too. After two volunteers deliver a table to the spot, I cover it with my table drapery and head back to my car. After all, it isn't even 8:30 a.m. I check my email, leaf through a magazine, and listen to the radio. After an hour or so I walk to a nearby coffeehouse to buy a drink and get change for a twenty (a vendor without change is like a golfer without tees).

When I return to the car I start to think about the best way to haul my stuff to the table. I could haul everything in one trip because I'm an efficient packer, whether it's clothes for a trip or books for a fair. I have three vintage hand-painted suitcases that fit nicely on a large-wheeled roll-cart. Since it is still early I decide to make two trips. Think of it as Exercise Rule #43: *If you can make two trips out of one, do it; the exercise will do you good.* So I do: I make two trips. When I arrive at my table I notice that the spot is no longer partially shaded; it's in full sun. But I don't think too much about it. After all, it's mid-September and in the low 70s. After I make a second trip and begin to set everything up, I start to feel the sun. It's hot, not uncomfortably hot, but it's hot, hot enough that I start to look around for a spot in the shade. I see one that might work. It's not as central, but there are two other vendors setting up nearby. I flag down one of the fair coordinators (the one who earlier said, "Great spot") and ask if I can get a couple of volunteers to help me move. She looks at me curiously and walks away.

Several minutes later a couple of volunteers appear, carefully lift the table at either end, and follow me to the new location. After I rearrange a few items that have fallen over, I introduce myself to the vendors on either side of me. On my left are two women selling books for a large distributor of children's books. On my right is mother-daughter duo, but I'm not sure what they're selling. As I talk to them I realize that they are selling a book that the daughter has self-published. The girl is nine years old and the title of her book is *My Day in the Library*. Unfortunately, it *looks* like a nine-year-old child wrote and illustrated it. It's emblematic of what authors face today: everyone, and I mean *everyone*, is getting in on the publishing act.

Alter Ego: "But isn't that what you're doing?"
Ego: "Well, yes, but I'm an adult, not to mention a published author."
Alter Ego: "But if you can self-publish a book, why can't this young girl, or anyone else for that matter?"
Ego: "Yes, I understand what you're getting at, but…"
Alter Ego: "I've heard you say it yourself: *Let the free market sort things out.*"
Ego: "Yes, and I believe that. If you don't like a book, don't buy it. It's pretty simple."
Alter Ego: "So why are you getting worked up over this girl's book?"
Ego: "It's the idea that anyone can write a book. It creates a false sense of accomplishment."
Alter Ego: "False sense?"

Ego: "Yes. Years ago, I read a newspaper editorial that really nailed it titled 'Feeling Good, But Doing Poorly.'"
Alter Ego: "But don't we want kids to feel good?"
Ego: "Of course we do, but not at the expense of a healthy sense of accomplishment."

As I'm having this internal dialogue—Chautauqua—a mother and her son walk up to my table to check out my books. I smile, introduce myself, say something about this or that book, and then I notice the t-shirt that the boy is wearing. Emblazoned on the front of it are the words: *I am your future president!* Maybe I have it all wrong. Maybe we should encourage everyone to reach for the stars. If they fail, well, they fail. What's wrong with that? I extend my hand to the boy and say, "Hello, young man, do you mind if I shake the hand of a future president?" His mother smiles as we shake hands. Not ten minutes after they leave a family walks by and emblazoned on their son's t-shirt is the slogan: *Someday I'm going to discover something incredible!* Wow, I think, it sure is a different world. When I was young, I didn't get a lot of encouragement; in fact, most of the time my stepdad just beat the crap out of me. I mean, what if he actually encouraged me? Maybe I could have been president, instead of the author of a measly two-dozen books.

I should be used to it. After all, it *is* Hyde Park. I relax a little, look around, take in the scene, and note the variety of people strolling through the park. There's the local high school drum corps. Cinderella and Goldilocks (two face painters across the main aisle from me). A rather tall man with a wooden "cobra" wound around his neck. An overly jolly clown named Simon. Several prepubescent girls in tutus working their way to a makeshift stage. The usual storybook characters—Curious George, Winnie-the-Pooh, and

Clifford the Dog—milling about in the crowd. An elderly woman dressed as Mother Goose holding a Mother Goose puppet.

And then there's Crazy Man.

Crazy Man is a wild-eyed, single-toothed, middle-aged man with long, straggly hair (an ex-chess champion or nuclear physicist, I'm guessing). When he steps up to my table everyone else steps back and leaves. He stares at me, then at my books, then at my table sign: *Get your autographed books here*. With the hint of a twinkle still remaining in his one good eye, he intones: "Why limit it to books? How about signing my jacket, or my pants, or my shoes?" He laughs. I smile. Then he launches into a serious monologue about a manuscript that his one-armed ex-girlfriend left him. It is an unpublished manuscript that his ex-girlfriend's mother had written about how she survived World War II, Nazi concentration camps, and the Communist purges during the McCarthy era.

"Really?" I gasp, not knowing what else to say.

Finally, after fifteen minutes of ranting and raving, he pauses and says that I should contact him because he needs help publishing the manuscript and that I just might be the right person to help him publish it. Then he takes out a crumpled sheet of paper and proceeds to write down his contact information. When he hands it to me I can't make out a single word. Absolutely nothing makes sense. His scrawl looks like writing, but I can't read it. I do recognize some numbers at the bottom of the page. As I study them he says, "That's my phone number. Call me. When I answer say that you met me at the book fair. And say it quickly. I get a lot of crank calls, hundreds a day. When the phone rings I don't know if I'll be speaking to a human or an alien."

"Really?" I repeat, as Crazy Man turns and walks away.

About a half hour later I see Crazy Man again, bending the ear of an Eagle Scout a couple of tables down from me. He's hovering over a handmade telegraph set that is hooked up to a 12-volt battery, mesmerized by the click-click-clicking of the contraption. I'm sure he's telling the Eagle Scout, who made the telegraph from scratch, that he's receiving a message from an alien ship hovering over Hyde Park. I have time to observe them because even though it's a gorgeous day on the south side of Chicago, it's been a pretty paltry day in terms of sales. I've sold a few books, but not much. One of the reasons is that there are several non-profit organizations here that are giving away books for free. *What? No wonder I'm not selling any books.* But it's not a total loss. By the end of the day I've sold enough to cover my costs. Not only that, but I do a good deed.

Across the grassy aisle from me—where Goldilocks and Cinderella have staked their ground—there's a line of families queuing up to get their child's face painted. It's a really long line and it's moving very slowly. Seeing the frustration of many parents, I hold up a permanent marker and say, "Parents, don't wait any longer. Come over here and I'll paint your child's face with my permanent marker for free." There are lots of chuckles, but no takers. Then, a little girl loses her balloon. As it sails skyward, she goes bonkers. I mean, she lets out a series of wails that turns everyone's head. She cries and cries—more screams than cries—while her flustered parents stand helplessly by. I look around, thinking: *We've got to get this kid a balloon and fast.* I quickly scan the area and see a balloon tied to an empty chair on the far side of the park. Since no one is at my table, I jog over to the chair, unfasten it, and head back to the couple trying to console their now totally hysterical child.

"Hello," I say as I approach the threesome. "You won't believe it, but I found this balloon floating by and thought that your daughter might like to have it."

The parents, at the point of exhaustion, are speechless. They take it, thank me profusely, and tie the ribbon dangling from the balloon to their daughter's wrist, which instantly calms her down. Now I'd like to say that it was a noble act, but it was either listen to the girl scream for another half hour or die from the boredom of no sales.

43 | Fire in the Belly

SOME DAYS IT'S INESCAPABLE. Some days my work list is so long that I have to devote an entire day to it. And that's what's happening today. I thought I'd spend at most an hour or two on it this morning, but it's already lunchtime and I still haven't finished half of what I need to do. And what do I have to do? Here are a few things on my list:

1. Update Rates and Availability page on website.
2. Revise author profile on Amazon's Author Central Page.
3. Email book order form to schools in Bloomington and Crown Point.
4. Order books from university library on self-publishing and marketing.
5. Add Children's Book Fair to website's Calendar of Events.
6. Get *Shark Man* ready to send to Florida distributor.
7. Take books culled from bookshelves to used bookstore.
8. Stop at post office to put *Shark Man* in the mail.
9. Head to office supply store to buy more mailers and packaging tape.

It's almost three o'clock in the afternoon when I finally make it to a coffeehouse to have my "morning coffee." I open my computer ready to write and realize that I have to create an invoice for a school that I'll be speaking at in October. *Argh!*

I think this is why many successful authors have office managers, booking agents, publicists, and any other odd number of assistants–virtual or otherwise–to help them manage their affairs so they can concentrate on writing. My wife talks about this all the time. After reading the latest issue of *Sculpture Magazine*, she often points out the big players in the field, never failing to note the half dozen or more assistants standing around in the background of each artist's studio portrait. How on earth can one person do it all? Especially in today's big money, multimedia, social networking, digital world? DIY it is not. But the fact of the matter is that most artists do most things themselves.

I do. My wife does. So do many of our artist friends. We do it all—idea development, production, marketing, sales, you name it. It comes down to one thing—drive, or as my wife likes to say *fire-in-the-belly.* If you don't have that fire-in-the-belly about your work you might as well hang it up and move to Florida. It's about staying focused, moving forward, working steadily, even during those facets of the work process that don't exactly excite you, like managing your website, ordering new inventory, creating an ad campaign, or packaging books to go out in the mail. If you can do that, stay focused from one high to the next, ignoring the troughs in between, then you have a chance to succeed, or at least sustain that fire-in-the-belly about your work.

Tommy Hilfiger's got it. He's got that fire-in-the-belly. I know he does because he was just on the *PBS Newshour* talking about *American Dreamer*, a memoir of his life as a fashion designer and businessman. When the commentator asked him if there were times when he wanted to give up and walk away from it all, Hilfiger replied that there were several times he felt like this, when things just weren't going exactly the way he thought they should. But he didn't give up: he persisted. That's fire-in-the-belly. As long as I have it, I'll keep writing and publishing and promoting my books. Only right now, I'm in a trough, a really deep trough of my own doing.

REMEMBER THE STORY I told you about Nick Cooper, the alias that I used with contractors after my wife and I bought our house. Remember that my name—W. Nikola-Lisa—is not so easy to figure out. Remember that my wife said that I should have changed my name to Nick Cooper when we married, that it would be easier all around (not to mention that Nikola Cooper would make a great writer's name). Remember that? Well, forget it! *No way, José. Not now. Not ever.*

Unfortunately, it turns out that she was right. I should have ditched W. Nikola-Lisa. But rather than change my name to Nick Cooper, I should have returned to my given birth name. I would have avoided a lot of hassle. In the age of heightened national security, when old people can't get on an airline without being strip-searched, and toddlers are fondled just in case they have a bomb tucked away in their diapers, using an official, government-approved name is a must. And neither Nick Cooper nor W. Nikola-Lisa is such a name. Only my birth name will do: William John Nikola.

Welcome to the 21st century.

Welcome to increased government scrutiny.

Welcome to TSA and the pre-approval process.

Since William John Nikola is on my birth certificate and on my passport, that's the only name that TSA will accept in order to get my Known Traveler Number (KTN). And getting your TSA KTN means that you can whisk through security without taking off your belt, your shoes, your watch, your pants, and anything else that's not riveted to your body. It also means that you can sleep in a little later on the day you plan to travel.

But try getting your TSA KTN when your name doesn't match your paperwork.

TSA Agent: "So, you want to do what?"
Me: "I'd like to apply for TSA Pre Approval, only the name I use for most things is not my given birth name."
TSA Agent [leaning forward]: "The name you use for most things? And what is that name?"
Me [shoving my driver's license toward the official]: "W. Nikola-Lisa."
TSA Agent: "You can show me anything you'd like, but what I need to see is your birth certificate and your passport if you have one. And if you've changed your name, I'll need to see an official, court-approved Change of Name form."
Me: "But I never changed my name legally. But I do have a valid driver's license, an insurance card, and my latest gas bill all with the name W. Nikola-Lisa printed on them. Even my social security card lists my name as W. Nikola-Lisa. Can't I use W. Nikola-Lisa for my TSA Pre Approval name?"
TSA Agent: "Not unless you legally changed your name. For TSA purposes, you are William John Nikola, until otherwise informed. And, by the way, why do you attach 'Lisa' to your last name?"

Me [squirming in my chair]: "Well, it's my former wife's last name. We put our names together when we married. 'Nikola-Lisa' sounded so, so musical."

TSA Agent: "*Musical?* That's why you took your former wife's last name? It sounded musical?"

ME: "Yes, and I'd like to keep using it, you see…"

TSA Agent: "Look, buddy, you've been divorced for thirty years. Get over it. Drop 'Lisa' and go by your given birth name, unless you'd like to spend the next few months changing your name legally through the court system."

Me: "No, sir, William John Nikola will be just fine. Thank you."

TSA Agent [smiling]: "Next in line."

If there's a silver lining in the process, it's that I'm a writer. And it's a good thing that I am because it looks like I might have a ton of paperwork to complete in the coming months because once I change the name on my driver's license, which needs to conform to my TSA Pre Approval name (or I'll have to carry my passport around with me every time I fly somewhere), I'll need to change the name listed on my car title, and on my car insurance policy, and on my voter registration card, and on the water bill, and on the electric and gas bills, and on my home insurance policy, not to mention the cards I get from Social Security and Medicare, *and…and…and…*

What was I thinking—*W. Nikola-Lisa?* It doesn't even make sense.

Argh!

44 | Bicameral Mind

> Having just finished *The Origin of Consciousness*, I myself feel something like Keats' Cortez staring at the Pacific, or at least like the early reviewers of Darwin or Freud. I'm not quite sure what to make of this new territory; but its expanse lies before me and I am startled by its power.

THAT'S WHAT EDWARD PROFITT, writing in *Commonweal*, had to say about Julian Jaynes' 1976 groundbreaking book, *The Origin of Consciousness in the Breakdown of the Bicameral Mind.* Profitt's quotation could equally describe the current bicameral nature of the publishing industry, with physical books residing in one house and e-books in the other.

The physical book, a direct descendant of the Roman codex, the book-like form that we use in the West, has dominated the scene for centuries, made even more present by Johannes Gutenberg's "invention" of moveable type. Of course, we ascribe to Gutenberg that invention even though we know the Chinese invented it prior to him (in the same way we ascribe to Christopher Columbus the "discovery" of North America). Origins notwithstanding, what Gutenberg did for the physical book, Jeff Bezos did for the e-book: each one providing a radically new means of production (and, in the latter case, a corresponding means of promotion, distribution, and consumption). As a result, we live in a new world, a world or house with two chambers, a bicameral house that allows us to tote around the remnants of a pre-industrial invention and the ephemera of a post-industrial revolution.

The physical book or the electronic book? Take your pick. Many people do, preferring one medium over the other, or, in just as many cases, splitting the difference and using them both. But now there seems to be another choice. To use a term often applied to Chicago, my hometown, there is now a "third coast" of book formatting—the audiobook. With e-book sales flagging, the audiobook appears to be ready to step in and take up the slack. In fact, according to Luke Graham of *CNBC News*, audiobooks are the fastest growing segment of the book industry, outstripping both physical and e-book sales.

Is this the new frontier, the third coast, if you will? On our trip to Penland earlier this summer, my wife and I consumed 17 disks of Peter Matthiessen's *Shadow Country*. Seventeen disks! My God, you almost need to hire an administrative assistant to help keep track of the disks and their whereabouts. For most people, physical disks are a thing of the past (especially for people with Bluetooth-enabled car stereo systems). We're hoping that it will soon be the same for us; that we can go digital (that is, if our new car has a Bluetooth-enabled car stereo system). Then all we have to do is switch on our smartphone, dial up an audiobook, and sit back and enjoy the story.

Of course, I'm hoping it will be one of my books because that's exactly what I'm doing right now: I'm in the process of recording *Dragonfly: A Childhood Memoir* in order to make an audiobook out of it. Well, I'm not recording it. A friend of mine is, but not just any friend: Victor, a professional musician and sound engineer extraordinaire, is recording it. We're holed up on the third floor of his house where he has a state-of-the-art recording studio. It's where he records most of Chicago's Irish musicians. When I ask him why, he just smiles. Victor doesn't say much, but he hears everything. While Victor tests microphones and adjusts the sound level, I huddle over my computer creating an account with Audible, an Amazon subsidiary. Amazon—you just can't seem to get away from the monolith, especially when it comes to books (or shirts, or shoes, or yoga mats, or frozen food).

After Victor's wife delivers a pot of herbal tea to us in Victor's attic-turned-sound-studio, we start to record. I'm situated in one room; Victor's next door in control central. But I can't see him: there's no wall of glass letting us see each other. You've seen this on television or in the movies hundreds of times: the musicians are in a sound-proof room playing their hearts out while the producer and recording engineer are in an adjacent room, studying the artists' every move through a large glass window. Not in Victor's studio. I ask him about it. He replies, in his usual Zen obfuscating manner: "Don't need to see you. Just need to hear you."

The recording goes remarkably well, even easy, but then I've always thrived on a stage, any stage, and the recording studio is just another stage. We record the entire book in less than three hours. After another break for tea we move on to the mixing and mastering phase. This is where Victor's real genius resides. He hears every little glitch and, just as importantly, knows how to fix each and every one of them. Fortunately, there's not too much to adjust. We add the intro and the outro, mark one of the chapters as the Audible "sample chapter," and before you know, I have an audiobook (and Victor's wife has lunch ready and waiting).

We go downstairs and over lunch Victor mentions that since I have mp3 files for the book I should use them to make a CD. I think about this, but not for long. I'm not sold on the idea.

"I don't know, Victor. What if they end up like the last project I did (a music CD), and just take up room on my already overcrowded bookshelves?"

"You could sell them at schools and book fairs. People would jump at the chance to have a CD of your book."

"First of all, they have to 'jump at the chance' to have the physical book. That doesn't seem to be happening to any great degree at the moment. How can an audiobook change that?"

You've heard the old adage "less is more." In the DIY world of independent publishing it appears that "more is more." The more you do, the more formats you have, the more platforms you create, the more media space you inhabit, the better the chance that your book will be discovered which, of course, increases the likelihood that it will go "viral." And "going viral," after all, is the name of the game.

But some days I don't want to go viral. I don't want to do more. All I want to do is write, and after I've finished writing I want to read a good book. And that's what I want to do right now. Unfortunately, I have to paint my bicycle helmet. No, I'm not just freshening it up: I'm changing the color from yellow to orange. And not because orange is the new black. It has nothing to do with that. It has to do with my wife. Well, not actually my wife, but my wife's bicycle helmet. But, then, I'm getting ahead of myself.

Several years ago I had a very bad bicycle accident. While biking one day, my wife and I stopped on a city street near our house. As we stood straddling our bicycles, my wife casually pointed at a house slightly behind me, saying that she wanted me to look at the color of the trim. So I did, I turned and looked at it, but I lost my balance, and when I lose my balance, I lose my balance (the result of contracting a snarky virus after eating a bad burrito). So, I went down hard. I must have gone down hard because the impact of the helmet hitting the street split the back of the helmet like a knife splitting a ripe watermelon.

This, of course, caused me great alarm. I mean, if falling off my bicycle while I'm not even moving can cause such an impact, imagine what a *real* accident can do. So the next day I ran out and bought a new helmet. It was thicker, better padded, and covered more of my head, but it only came in one color—army green.

Wait a minute. Earlier, you said that your helmet was yellow.

It is, or was, but now you're getting ahead of me. Let me explain. You see I bought this really goofy-looking army-green helmet and rode around with it for several weeks until one day some guy in a beat-up truck passes me and yells, "You shouldn't wear an army helmet if you've never been in the army." Unsettled by his harangue, the first thing I did when I got home was to march into my wife's studio and rifle through all of her oil paints until I found a really brilliant yellow. "That's Winsor Lemon," my wife informed me. "I don't care if it's Papaya Purple. I just don't want army green." So I painted the entire helmet bright yellow—I mean, Winsor Lemon.

Everything was fine, terrific, even though when I rode my bike I looked like a smudge of lemon sorbet. But I didn't mind. There was only one problem. My wife's helmet was also brilliant yellow. Not only that but we both wore yellow reflective vests when we rode at night. More times than naught people mistook us for a pair of bicycling policemen (or worse, parking meter patrolmen, the bane of every Chicago driver). But the clincher came last night when we were out in a very hip neighborhood—Lincoln Park on Chicago's north side—and while we were stopped at a light near an outdoor bar and grill some drunk dude started yelling, "Hey, Mom. Hey, Dad. You look cute in your little matching outfits." Judiciously, my wife ignored his rant. Not me. I started fuming and was about to jump off my bike and clobber the kid with my brilliant Winsor Lemon bike helmet when the light changed.

And that's why this morning I'm home in my wife's studio about to paint my bicycle helmet flaming orange, or, as my wife informs me, Cadmium Yellow Deep.

45 | Concord Dust

DO YOU REMEMBER WHEN I wrote in Part I that I'm not a bibliophile; that is, in the technical sense of the word: one who loves and collects rare and exotic books? I also mentioned that I don't have any first editions, at least any that are worth mentioning. Then, I ended my confession with the following: "Moreover, I'm not a collector of fine literature: you'll find very few books by Shakespeare, Dickens, or Dostoevsky; no volumes by Keats, Wordsworth, or Coleridge; and not a lick of Longfellow or Thoreau."

Remember that? Well, forget it. I just bought Robert Sullivan's book *The Thoreau You Don't Know*. I bought it sight unseen from the Daedalus book catalog. I thought it was a catchy title. I also thought that it might be a unique spin both on Thoreau and on how to tackle a biography. It's not the first time I've come across Thoreau however. I was introduced to the nature writer (of course, Sullivan would shudder at my description of Thoreau) in my undergraduate days while studying comparative religion. I took a seminar on the life and work of Mahatma Gandhi. Each week, we read two or three books. Yes, you heard me right. Each week, we read two or three books (only one if it was over 400 hundred pages). Thoreau started us off. To understand Gandhi—and, for that matter, Martin Luther King, Jr.—you have to understand

Thoreau's essay "Civil Disobedience" (which came bound with *Walden*, his most famous piece of writing). So, yes, I'd come across Thoreau, but I can't say that I was enamored of his writing. Like many 19th-century writers, I find him dense and his thinking—though lucid at times—quite round about. In short, I dumped Thoreau at the end of the semester (I think I got enough for the book to eat lunch the next day). Years later I came across the same book in a used bookstore, picked it up, thumbed through it, and then I put it down: in my mind the writing was still a bit too dense for my taste.

But there was something about Sullivan's title (and the book's cover art) that caught my attention—*The Thoreau You Don't Know*. I don't know, it just caught my eye and I bought it. Not only that but I took it on our trip to the Pacific Northwest. I figured if I had to read a book while exploring Vancouver Island, a book about Thoreau was as good as any. Certainly, the opening lines led me to believe this:

> I'd like to introduce the Thoreau you don't know, or don't necessarily know, or know but perhaps never hear people talking about when people talk about Thoreau. People talk a lot about Thoreau in America—they reference him in these days of ecological awareness, in these green times, in times when, as people all along the political spectrum agree, we care about the earth, the wilderness, what's wild. But when we talk about Thoreau, we talk about a particular Thoreau who I would suggest has more to do with us than Thoreau. The Thoreau we already know is, for instance, not here. He's out, away, off in the woods most likely, on the shore of that lonely little pond or ascending a faraway mountain.

The writing was snappy, alluring, full of guile and intrigue. It also had a certain lilting, poetic quality to it, which we hear in the first phrase: "I'd like to introduce the Thoreau you don't know, or don't necessarily know…." Unfortunately, like many books, the writing didn't sustain itself. By the third chapter, Sullivan's writing had lapsed into a slower—even sluggish—pace. By the end of the fourth chapter I found myself leafing through the book, literally leapfrogging over long academic passages, looking for tidbits of information or insight that might justify reading the book in its entirety.

It's a shame. Here I am in the middle of the woods reading about a man who truly loved nature (Thoreau was a nature-lover and a walker; every day he set out, often walking miles through the woods alone or with a friend), and I find myself turning away from his writing—well, not his, but Sullivan's prosaic text about him. It reminds me of an incident I had with a literary agent. I've had only one agent in my writing career. I forged a relationship with her after we met at a writing conference. Although she represented romance writers (Christian romance writers specifically), as well as a few Hollywood screenwriters, she occasionally took in a children's book author or two. I was one of the latter that she took in. But it was at a time in my writing life when I was trying to make a change: I wanted to get out of the business of writing for children in order to tackle more content-heavy stories for the adult market. To that end, I had been writing—and rewriting—a piece of nonfiction on the early history of the Harvard College Observatory. I shared it with my agent and then showed up for a one-on-one conference. After she reamed me out for my dull prosaic writing, I collected my things and walked out—no, I stomped out—of her office. As I reached the door, she chastised me one last time: "And no one, and I mean *no one*, wants to read an encyclopedia entry!"

Okay, I get it. The writing was dead, dead in the same way that Sullivan's writing became stultifying by the third or fourth chapter.

AS I'M WADING THROUGH Sullivan's text, catching a glimmer of brilliance every thirty pages or so, I'm thinking that this is exactly what is going on outside the car window as my wife and I drive through the Pacific Northwest. Every so often we stop at a *Point of Interest* sign. Most of the time the sign explains some unique historical feature: the foundation of an old settlement, a small fishing village that has long since been abandoned, or, more poignantly, a farm that was once owned by a Japanese family interned during the Second World War. Occasionally, however, the sign simply says *Old Spruce Tree.*

The "old" in the sign usually means a tree from an Old Growth forest. Such forests covered the Pacific Northwest before the arrival of European settlers. Once they arrived, all bets were off; they felled every tree in sight. First Nation people also cut down trees—Giant Red Cedars most often—but they took only what they needed and gave plenty of thanks before and afterwards. European settlers took as much as they could—for the burgeoning lumber and paper industries—and rarely stopped to say thanks. Oh, they did, occasionally, setting aside a few "points of interest," but only after they had made a fortune harvesting most of the trees in an area.

Actually, that's how we found ourselves in the Pacific Northwest in the first place. My wife was offered a residency at the Bloedel Reserve, a 150-acre natural preserve at the north end of Bainbridge Island just west of Seattle. Prentice Bloedel established the nature preserve on the site of his family estate toward the end of his life as a place of contemplation for anyone so inclined. He could do this because at one point his family owned most of the logging rights in northwest Washington State and western British Columbia.

This thought brings me back to the occasional roadside sign. Whereas you will not find one single sign on the Bloedel Reserve (Bloedel didn't want any identifying signage to distract from nature's beauty), you do find *Point of Interest* signs every so often as you drive through the heavily logged areas of Vancouver Island (where the Bloedel-McMillan Corporation had a large portion of its logging operation). The signs direct you to stop, get out of your car, and walk a few hundred yards to the one remaining Old Growth tree in the area (sometimes it's a Blue Spruce; sometimes a Douglas Fir; just as often a Giant Red Cedar). But it's the *only* one, unless you stop at Cathedral Grove, just east of Port Alberni, where you can walk through an entire grove of Old Growth trees.

It makes me think of Thoreau's experience at Walden Pond. The pond, and the woodlot that surrounded it, was a small sanctuary at the edge of Concord, a town that Thoreau just couldn't seem to stay away from: *[Am] I not made of Concord dust?* He loved Concord (even if many of the townspeople didn't love him). For the two years or so that Thoreau claimed Walden Pond his home, it was far from a hermitage, a rocky grotto in the middle of nowhere, a stopping point on his way to literary sainthood. Why, it wasn't even his exclusively: several men lived and worked near the pond. And even if they hadn't, every other day one or more of his friends—namely Ralph Waldo Emerson and Ellery Channing—dropped by for a chat. And on days when he had no visitors, Thoreau usually headed off into the woods or, just as often, to his mother's house to deposit his dirty laundry.

As uninspiring as Sullivan's *The Thoreau You Don't Know* is, once we return home from our sojourn to the Pacific Northwest, I do two things: first of all, I get out my birdfeeders because winter is around the corner, or will be soon. I keep a birdfeeder filled with thistle up all year long. Migrating flycatchers, warblers, and nuthatches occasion the feeder in the spring and early fall. Black-capped chickadees take over after that, teasing out the fine thistle seeds during the long winter months. As winter approaches I put up two more feeders: one filled with suet for several woodpeckers that inhabit the neighborhood and one filled with black sunflower seeds for the sparrows, juncos, and cardinal pair that have been hanging around the yard for several years.

The other thing I do is to pick another book to read. (I hurriedly finished Sullivan's book on the flight home, though I did linger over his *Notes* section that I found quite informative.) Thumbing through two rows of books I settle on William Finnegan's *Barbarian Days: A Surfing Life*. First of all, it seems an appropriate follow-up to Thoreau. Secondly, it got rave reviews last year and was a *New York Times* bestseller. Finally, as you know, like Finnegan, I was once addicted to surfing (although I don't think Finnegan would consider surfing up and down the east coast of Florida "real" surfing).

46 | Showstopper

IT'S A CHILLY FALL day in Chicago. I don't think winter is around the corner, at least not yet, but the signs are mounting—a noticeable drop in air temperature, a darker blueness to the sky, increasingly shorter days; and then there are the trees. In our part of the universe—Zone 5—the first tree to lose its leaves is the neighbor's scraggly locust tree. It turns a shimmering yellow long before any other tree, then in the blink of an eye drops its leaves, covering their backyard—and ours—with tiny splashes of yellow. Following right behind the locust tree is the sumac just over our other neighbor's fence. It, too, turns brilliant yellow, with splashes of red and orange, before turning the ground into a colorful carpet of saw-tooth-edged leaves.

These, of course, are the more showy displays of color. The serviceberry and Japanese maple at the back of our property, on the other hand, morph slowly from green to red to dusky purple. It's a slow, almost imperceptible change, but then all of a sudden there they are, throbbing with deep, dark, rich color. By the time they reach their place on the color spectrum, the dogwoods, the witch hazels, the viburnums, and the newly-planted ginkgo tree start to flash red, yellow, and orange.

The last holdouts are the Siberian elms that arch high above the backyard. They stand tall and stately and fully green, watching every other tree and bush go through the color wheel before they even think about turning. Then, after most trees and bushes are nothing but thin skeletons against the graying sky, the great Siberians begin to drop their small splotchy, oblong leaves clogging the gutters, adorning the rain barrel, covering the back patio, and generally turning the slate-gray walkways around our house into a Jackson Pollock painting.

I could easily spend all day pondering the magic of fall, but I can't: Halloween is around the corner and that means it is time to *Shake Dem Halloween Bones*. Published in 1997, *Shake Dem Halloween Bones* has been a perennial favorite of readers for over two decades (along with *Bein' With You This Way*, it's also been powering my writing career for about the same amount of time). And it's not just a winner with families with young children. Teachers love it too. I know this because by mid-October I start to get emails, tweets, and Facebook posts from teachers around the country extolling the virtues of the book after they read it to their students. I also get something else: the early morning phone call from a teacher desperate to know how I sing the book so she can sing it to her young charges later that day.

The most humorous example of this occurred several years ago. I had just stepped out of the bathtub and was dripping wet when the phone rang. As my wife was still asleep, I answered it. On the other end of the phone was a teacher from a small town in Florida who wanted me to sing a few verses of *Shake Dem Halloween Bones* to her, so she could read it to her little charges later that day. I complied, of course. Why not? It's a terrific book. So, while wrapped in a towel outside our bedroom door, I launched into a few bars of *Shake Dem Halloween Bones*. I must have really gotten into it because after a couple of stanzas I hear my wife bellowing from behind the closed door, "What on earth are you doing?"

Yes, *Shake Dem Halloween Bones* is a showstopper, a real barn-burner—and that means I'm about to go on the road. It's weird too, because my wife and I don't even like Halloween. It's the one holiday that we totally despise: way too much sugar-saturated candy and non-recyclable plastic. It's also dangerous—that is, if you live in Chicago (or New York or L.A.). About six weeks out my wife and I start to Halloween-proof our house: we don't decorate (our neighbors do), we keep the front gate closed (no one else does), and on Halloween night we lock the front door and turn off the porch light (no one else does that either). Then we hunker down, which means we don't leave the house (we don't leave it on New Year's Eve and the 4th of July either). I mean, you could get knocked out by a stray bottle rocket or, worse yet, get shot by a misguided celebrant. So, we hunker down, or at least my wife does: I'm usually on the road visiting schools and public libraries.

This year I'm headed to Bloomington-Normal, about two hours south of Chicago. I've been to the double city more than a handful of times in the last 20 years, usually to visit area schools, but also to give programs at the main public library in Normal. My first visit to the library is still quite memorable: I was greeted with a bit of local lore that the librarians—and I assume most residents of Normal—enjoy sharing. The story goes something like this: when a man from Normal married a woman from the nearby town of Oblong the local newspapers ran the following headline, "Oblong Woman Marries Normal Man." All of the librarians laughed, even before the teller got to the punch line, as I assume they do every time they hear the story.

This year's visit to the area reminds me of another story—one that involves me. On one of my first visits to the public library in downtown Normal, I received an email from the librarian who was arranging the event requesting that I forward a headshot to her before my visit so she could circulate it among the other branch librarians. Since this was before the advent of hi-res JPEGs, I faxed a black-and-white headshot to her and forgot about it. During my lunch break on the day of my presentation, I found myself chatting with a handful of librarians and somehow the conversation turned to the fact that some of them thought that I was black. I instantly jumped into the conversation, explaining that this happens on a regular basis because of a handful of books that I published in the mid-1990s that feature either children or families of color.

"No, no," one of the librarians interrupted. "That's not why we thought you were black."

"It's not?" I replied.

"No, as we copied your photograph and sent it around, it kept getting darker and darker until you looked like you could have been a member of The 5th Dimension."

As we laughed at the improbability of this, I wondered which story they would tell more often: the one about the Normal man marrying the Oblong woman, or the one about me. No matter. That was then and this is now.

Now I'm sitting at a table in my on-the-road office (a.k.a. Starbucks) just north of the Bloomington-Normal city limits thinking about my next two days. It's a light load, so to speak. I give two evening family literacy programs at two different schools, leaving me a day to myself in between. A day to myself—that sounds like a writing day, which I'm sure it will be. As for the evening programs, I can almost do them in my sleep I've been doing them that long. Not that I do them in a rote manner (if I did, I wouldn't be on the road in the first place). It's just that I'm a natural entertainer. It's where all of my native talents come together—music, writing, storytelling, and humor. I have a small briefcase (circa 1950 that was probably used by an IBM executive) that I fill with books, props, and simple musical instruments. I don't have a set agenda or, in modern parlance, a playlist: I start and then let the audience take me where they want to go. I usually know from my experience where they want to go: a rousing song, a quiet story, a participatory experience, or a soothing lullaby. I just ride the group's energy, letting it direct the show, while I do the work. But work it is not, not when the end result is a roomful of smiles, approving applause, or, best of all, a hug from a child.

AS I FINISH THIS writing I get an email from a librarian in Appleton, Wisconsin. I'll be visiting area schools there at the end of February. As I already mentioned, I've visited Appleton before, and I've visited this librarian's school. It was at his school that I almost embarrassed myself by not bringing the Golden Archer Award, which I won in 2001 for *Shake Dem Halloween Bones.*

The librarian is writing to me, four months before my visit, to remind me to bring the Golden Archer Award. I have a sneaking suspicion that this won't be the only reminder I get from him. But it's a good thing he's giving me this much lead-time: I'll need it, since I'm not exactly sure where the medal is at the moment. But I won't let him know that. I'll just scribble a note of encouragement back to him: *No problem. Of course I'll bring it. It's in my office… somewhere.*

47 | Old Possum

I BUY A LOT of books. I also get a lot of books for free—advance reader copies—one of the perks of being a university professor (though now emeritus). They usually arrive a dozen or more to a box. I pick through them, scan several of the more interesting titles, and then shelve the lot. If I take a book down for a second or third look, it's usually because it's germane to something I'm working on. That's what I did with Nikki Giovanni's book *The Genie in the Jar*. I received an advance copy and read it a couple of times, admiring both Giovanni's fresh poetry and Chris Raschka's vibrant illustrations, and then I shelved it.

Several years ago when I was studying Raschka's work for a project, I pulled the Giovanni book off my bookshelf. But a strange thing happened: as I pulled the slim volume from its place, the book came apart in my hands strewing its contents—dust jacket, boards, and inner leaves—all over my office floor. As I stared at the scraps of paper and cardboard littering my floor, I began to focus on the dust jacket. I don't know why, as I'm sure the exposed boards and loose inner leaves were just as interesting. For whatever reason, I just couldn't stop looking at the dust jacket.

The purpose of a dust jacket—as its name implies—is to protect the underlying hardback cover. Originally, the dust jacket was used temporarily, in the transit of a book from publisher to book-buyer, at which point it was removed and discarded. (Why not? In most cases it was only a brown paper wrapper.) That was its original intent: to protect the more durable cover beneath it from dust, dirt smudges, and scratches while in transit. That is, until the early 20th century when publishers noticed a correlation between a smartly designed dust jacket and book sales, whereupon dust jacket design became an art unto itself.

The jacket has several distinctive parts: the front, the back, the spine, and the front and back flaps. The front cover is especially important, functioning as the book's main marketing tool. Generally, the front cover contains the title of the book and the name of the author. The most important element, however, is not textual; it's visual. The front cover image is crucial in attracting the reader's eye. It has to be both informative and alluring (like a pitcher plant that uses its exquisite beauty to attract—and trap—its prey).

The same is true of the back cover: only here there is more room for variation. The back cover image could simply be an extension—a wrap-around image—of the front cover, spanning the front cover, spine, and back cover. It could be a new or unique image related to, but not necessarily a duplicate of the front cover image. More frequently, the back cover contains textual features not found on the front cover: blurbs about other books by the author; critical reviews or testimonials of the book; a full-page ad or pitch for another book by the same author; brief descriptions of several recently-published books by other authors; a list of books comprising a well-known publisher's series; or, in a few cases—though highly unlikely nowadays—an empty or blank page.

Connecting the front and back cover to each other is the spine, which typically lists the author, the title of the book, and the publishing company, including—though not always—the company's logo. The most important aspect of the spine is both the position of the text and the selection of the font style, size, and color.

If we were talking about a paperback or a case laminate hardcover, we'd end our tour here. But with a hardcover's dust jacket we have two additional areas to consider: the front flap and the back flap, which contain more detailed information about the contents of the book (front flap) and the book's creators (back flap). For instance, in the case of Nikki Giovanni's *The Genie in the Jar*, we learn from the front flap's "blurb" (usually a commendatory, if not overly embroidered, description of the book) that the book "is a poetic picture book, a hymn to the power of art and of love." As such, we are invited to "read it carefully, for each spinning word and each vibrant color has many stories to tell." From the back flap we learn that Nikki Giovanni originally dedicated the text to the singer Nina Simone, and that Chris Raschka illustrated the book while listening to Ms. Simone's recordings.

Publishers, booksellers, and the buying public aren't the only ones who pay attention to the dust jacket of a book. So does the British Library. Since the early 1920s the British Library has collected over 11,000 book jackets, mostly by British publishers, making the British Library Dust Jackets Collection, currently available at the Albert and Victoria Museum's Blythe House Reading Room, the largest in the world. It started selectively, in the early 1920s, with the collection of a handful of highly evocative dust jackets. Each year more jackets were added to the collection—again selectively, based on their unique graphic appeal—until the mid-1950s. From 1956 to 1991, the British Library retained all dust jackets from books published in Britain, as well as some foreign language volumes.

An important, but often overlooked, factor in the evolution of the dust jacket, especially during the early 20th century, is the influx of fine artists into the world of commercial art, specifically trade book publishing. If good book design sells books, which apparently it does, then hiring good book designers and illustrators is an essential ingredient to that end. In other words, the works of great authors sell best when great artists are employed to package their work. Some publishers recognize this more than others.

One publisher is Faber & Faber of London, founded in 1929 by Geoffrey Faber (after the firm Faber & Gwyer was dissolved four years after it had been formed by Faber and Lord Maurice and Lady Gwyer). Faber & Faber soon became known for its stable of writers—many of them poets, including T. S. Eliot, who joined the company during its first season as a literary advisor. Other notable poets included Ezra Pound, W. H. Auden, Marianne Moore, and James Joyce. In the Sixth Dent Memorial Lecture given in London on October 23, 1936, Faber & Faber board member Richard de la Mare discussed the elements of good book design, which included a brief discussion of the dust jacket. Curiously, de la Mare's address begins with the admission of a certain amount of ambivalence about these "ephemeral wrappers":

> The history of the book-jacket is a strange one. The wretched thing started as a piece of plain paper, wrapped round the book to protect it during its sojourn in the bookseller's shop; but it has now become this important, elaborate, not to say costly and embarrassing affair, that we know to-day, and of which we sometimes deplore the very existence. How much better might this mint of money, that is emptied on these ephemeral wrappers—little works of art though many of them may be—be spent upon improving the quality of materials that are used in the making of the book itself! I fear, however, that we must

> consider ourselves wedded to the innovation; for there can be no question that the well-designed book-jacket, *rara avis*, can be a real help to the intelligent bookseller.

Despite the author's reluctant appreciation of the role strong dust jacket design plays in the book-selling enterprise, it was not de la Mare, a former Faber & Faber production manager, who gave Faber & Faber's catalogue its distinctive look. It was Berthold Wolpe, Faber & Faber's longtime artistic director.

Berthold Ludwig Wolpe was a German calligrapher, typographer, book designer, and illustrator. Born in 1905 in Offenbach am Main, Germany, Wolpe studied with Rudolf Koch at the Offenbacher Werkstatt, which Koch founded in 1921. In 1935, Wolpe immigrated to England, joining the design team at Faber & Faber six years later. Wolpe worked at Faber & Faber for 34 years, serving as its artistic director until he retired in 1975. Interested in type design as much as he was book design, Wolpe invented seven typefaces, including *Albertus*, which was issued by the Monotype Corporation of London as a full alphabet in 1938. It was an immediate success and ultimately became Wolpe's best-known typeface (aided in part by Wolpe's constant use of it on many Faber & Faber dust jackets).

What makes a Wolpe typeface distinctive is the uncanny balance Wolpe maintains between the sculptural form of a letter and its functional use. To achieve this end, Wolpe often concerned himself less with how an individual letter looked, and more with how the entire alphabet in question worked with other letters in a word or block of text. Wolpe, who became a naturalized British citizen in 1947, was named a Royal Designer for Industry in 1959 after designing hundreds of books and dust jackets, as well as—at least up to that point—six distinctive typefaces. In 1982, Wolpe received the Order of the British Empire, seven years before he died at the age of 84.

READING ABOUT BERTHOLD WOLPE and the design work he did at Faber & Faber got me to thinking: Do I have any books published by Faber & Faber hidden away in my bookshelves? Curious, I set up the six-foot ladder and start to scan my bookshelves for a sample. I find books published by Oxford, Tarcher, Doubleday, Viking, Simon & Schuster, Dorling Kindersley, and Philomel, among others; but none by Faber & Faber.

No, wait. Just a second. Over there. No, a bit further.

I lean precariously to the left, perhaps more than I should, and grab a volume off an upper shelf. I can tell instantly that it is a Faber & Faber book just from the spine: strong geometric shapes paired with a distinctive typeface. Since the bottom of the spine is torn (the place where the publisher's name or logo typically resides), I can't tell immediately if it's a Faber & Faber book, but turning the book over and over in my hands I know it must be: geometric shapes appear on the front and back cover as three-dimensional prisms, each prismatic shape containing a word from the title—*The Looking Glass Book of Stories*—and at the bottom of the cover the author's name: Hart Day Leavitt. Looking closer, I also see the words: Looking Glass Library.

So it's not a Faber & Faber book. But, then again, it is of sorts. Looking Glass Library was a venture started in 1959 by Edward Gorey, Jason Epstein, and Celia Carroll. The trio's intent was to repackage classic children's books with—at least given the era—a modern look. The venture produced a shelf full of books, most of them reflecting Gorey's quirky artistic vision. Then, in 1962, after only three brief years, the company folded. That each book reflected Gorey's personal taste is important, because I've seen that look before—on one of my bookshelves.

I know it's here somewhere. I can see the cover, vaguely (I inherited some of my father's photographic memory, but not all of it). It has black-and-white ink drawings on the front cover with very distinctive typefaces proclaiming the title of the book and its author. Come on. Think harder. Where is it? *Yes, here it is!* T. S. Eliot's *Old Possum's Book of Practical Cats*, with drawings by Edward Gorey. *Edward Gorey?* That means that it could just as well be another Looking Glass Library volume. But it's not. I recognize the Harcourt Brace Jovanovich logo on the spine instantly. And the pub date is 1982. No relationship to either Faber & Faber or Looking Glass Library.

But wait! There's another copyright date, 1939, held by T. S. Eliot. *T. S. Eliot?* Wouldn't that be the same Thomas Stearns Eliot who worked at Faber & Faber in London as a literary advisor? Thinking about it, he would have been working there in 1939 when the book was first published. *Interesting*. No, wait, more than interesting: look at this. On the front flap of the dust jacket there's an arresting bit of information:

> These playful verses by a celebrated poet have delighted readers and cat lovers around the world ever since they were gathered for publication in 1939. As Valerie Eliot [T. S. Eliot's second wife] has pointed out, there are a number of references to cats in T. S. Eliot's work, but it was to his god-children, particularly Tom Faber and Alison Tandy, in the 1930s, that he first revealed himself as "Old Possum" and for whom he composed his poems.

Tom Faber? That must be a reference to Thomas Erle Faber, son of Geoffrey Faber, founder and president of Faber & Faber. Yes, it makes perfect sense: T. S. Eliot was close to Geoffrey Faber and his family, close enough to be named Tom Faber's godfather, which means that *Old Possum's Book of Practical Cats* must have been published originally by Faber & Faber. But a cursory search of the Internet reveals that Harcourt, Brace and Company published *Old Possum* in 1939.

I think we'll need to consult an expert.

I turn to Caroline Behr's *T. S. Eliot: A Chronology of his Life and Works*, and here it is on page 91, an entry for *Old Possum's Book of Practical Cats*. In black and white Behr states that Faber & Faber Ltd. of London published *Old Possum's Book of Practical Cats Possum* in 1939, revising and enlarging it in 1953. However, Behr states that Harcourt, Brace and Company also published *Old Possum's Book of Practical Cats* in 1939, which it revised in 1968. In other words, Faber & Faber and Harcourt, Brace and Company each published Eliot's romp through the feline world in 1939 (one for the English market and one for the American market). But why does my edition, published by Harcourt Brace Jovanovich in 1982, have the look and feel of a Faber & Faber book?

Digging a little deeper, I find out that Faber & Faber published Eliot's jaunty rhymes in 1939 with pen-and-ink drawings by the author himself. A close look at Eliot's drawings shows an uncanny resemblance between the poet's renderings and Gorey's illustrations (much more so than Axel Scheffler's illustrations adorning the latest edition of Eliot's book). In other words, Gorey was the perfect choice—stylistically—for the 1982 makeover of Eliot's book. (Of course, it didn't hurt that by the 1980s Gorey was a hot item: an extremely gifted and popular illustrator whose quirky and often macabre drawings matched perfectly Eliot's whimsical rhymes.)

And that's why my 1982 Harcourt Brace Jovanovich edition has the look and feel of a Faber & Faber book.

AND WHAT ABOUT FABER & Faber today? Today, Faber & Faber is an imprint of Farrar, Straus & Giroux, which in turn is owned by Macmillan Publishers, which in turn is a subsidiary of… which in turn is controlled by…which in turn is…

But that's another story.

48 | Cease and Desist

AS INTERESTED AS I am in T. S. Eliot and Faber & Faber, this is not what preoccupies me now. What I've spent the last several days doing is overhauling my website. Actually, "websites" would be more appropriate since I maintain two of them: one for my traditionally published books (under the name Nikola Books) and one for my independently published books (under the name Gyroscope Books). Remember, I'm a double Gemini. Under the influence of the Sign of the Twins, I'm always pulled in two directions. In this case I got it into my head that I wanted to separate my traditionally published books from my independently published books. It seemed like a good idea at the time. I was looking long term: in ten years will I really want to be on the author visit circuit? Probably not. So I thought that over the next few years I'd shift everything to my Indie site, emphasizing online sales over direct sales to schools and public libraries (where I still make most of my income).

But that was then and this is now. Now, it's turned into a headache. The reason it's turned into a headache is because I just found out that I'm not the only person who uses the online URL handle "Gyroscope Books." And to add insult to injury, I found this out *after* I received notice from the pro bono lawyer I was working with that my trademark application had been successfully processed.

Okay, stop. I think we're all ears. But for the record, could you open your web browser and do a quick search? Type "Gyroscope Books" into your search engine's dialog box and tell us what you find?

Sure. Since I use Google for my search engine, the first thing that pops up is a Google ad: *Shop for gyroscope books on Google* (and Google doesn't mean shop for books on *my* website, or even on the other party's Facebook page; it means—literally—shop for books about gyroscopes listed on a variety of Google's ad-sponsored sites). I am happy to report, however, that the first link listed after the Google banner ad is my website—Gyroscope Books. Yes, it's at the top of the list—that's good news. The next link is for James Scarborough's book *The Gyroscope Theory and Applications*, offered for sale on Amazon. After that, there's a link to www.gyroscope.com, a site that hosts general information about gyroscopes.

It's the next link that disturbs me: *Gyroscope Books – Facebook*. I open the link only to find out that it's run by someone like me: an independent author/publisher who's just trying to get her work out (her work being "Sci-fi from a Christian Perspective"). The author is Julie Rollins and, yes, she uses Gyroscope Books as her handle, as do I. So, what should I do? Should I call up Bryan, the pro bono lawyer, and have him send a threatening letter to her? *Cease and desist, or my client will…* What would any CEO worth his salt do in such a case? After all, the United States Patent and Trademark Office granted me—not her—trademark status for Gyroscope Books (and it says so right on my website: I put the little ™ symbol after the name).

Before I work myself into a complete dither, I need to slow down, take a deep breath, and figure out just who this author is. The first two books in Rollins' Vadelah Chronicles (that's the name of her Christian fantasy series) were published as physical books in 2005, but not by Gyroscope Books. The publisher's name is Essence Books. Then, there is a seven-year hiatus; no books in physical or electronic form at all. In 2012, however, Rollins begins to release a book or two in the Vadelah Chronicles series almost every month. They're in e-book format exclusively. She's up to #15 right now: all e-books, all available on Amazon.

That's why I didn't run across Rollins' Gyroscope Books imprint when I was doing my search. I was doing my search in 2010, during her publishing hiatus. Hence, I found no online entity using the handle Gyroscope Books. I was free and clear, or so I thought at the time. But not now: now there are two of us—Julie Rollins and me.

I dial up Bryan. "Bryan, what should I do?" I implore, after explaining my conundrum. For a young guy (junior partner and all that), he's very judicious:

Bryan: "First of all, take a deep breath or two."
Me: "Okay, okay, I've heard that before."
Bryan: "Look, you're both independent, self-published authors, right?"
Me: "Well, yes."
Bryan: "Moreover, your work doesn't overlap, I mean, not even in the slightest."
Me: "True."
Bryan: "Now, if you were 25 years old and at the beginning of your career, I'd say *Fight it! Lawyer-up and fight it.* But, you're not 25. You're 65 and most of your writing career is behind you."
Me: "Hey, wait a minute…"
Bryan: "Sorry, but in historical time, that's just the reality. Isn't it?"
Me: "Yeah."
Bryan: "So, my advice to you is simple: ignore her and carry on."

Me: "Ignore her?"
Bryan: "Yes, ignore her and carry on. Look, you could spend a lot of time and energy—not to mention money—fighting this thing, but what would you achieve in the end? That's what you need to ask yourself?"
Me: "Okay, you're right. Besides, what's the harm in having two Gyroscope Books in the world anyway?"
Bryan: "Now you're talking sense."

I hang up with a new appreciation of Bryan's counsel, but what I'd really like to do is call up Julie Rollins and ask her how things are going:

Are you selling any books?
Are you happy with Amazon?
Do you use other sites to advertise and sell your books?
Has Facebook been a good vehicle for you?
If you could do it all over again, what would you do differently?
Is self-publishing rewarding?
Or is it a struggle filled with self-doubt like it is for me?

Of course, I don't call her up (Bryan told me not to). What I do is go online and sign up for an account at every major social media site that I can think of under the user name "Gyroscope Books." It's the 25-year-old in me that wants to fight, just not in a court of law. Julie Robbins might have a lock on Facebook, but I've got a lock on every other social media site in the universe.

GREAT NEWS! I JUST got my TSA pre-approval confirmation letter in the mail with my "new" name: William John Nikola. Technically, I'm no longer W. Nikola-Lisa; I'm William John Nikola. There's a certain relief in changing my name back to my birth name: I feel whole, more integrated, less divisible. It makes me think about my websites. Why should I keep two of them: one for Nikola Books and one for Gyroscope Books? It would be much simpler if I kept one site with all of my work on it. Why separate my trade books (listed on my Nikola Books site) from my self-published books (listed on my Gyroscope Books site)? That's it. I'm ready to consolidate, ready to integrate: I'm ready to be one whole entity. But which site should I keep: Nikola Books or Gyroscope Books?

It's a no-brainer, really: Nikola Books is where the body of my work resides. It's where I list most of my books, where I advertise myself as an author and a storyteller, where I list my programs, rates, and availability, and where I post testimonials from teachers and parents. In short, it's who I am and have been for most of my writing life.

Realizing this, I decide to move everything from gyroscopebooks.com to nikolabooks.com, leaving only one paragraph on the former website's home page:

> Gyroscope Books™ is the independent publishing arm of author/storyteller W. Nikola-Lisa. For more information about Mr. Nikola-Lisa's background, published work, and school and library programs please click here.

And, of course, by clicking "here" you will be redirected to my primary website where you will find me (and my work) in a straightforward, uncomplicated form. Something my wife has been hoping for throughout our thirty-year marriage.

49 | Paperwhite

THE LAST FEW DAYS in Chicago have been glorious with clear blue skies, and not even a hint of the usual mixture of low-slung clouds and factory smog. Against the sky, trees linger in a state of suspended animation, waiting for their first brush with winter. It's as if they're in some deep yogic pose—*breathe in, breathe out, slowly now, hold that pose.* As they stand still as statues, with only an occasional gust to rattle their leaves, they continue to cycle through the color wheel. Most of the backyard's low-lying bushes have traded in their lush green foliage for various shades of brown and yellow. The stately ginkgo tree—stately, that is, until several young and overly-exuberant raccoons playing a game of tag earlier this fall broke the leader—is holding on to most of its greenery, with only spikes of yellow showing through. Overhead, the Siberian elms continue to hold onto their full summer regalia.

With November on the new calendar page, the end of the year is now in sight. But there's still work to do. Although this project takes most of my writing time, other projects rear their head demanding attention here and there. Right now I'm about to pick up the phone and call one of the POD publishers that I work with. I'm embarking on a new project and I want to get more information on options related to the weight of their cover stock and interior paper. The project involves publishing several short stories in small collections. What I can't decide upon is whether or not I want to "standardize" the trim size for these editions or publish each collection differently. The real question is whether or not I want to publish them in more than one format. I've decided that they are definitely not e-book material because I see a variety of design elements that won't work that well in e-book format unless each page is "fixed," which is not the typical way of formatting an e-book. So, the question is: do I want both paperback and hardcover editions for each collection, and, if so, how large of a trim size?

The first six books I self-published have all gone the same route: e-book, paperback, and case laminate hardcover (the latter being the standard format for school and public libraries). The project I'm working on—the one you're currently reading—will deviate from this: first phase, four separate e-books, one for each major part; second phase, completely revised and edited e-book containing all parts (mainly to serve as an e-galley for distribution to reviewers); third phase, completely revised and reformatted full-edition paperback for retail sales. I decided on this trajectory in order to break out of the previous routine; not that it wasn't working for me, rather experimentation in the independent world of publishing is a necessity given the ever-shifting ground of the publishing world. It also goes back to what is at the top of my tree of knowledge—creativity. I just can't do the same thing over and over again without getting bored (I'm sure I don't have a corner on this market). So, for *Dog Eared*, I was ready to experiment. And for the next set of books, each one containing several short stories, I'm ready to experiment again—with interior design, trim size, paper weight, cover stock, etc., anything that can be manipulated within the parameters allowed by a POD printer.

And I think I just answered my own question: I'm not going to standardize the trim size of these stand-alone books. I'm going to experiment.

It all sounds so easy, but it's not. Case in point: I just sent my graphic artist the revised EPUB file for Part 3 of this book. I was somewhat proud of myself because I figured out how to do the revisions directly on the EPUB file using Mac for Reader's highlight function, which means that I didn't have to create a separate word doc listing my edits line by line. I just added them into the EPUB file as a highlight with notes and that was it, done. At least I thought I was. After I made the edits and sent the EPUB file back to the graphic artist, she wrote to inform me that there *were* no highlights or notes.

What? No edits. I double-checked the EPUB file that I sent her and to my utter surprise I couldn't find the highlights there either. They seem to have disappeared, like that. *Poof.* What's going on? Why aren't they there? I checked the original EPUB file, just in case they migrated there. But no, nothing, not one highlight or edit, and my graphic artist doesn't have a clue either. *Argh!*

What is going on? I don't know, and I just don't have the time and energy to figure it out. It's probably just as easy to start over, which means editing the 80-page document line-by-line, writing down every edit on a separate word doc indicating which chapter, paragraph, and sentence the edit appears in along with an explanatory note.

Just another day in paradise, I guess.

OF COURSE, I'D RATHER not be doing this work at all (since I already did it once). I'd much rather shop. Now don't get me wrong, I'm a terrible shopper, hardly even step into a store. When Pea Pod announced its grocery-store-to-home food delivery service I was ecstatic. Now I didn't even have to go to the grocery store anymore (of course my wife nipped that fantasy in the bud pretty quickly: "And who's going to pay for the service, not me?"). Still, I try to shop online from the comfort of my home office as much as possible. Today, for some reason, I got it in my mind to buy a Kindle Paperwhite. A new version of the e-reader just came out and Amazon's knocked thirty bucks off the list price. All it would take is one click of the mouse and it's mine.

But I don't press the Buy-Now-With-1-Click button. Instead, I put the Paperwhite in my Amazon shopping cart and stroll into my wife's office and start talking about some things we should buy for the house: a new mat for the back door, a string of LED lights for the front porch, a set of measuring spoons, and a new mouse for her computer.

"Oh, and by the way," I say as an aside, "I think I'm going to finally get an e-reader. Amazon has a great deal…"

I don't get any further. My wife stops me midsentence to remind me—somewhat heatedly—that I've already had two of them. Yes, that's right, I've already had two of them, but not e-readers. I had two electronic pads. The first one, a retirement gift from work, was an Amazon Fire, the equivalent of an Apple iPad. I used it for several weeks and gave it to my niece. I just didn't like it—too cumbersome and way too slow. Several years later, I bought an iPad, but not to use as an e-reader, rather I wanted to integrate it into my electronic music setup (when I'm not writing, I'm usually upstairs playing around with a couple of analog synthesizers). But that idea soon went bust when the music apps that I thought

I'd use just didn't satisfy me. So, like the Amazon Fire, I gave the iPad away—to my wife, who uses it everyday to read *The New York Times*.

And that's why I want to get a Paperwhite: so I can catch up on the news and read books. According to the comparison chart on the Paperwhite's product page, I can fill this thing with a thousand, no, make that a million books. And I will, someday, just not right now. Right now, I need to return to my office, reboot my computer, and navigate to my Amazon shopping cart. Once there, I need to hit "delete" right after Kindle Paperwhite. You see, I just can't pull the trigger. I can't pull it for two reasons: first of all, I'd never hear the end of it from my wife if I bought it and then didn't use it; secondly, I'm halfway through Nicholas Basbanes' book *On Paper*, a marvelous account of the history, nature, and cultural uses of paper. Basbanes covers everything, and I mean *everything*: ancient papermaking techniques, the important role paper plays in the world of espionage, rare works of art made on all sorts of paper (including the endpapers of rare 17th-century books), and, of course, the profitable, but shady industry of forgery and counterfeiting. Basbanes also takes us deep into the "treasure vaults" of several private collections and national museums, including a scintillating look at the holdings of the Folger Shakespeare Library in Washington, DC. How on earth could I pull the trigger? Just imagine reading Basbanes' book on an e-reader? It would be an act of sacrilege.

So, yes, I need to delete the Paperwhite from my shopping cart—and it's not the first time I've done this. I did it last year, but more for political reasons: honestly, how can anyone justify carrying around three or four electronic devices? So I go to my Amazon shopping cart, click on the icon for the Kindle Paperwhite, and hit "delete." It's painful. I really wanted to buy an e-reader. But

I don't. Instead, I do the next best thing: I pick up last month's Daedalus book catalog, dial the 800 number on the back cover, and order four books that I earmarked earlier this week—three for myself and one for my wife (you know, it never hurts to get on her good side).

50 | Of Mice and Men

WRITING, REVISING, PRODUCING, AND promoting this project has convinced me that serial time is illusory even though the activities of my life appear to be linear, one event following on the heels of another. What happens in my head is quite different: it's a swirl of Einsteinian moments with thoughts constantly colliding into each other. When this happens, serial time flies out the window, making the mind more like a fully lit-up hologram than a series of neurons firing one after the other. It puts into question the very nature of time: what is past, present, and future when you're working in all of these realms at the same time?

This is particularly true of this project, especially now that I'm two-thirds of the way through the process that I've laid out for myself. The original intent of this project was to create a book in four parts to correspond to the four seasons of the year, tracking my office-cleaning project and my self-publishing activities. Now that I just posted the third part of this project online as an e-book, I find myself working in—or at least thinking about—the past, present, and future simultaneously. Take yesterday, for example. After posting the last chapter from Part 2 to my blog, I did a final proof of the MOBI file my graphic artist sent me for Part 3 and uploaded it to my Kindle account. As I waited for it to upload I began revising a chapter from Part 4, the final section that I'm close to completing now.

To keep all of this straight I maintain four manuscript files: one for the original raw chapter files, one for the e-book editions that I've been publishing separately, one for the fully revised and complete e-book edition; and one for the fully revised and complete paperback edition. Since the narrative arc follows the year through the four seasons, there's no let-up. None. I'm tethered to a timeline of my own creation. Seeing my increasing frustration and exhaustion, my wife advises me never to do this again: "That's the beauty of self-publishing, isn't it? To do it on your own terms and at your own speed." Yes, I guess so, but I'm committed; there's no going back. For the moment I'm resigned to live in both the lockstep motion of serial time and the undulating mishmash of psychological time, the two often competing for my attention.

Curiously, the most linear aspect of this project is not the writing of it, even though the book loosely follows the four seasons of the year. It is more the marketing plan that I've devised for myself. You read about this everywhere: *Before you write your next book, come up with a marketing plan!* Wait a minute. Did you say *before* you write your next book? Isn't that jumping the gun a bit?

Apparently not, at least that's what Jennifer Mattern says in her article "Book Marketing Timeline: From Pre-launch to Post-launch." Mattern offers a step-by-step approach to marketing your newest book that covers an entire year's worth of activities. No mishmash of psychological time here: Mattern's ideas come straight out of Marketing 101—create a plan and follow it, even *before* you begin to write.

Imagine John Steinbeck before he wrote *Of Mice and Men*. He's sitting around, munching on potato chips, watching TV, thinking about his next book: *Let's see, I'll need to contact research labs that use mice in their studies. Oh, and what about MICE, the international group that deals with large business meetings? They'll be interested. And let's not forget the Mickey Mouse Club. I'm sure Mouseketeers around the world will want to snap up a copy or two…*

Along with developing a marketing plan, Mattern advises the prospective writer to conduct market research to determine if there's a market for your book. That's weird because I don't know many authors who do this *before* they write a book. Sure, some market research is advisable. I mean, you don't want to write a book that's already been written, but to determine if there's a need for a book and then to write it: I seriously doubt it. Certainly no fiction writer does this.

Hi, John Steinbeck here, I thought I'd do a quick shout out. You see I've got a really great idea for a book, something about mice and men. If you have any thoughts about it, send them my way…

That's the "before you write your book" phase, now for the "while you write you book" segment. First up, finish everything you started in the first phase, and then set up your author website (even though you're not an author just yet), and start creating a presence on social media networks. Oh, and you'll also want to start blogging regularly to get the word out. This is how you start to establish your brand. It's very important to start building your brand early.

John Steinbeck reporting live from California where mice seem to be running amok. I've never seen it like this. I thought we had a mouse problem in Salinas when I was a kid, but now as I drop out of Stanford for the third time (or is it the fourth time?), I've never seen so many mice…

The most crucial part of the book launch cycle is six to nine months before the scheduled release of your book. Here are a few things to consider: sign up with an email marketing service and start blasting an email or two out monthly; build a list of "influencers" (these are key leaders in the field that can help you drive awareness of your book to the larger market); along with a list of influencers you'll also need a list of blogs, websites, and other media outlets to support your book launch publicity tour; oh, and hey, don't forget to get your headshot taken (a nice frontal view; nothing too fancy-schmancy), then upload it to all your social media accounts.

Excuse me, Mr. Steinbeck, could you turn a little this way, toward the camera? And could you please stop playing with that pet mouse for a moment? Thank you, that's much better…

Now you've got about three months before your book is released (and you probably don't have any fingernails left). If you haven't rolled up your sleeves, it's now or never. So get to work: create a marketing calendar with explicit tasks; reach out to media outlets for guest posts, interviews, or live appearances; and don't forget book reviewers, you have to reach out to them as well; send an advance copy to any key reviewers who express an interest in your book; post updates to your blog (anything to keep you and your book in front of the media); create a professional-looking book trailer.

I think we can handle the background shots you'd like, Mr. Steinbeck. But filming you with mice crawling all over your body? Maybe we should talk about that a little more…

You have only one or two months to go: crunch time. Have you created a sales page for your book? Have you created a media kit? Have you written your launch day press release? Have you sent advance copies to all reviewers? Have you prepared your 30-second elevator pitch? Are your bookmarks printed and ready to distribute? And what about your pre-launch contest or giveaway? How's that going?

I'm sorry, Mr. Steinbeck, but we just can't give away live baby mice. The animal rights coalition just wouldn't take kindly to it. And, besides, don't you think it would involve some liability issues? I mean, the little rascals bite, don't they?

The week before your book launch don't forget to update your social media sites, and don't forget to blog, blog, blog… And while you're blogging, don't forget to monitor any and all comments from your readers. Are there additional reviewers you need to contact? Finally, when you do get a much-deserved break, post an excerpt from your book, maybe the first chapter, or something similar to it on your website, and then brag about it… I mean, blog about it. As the day of your launch approaches, check your book information for accuracy. Make sure it's correct on all your distribution delivery sites. And while you're at it, create author pages on those sites if you haven't already. Then make sure your website's "buy now" links work.

Yes, Mr. Steinbeck, I think we can use the image of a mouse for your "buy now" button. I'm just not sure we can have it peeping out of a mouse hole…

The day you've been waiting for has finally arrived—your long awaited book release day. It's time to make that last push. Post an official release statement on your blog, your website, and any relevant social media networks. Encourage people to share your exciting news (and then thank those who do). Send out your launch day press release to more formal news organizations. Add a link to your book's sales page to your email signature. Send out another email blast with links to your website and your book's sales page. And then cap it all with a book launch party at your local independent bookstore.

Napkins in the shape of a mouse? No problem, Mr. Steinbeck. I just don't think we can do the same with the cupcakes…

Whew, you did it. You ground it out through the last nine months of marketing tactics, capping your Herculean efforts with a smashingly successful book launch party. Now it's time to collapse.

Oh, no it isn't. Just because you've released your book doesn't mean that you can relax. You've got at least six months of post-launch work ahead of you (at least that's what Jennifer Mattern says). So get up and strap on those mouse ears, Mr. Steinbeck.

You've got work to do.

51 | I Love Brown

IT TURNS OUT THAT the frigid temperatures of late November were just a tease: it's the last week in December and it's in the mid-50s. There's not a trace of ice or snow, making it difficult to know what to wear: long-sleeve shirt, turtleneck, or pullover sweater. Who knows what's around the corner? Usually at this time of year I load up my backpack with several clothing accessories: light woolen cap, extra pair of biking gloves, rain pants, and windbreaker. You just never know. You can leave the house in what looks like a temperate fall day and return in a blizzard. So, like every Boy Scout, I'm prepared for the worst.

Today's "worst" isn't what's happening outside, however; it's what's happening inside. I've got several piles of stuff on my work desk to sort through. But once I deal with these, I'm finished. I will have sorted through, culled out, cleaned off, straightened up, and reorganized the entire contents of my office, which was my plan this year. So I roll up my sleeves (metaphorically, that is: I decided to wear a short-sleeve shirt) and start to sort through the piles of papers, stacks of catalogs, mounds of professional magazines, remnants of student work, and God knows what else on my desk.

Book Contracts. The first pile I come across is small, but very important: two manila folders filled with contracts from my traditionally published books—twenty or more of them. The folders are labeled "still in-print" and "out-of-print, rights reverted." Publishers don't necessarily give book rights back to the author when the book in question goes out of print. You have to contact them and officially request a reversion of rights. It's more pro forma than anything, but the onus of responsibility falls squarely on the shoulders of the author, which means you have to comb through your semi-annual royalty statements looking for inactivity. Often when a book hasn't sold for several royalty periods that's a pretty good sign that the book is out-of-print. But not always; sometimes, an inactive book will be designated "temporarily out-of-stock" rather than out-of-print. Of course, what "temporarily" means is the question: this is often a way for a publisher to hold on to the rights in perpetuity (because, technically, if the book has not been deemed out-of-print, the author can't request a reversion of rights). And, of course, in the digital age a book can "sit" in a digital server for eons and not cost the publisher anything, which means they are even less likely to deem the book out-of-print.

After looking through the two files, I realize that I'm missing a file, the most important file: the one labeled "out-of-print, request reversion of rights." I counted nine contracts in the first file and seven in the second file for a total of 16 book contracts. That means I'm missing four contracts. These should be in a file labeled "out-of-print, request reversion of rights." But, take heart, I know exactly where it is: *It's in my office!* Of course you know what that means: *I've gone and lost it. Dang.* But how can I lose it in my office? I just finished cleaning the whole thing out.

Postcards. Another item staring at me from my work desk is a box of postcards. No, these aren't postcards that I've collected over the years from exotic places that my wife and I have visited (although I do have a box of those). Actually, it's not a box; it's an old leather binocular case circa mid-1950s. It's filled to the brim with postcards that sport a vintage black-and-white photograph of some bizarre image on the front side. One postcard shows half a dozen people with their heads stuck in the ground. Another postcard shows two tightrope walkers—a bride and groom—tiptoeing toward each other high above the ground. Another postcard depicts a horse reared up on its hind legs sparring with a man. Then there's my favorite postcard: a man and a baby elephant crowding into a small telephone booth.

But these aren't the postcards that catch my attention (well, they do, but not for long). The postcards that grab my attention are the ones that I've created over the last few years to advertise my self-published books. I keep these in a bigger box labeled "postcards"—what else? For *The Men Who Made the Yankees*, I made several dozen two-inch square postcards that I sent to all of the bars surrounding Yankee Stadium. I also made a standard postcard that I sent out to all of the bookstores—chain and otherwise—in the greater New York City area at the start of baseball season. Finally, I sent postcards to all of the concession stores at Yankee Stadium, to the Babe Ruth Museum in Baltimore, and to the Baseball Hall of Fame in Cooperstown, New York.

I made similar postcards to advertise the release of *Dear Frank*, *Shark Man*, and *Gaya Lives in a Blue House*. It's not hard to make a postcard. The bigger issue is: Where do you send them? For *Dear Frank*, since it is a piece of historical fiction set in Boston in 1918 when Babe Ruth pitched for the Red Sox, I saturated the greater Boston area with postcards announcing its release. *Shark Man*, too, was a no-brainer: it went out to surf shops, libraries, and middle schools up and down the Florida coast. The stumper in the group was *Gaya Lives in a Blue House*. It's a beautiful book, a new-age story about reaching your potential, illustrated by my wife with her distinctive collage and Sumi-e ink drawings. It's one of those "picture books for all ages" that publishers detest. I mean, how do you market a book if it's for all ages? Well, I didn't know either until our oldest daughter told us that she reads it at the end of all her yoga classes, especially her classes for families and kids. *Bingo!* The light went on and I sent out a ton of *Gaya* postcards to as many yoga studios as I could find.

The last set of postcards in my postcard box is the one that I bring to all of my direct sales events because it advertises more than my books. It advertises *me*—as an author, storyteller, and musician.

Pendragon. The next file I pick up takes me back in time. As I flip the file open I'm met with a faded ink sketch. It's a line drawing of a dragon whose serpentine body spells the word Pendragon, a reference to Uther Pendragon who ruled pre-Roman Britain (although a wise ruler, he is primarily known as the father of King Arthur). Uther's surname, derived from Old Welsh, means "chief" (*pen*) "warrior" (*dragon*). I know this because Pendragon was the first pseudonym that I considered at the start of my writing career. I was quite serious about it, so I asked my girlfriend to design a logo that incorporated the image of a dragon into the name Pendragon. She did—and then she left me. She decided to date the astrologer who had earlier told me that I had all of the writer's destiny marks except one—contact with publishers. (It looks like he could have added another exclusion to the list—"contact with girlfriends.")

Dummy Books. After filing the Pendragon folder in my two-drawer filing cabinet, I pick up a stack of plastic folders, each one containing a "dummy book" for one of my early manuscript ideas. These are not to be confused with the "proto-books" that I described in an earlier chapter. Whereas proto-books are fully illustrated picture book mock-ups meant for an editor's eye, dummy books are small handmade books that help me with text placement and are only for my eyes.

When I started writing picture book texts for young readers back in the 1980s, there were a few things that you had to keep in your head: the most important—aside from the writing itself—was the number of pages that made up a picture book. Since books were printed in large runs using an offset printing press, they generally contained 32 pages because that's how a "galley sheet" came off the press; namely, 16 pages printed back and front. When the galley sheet was folded and trimmed, it created a 32-page picture book. (The process is the same for 40-page and 48-page picture books as well.) Knowing this, I made 32-page dummy books to help me visualize how my story flowed across this space. It also helped me understand—and revise—the words on each double-spread.

I don't make dummy books anymore, however—for two reasons. First of all, after publishing 20 or more picture books, I've pretty much internalized the process: I don't need to hold a physical dummy book in my hand in order to "see" the flow of my words across a 32- (or 40- or 48-) page space. Secondly, in the age of print-on-demand publishing, page count is a thing of the past since a print-on-demand printer doesn't produce a multi-page galley sheet; it prints a book in much smaller page units, which means that a self-published book is not limited to the same page count as a traditionally published book, especially one that is produced by an offset printer.

Knowing this, and the fact that I'll probably never produce a traditionally published book again, still I just can't seem to throw away the dummy books that were instrumental in getting my writing career off the ground. "Be careful," I hear my wife saying. "Pretty soon you'll be turning the house into a museum of oddities."

No, I doubt it. But still, I just can't trash these dummy books (or the even earlier proto-books that I still have). What I can trash is the stack of book ideas and early drafts of stories that I no longer intend to work on. I imagine it's the same for every writer: you have a large story file that is divided into various sections: book ideas, story starts, completed drafts, revised manuscripts, manuscripts ready for submission, manuscripts in need of major revision, manuscripts on hold (for whatever reason), and the "kill file." Like anything that sits around accumulating more and more stuff, it needs an occasional going-through, a spring cleaning, if you like. And that's what my story file needs (mainly because it's no longer contained in one place, but has been spilling out into my office over the last few years). Believe me, it will be a pleasure to cull out unnecessary and unwanted drafts of stories I'm no longer interested in.

Actually, I don't jot down book ideas that much anymore at all. It's not that I don't have them. Rather, it's because I've learned over time that good ideas just don't go away. They tend to hang around, pestering me here and there. That's when I know that an idea is ripe for picking—when it just won't recede into the background. Story ideas are like seeds: throw them out, give them some water, and watch them grow. But don't tend to them too much. Just let them grow naturally, of their own accord. The good ones, the ones that have substance, will continue to grow and at some point capture your full attention. I have lots of book ideas swirling around in my head; they pop up and recede, pop up and recede, until one of them finally jumps up, grabs me by the collar, and says, "Work on me." Lately, as I come to the close of this project, some of these nascent book ideas have been popping up, trying to capture my attention.

Student Work. Not jotting down every idea that I get is only one way that I've begun to limit the amount of paperwork in my office. Another way that I've been reducing it is by scanning everything into my computer that I need to save but don't need a physical copy of: office receipts, check stubs from school and library visits, catalog ads, invoices of purchased books, inventory lists, editorial and non-editorial correspondence, relevant articles from monthly professional magazines. It's a long list. But over the last few months I've been faithfully scanning everything possible. Not only do I find myself with less stuff in my office, but thanks to my computer's search function I tend to find things a whole lot quicker. And that means, no more "It's in my office, honey!" Just the occasional "It's in my computer! I think."

But I can't scan everything, nor do I want to. This includes the hundreds of responses I get each year from students who've either read my books or who have attended my school or library presentations. Even though the responses take up two large boxes in my office, I just can't seem to get rid of this work. They include such things as retellings of *Night Is Coming*, *Storm*, and *Summer Sun Risin'*, new stanzas written to supplement the verses found in *Tangletalk* and *Shake Dem Halloween Bones*, poetic responses to the diversity theme in *Bein' With You This Way*, and personal essays by intermediate and middle grade students in response to reading *How We Are Smart*. There are also reams of *Thank You* notes from students and teachers, stacks of 3x5 cards filled with questions about what it's like to be an author, and a manila envelope filled with students' drawings, many of them attempts to draw my portrait (where I look like anything from a dapper college professor to a Mafia hit man). And then there are the entirely unsolicited and quirky—and just as often unintelligible—responses from students, like this young girl's sweet but entirely indecipherable response to my visit to her school: *I love brown*.

That's it: *I love brown*. When I first read her note, I stared at it for a long time. I hadn't a clue what she was thinking about. Was she commenting on the color of my shoes? Was she thinking about the trees outside? Is her dog some shade of brown? What on earth did she mean: *I love brown*. But then it hit me. She was trying to write "I love the way you sang *Brown Bear, Brown Bear, What Do You See?*" This is a favorite book of mine written by Bill Martin, Jr. It's a pattern book with a very steady rhythm, so I "sing" it, accompanying myself with a blues harmonica. What makes the performance even more memorable is that I wear a fedora and sunglasses—a tip of the hat, so to speak, to Chicago's Blues Brothers.

Yes, I'm sure that's what she was thinking. To quote a popular ad campaign for a major credit card company, her note was, well… *priceless* (so priceless, in fact, that I think I'll keep the original, along with dozens of other student responses to my work).

52 | So Many Books

IT'S THE 31ST OF DECEMBER—the last day of the year. The temperature's in the mid-30s and except for a brief snow flurry yesterday there's been very little precipitation. After an early morning round of Tai Chi exercises in the kitchen, synchronized to Rachel Martin and Steve Inskeep's NPR reporting, I eat a hurried breakfast (fried egg on English muffin washed down with black coffee), put on another layer of clothes, and take off for a morning ride.

The air's crisp, but refreshing. I learned how to ride a bike as a kid growing up in Texas. If you wanted to get to a friend's house, you walked, rode a horse, or took your bike. No Soccer Moms to bus us around. It was when I moved to Montana after graduating from college that I really got into biking. I'd ride my bike to work as long as I could until it started to snow. Then, when it was just too darn cold and snowy to ride a bike, I'd switch to cross-country skis. I like road trips, but I detest being stuck in a car in city traffic—so I ride a bike, everywhere.

Right now I'm headed to the lakefront, an easy mile or so with very little traffic. I head south on the lakefront bike trail. After passing a few empty playgrounds Montrose Harbor appears on my left (a great place to go birding, especially in spring and early summer). The Sydney Marovitz Golf Course is next. I trail my hand along the 12-foot-high chain-link fence that keeps golfers' golf balls from pelting passing bikers. But there are no golfers today; it's the end of December. Next, I zip by Belmont Harbor and the Diversy Parkway cut-off, heading slightly uphill toward the newly developed Fullerton Avenue cut-off. This stretch of bike trail is usually packed, but today there's just a handful of bikers and joggers. I take the Fullerton Avenue cut-off and head west, under Lake Shore Drive, past Lincoln Park Zoo, to the back of the Peggy Notebaert Nature Museum, where I hang a right and follow the walking path as it curves around North Pond. I emerge on Marine Drive, but continue west, threading through several upscale Lincoln Park neighborhoods, until I hit Lincoln Avenue, south of Sheffield, which takes me to the intersection of Lincoln and Southport, and to one of my favorite coffeehouses.

The sign on the door—Heritage General Store—seems misleading at first, but the more I think about it, the more I realize that it's the perfect sign for the store, which is half coffeehouse, half bike repair shop. To emphasize the "general store" nature of the place, it's decorated with funky items like shiny-metal canister lighting, a handmade incandescent-bulb chandelier (made from old bike rims), a single-speed bicycle suspended from the ceiling, and an ancient gramophone perched on a shelf high above the cash register (which isn't a cash register at all, but a snazzy Square Reader that swivels 180 degrees). And did I mention that the Heritage has a working Underwood typewriter—circa 1930—at the end of the counter? I've seen more than a handful of people pound out a line or two of poetry while waiting for their morning coffee.

By the time I arrive, morning is almost over. But I stop, grab some coffee, and find a table in the window up front. One of my favorite songs is playing in the background—Jackson Browne's "Sky Blue and Black." While I wait for my computer to boot up, I start to think about what I'll do the rest of the day. Since it's December, there's not a lot of writing in me, at least as far as this project is concerned. I've written all of the chapters (except this one), and since I've decided not to post Part IV as a separate e-book, choosing to skip it and move on to the Advance Reader Copy, there's not much left to do. Well, that's not really true: there's the onerous task of revising. And I'll get to it; it's just that I'm an idea person and that means that I'd much rather start a new project than revise an old one.

When I was younger, that was exactly what I did. I was always moving on to start a new project before I had finished the one I was working on. Now that I'm older and a bit wiser, I don't pull up stakes and move on as quickly. I tend to sit on a project longer, consider it more thoroughly, and let it sink in until I'm completely satisfied with it. It's not just a function of age: since I've made the transition from traditional author to independent author/publisher I find myself slowing down, focusing more, making sure that what I've created is what I want to put into the world. Years ago I had a Kung Fu instructor who told his students that when we participated in a Martial Arts tournament we were not representing ourselves; we were representing him. What he meant is that when we stepped onto the mat, *his* reputation was on the line, not ours. That's how I feel now: I'm not just putting another book into the world, I'm putting my reputation as a writer into the world.

After rifling through my email inbox, reading a few online marketing newsletters, and checking my websites for traffic, I gulp the last sip of coffee, pack up my things, and head home. It's time for lunch. It's also time to get to work. Although nine-tenths of my bookshelves are cleaned, sorted, and restocked, I still have a few things to sort through—some odds-and-ends promotion materials, student artwork from my days teaching second grade in Montana, a box of miscellaneous office supplies, several artist drawing pads that I thought I'd use for a book illustration project, a small box filled with an assortment of handwritten notes (half of which don't make any sense), and a stack of books at the far end of my work desk.

During my yearlong office-cleaning project I've been pulling books aside, hoping to read them once this project is over. Some of the books, like Jack Gantos' *Dead End in Norvelt*, I've read before; others, like Michael Blanding's *The Map Thief*, I've not. It's an eclectic bunch, a combination of fiction, nonfiction, memoir, poetry, and biography. Every reader has one, his or her "want to read" list (just log into Goodreads and you'll see thousands of them). Like every reader's list, mine is ever-changing: Do I really want to read Sophie Divry's *The Library of Unrequited Love*? (I don't know, maybe not.) And what about Amy Leach's *Things That Are*? (Yes, that's definitely a keeper.) As the improvisational guitarist/composer Frank Zappa once said, "So many books, so little time."

He's right, of course. There are so many books (not *too* many, so many), but never enough time to read them all. Maybe that's how I should end this piece of writing: by reading a book. The urge is strong, very strong. As I luxuriate in the idea of reading a book in a tubful of hot water upstairs, something else pulls at me—the date, December 31st. Shouldn't I be getting ready for Inventory Counting Day? After all, tax season is around the corner (my graphic artist always commends me for being the first of her clients to initiate the 1099-Misc process). With this thought in mind, I stroll into my office and start to think about what I'll need to count my book inventory. Let's see, I've done this before. I'll need a pad of paper, a calculator, an ink pen, a black magic marker, a pad of post-it notes, Scotch tape, and a flashlight. As I mindlessly start to gather these items, I catch a glimpse of the stack of books perched precariously at the end of my work desk.

Wait! Stop! This is insanity, my mind explodes. *You can't end this project with the mundane, mind-numbing, meaningless (well, meaningless to me, but not to the IRS) task of counting book inventory. It's just not right.*

I glance at my watch. It's not 4 p.m., but it is cold outside and a good soak in the tub upstairs would do me good after my morning bike ride. Yes, that's how I'd like to bring closure to this project—by slipping into a bathtub filled with steaming hot water and losing myself in a good book. *Ah, is there any greater pleasure?* But what should I read? The stack at the end of the desk has been growing steadily. Well, I better get to it before I fritter away another day (or the stack—another one of my Leaning Towers of Pisa—falls over). So, let's see, what will it be…

Hugh Aldersey-Williams' *Periodic Tales*
Carol Fisher Saller's *Eddie's War*
José Saramago's *Small Memories*
Dava Sobel's *The Glass Universe*
Karen Hesse's *Aleutian Sparrow*
Joseph Dane's *Dogfish Memory*
Katie Waldegrave's *The Poets' Daughters*
George Johnson's *Miss Leavitt's Stars*
Philip Schultz's *Failure*
Martin Sandler's *Trapped in Ice*
Neil Gaiman's *Norse Mythology*
Clayton Smith's *Anomaly Flats*

After pondering the titles in the stack, I pull Neil Gaiman's *Norse Mythology* and Karen Hesse's *Aleutian Sparrow* from the stack and head upstairs. It's the Gemini thing, always laboring beneath the Sign of the Twins, always moving in two directions. I won't know which book I'll read first (or, if at all), until I settle into the tub. Then I'll reach for one of them and do what authors do to their great delight and satisfaction—*read.* Read for the sheer pleasure of it. Read until they are full. Read until that other urge—the urge to write—begins to nag at them. Once it begins to nag at them sufficiently, they'll return to their notebook, to their computer, their voice recorder, or typewriter: it's just the yin-yang of the consumption/production process constantly pin-wheeling along.

In my case, it's the Gemini thing, always laboring beneath the Sign of the Twins, always moving in two directions. Reading and writing (consuming and producing)—there's just no separation, just one long unending Mobius strip of activity. And like other writers, I'm a lifer, imprisoned in a house of words of my own design.

Source Notes

Front Matter

So many books... Frank Zappa: http://quotes.yourdictionary.com/author/frank-zappa/610999 [accessed 18 January 2016]. I don't know if Frank Zappa actually uttered these words. You can't find a definitive source on the Internet where his words first appeared. What you do find are pages and pages of websites and blogs using the quotation as a header, giving credit to Zappa but not the original source.

Reb Zebulun told... Isaac Bashevis Singer. *Stories for Children*, p. 173. I've had this book in my collection for more than 30 years, often reading stories from it for Hanukkah ("Zlateh the Goat" being my favorite). But what I found the most insightful is the commentary at the end of the book titled "Are Children the Ultimate Literary Critics?"

When I was... W. Nikola-Lisa, *personal notes.*

Part I

5 | An Award, Sort of

The author/illustrator shall... The list of six items outlining what publishers must meet to qualify for PAL status is taken directly from the Society of Children's Books Writers and Illustrators website: http://www.scbwi.org/about/pal-guidelines/ [accessed 04 June 2016].

6 | Sign of the Twins

"Why, yes," Narcissus... Hermann Hesse, *Narcissus and Goldmund*, p. 45. For many years, I reread several of Hesse's books annually, but not his most popular novels, i.e., *Demian*, *Steppenwolf*, or *Siddhartha*. I preferred the early and little known *Beneath the Wheel*, which is Hesse at his most melancholic.

Goldmund stood looking... Hermann Hesse, *Narcissus and Goldmund*, pp. 68–69.

10 | Temple of the Universe

cheapest drinks, best... Groghouse: http://www.groghouse.com [accessed 11 March 2016].

to provide an... Temple of the Universe: http://www.tou.org [accessed 13 March 2016]. Mickey Singer still presides over the Temple of the Universe. If you visit Gainesville, Florida, for any length of time, it is worth visiting on Sunday morning for prayers, chants, and community.

13 | $11.11

muddle-duddle, cribble-crabble... Hans Christian Andersen, "The Bog King's Daughter," *Hans Christian Andersen: The Complete Fairy Tales and Stories* (translated from the Danish by Erik Christian Haugaard). New York: Anchor Books, 1983.

Part II

14 | Buyer Beware

The art of... Angela Bole, "Choose Change," *IBPA Independent*. February 2016, Vol. 34, No. 2, p. 5.

failed to achieve... James A. Cox, Editor-in-Chief, *Midwest Book Review*, personal correspondence.

too many books... Ibid.

You know that… Kristina Radke, "Which Review Outlet Should You Target? *IBPA Independent*. July 2016, Vol. 34, No. 7, p. 17.

effective frequency… Ibid., p. 17.

16 | Medieval Cats
The sensational discovery… Susan Herbert, *Medieval Cats*, p. 5.

17 | Fool's Cap
Just as the… Jean Cocteau, as cited in Patrice Vecchione's *Step Into Nature: Nurturing Imagination and Spirit in Everyday Life*, p. 150.

20 | Authorpreneur
authorpreneurial… I've not taken this term from any direct reference; however, it is a term that has been gaining popularity with self-published authors to describe their position in the marketplace: as independent author/publishers with a healthy entrepreneurial spirit.

professional, unbiased book… Kirkus Reviews: https://www.kirkusreviews.com/indie-reviews/ [accessed 7 August 2016]. Kirkus has been the gold standard for the publishing industry for years. But like many historic review agencies, they have entered the self-publishing arena with a host of fee-based services.

the literary sensation… Guy Kelly, "Meet Mark Dawson, the Literary Sensation You've Never Heard Of." *The Telegraph*. 15 April 2016: http://www.telegraph.co.uk/men/ thinking-man/meet-mark-dawson-the-literary-sensation-youve-never-heard-of/ [accessed 8 August 2016].

22 | UpublishU
scholars, critics, professors… The Children's Literature Association: http://www.childlitassn.org [accessed 29 August 2016].

the largest publishing… BookExpo America: http://www.bookexpoamerica.com [accessed: 29 May 2016]. BookExpo, with its follow-up fan convention BookCon, is by far the largest celebration of books, book creators, and book publishing in the United States.

23 | Game-changer

a service that... Ingram Content Group: http://www.ingramcontent.com/news/ingram-acquires-aerio [accessed 18 September 2016]. Along with Baker & Taylor, Ingram is one of the largest book distributors in the nation; however, like many 21st-century publishing entities, Ingram has grown its business to include print-on-demand and e-book publishing, and has teamed up with other digital savvy companies, Aer.io being one of them:

curate... Ibid. It's a curious word. We usually reserve the word "curate" for the art world. But new technologies in digital publishing, such as Aer.io, allow us to sculpt (to use another term from the art world) a book list around a central product, whether that product be your newly published book or a set of Teenage Mutant Ninja Turtles.

A product of... Indiebound: https://www.indiebound.org/indiebound-faq [accessed 19 September 2016].

an independent publisher... paraphrased from Robert Gray, "The Optimistic Stochastics of Indie Publishing," *Fresh Eyes Now*: http://www.shelf-awareness.com/issue.html?issue=1305#m10529 [accessed 19 September 2016].

24 | Palimpsest

According to them... paraphrased from Lee Odden, "SEO Basics: Will Moving or Changing My Site Hurt Rankings?" *TopRank Marketing*: http://www.toprankblog.com/2008/10/seo-basics-change-site-hurt-rankings/ [accessed 12 May 2016].

Dear Mr. Nikola-Lisa... Bryan Munster, *personal correspondence.* Of course, Bryan Munster is not the real name of the pro bono lawyer that aided me with my trademark application. Since the real "Bryan" *is* a lawyer, I thought I'd play it safe and use a pseudonym.

a children's book… Home Page, Square Fish Books, Macmillan Publishers: http://us.macmillan.com/publishers/square-fish-books [accessed 12 May 2016].

unconscious plagiarism… Twain Quotes: Directory of Mark Twain's Maxims, Quotations, and Various Opinions: http://www.twainquotes.com/Plagiarism.html [accessed 14 May 2016].

Nothing is ours… Ibid.

If he takes… Ibid.

Night is coming… W. Nikola-Lisa, *personal notes.*

Night is coming… W. Nikola-Lisa, *Night Is Coming*, 1991. As a first book *Night Is Coming* was a painful experience. Three years in the making with numerous revisions, all prompted by the brilliant young editor Donna Brooks at Dutton Children' Books. Although I only published two books with Donna (*Night Is Coming* and *Tangletalk*), they remain two of my favorite books.

Part III

26 | Brilliant

Friedlander admits that… paraphrased from Joel Friedlander: thebookdesigner.com [accessed 23 May 2016]. If you want to learn about books and their creators, *The Book Designer Blog* is the place to go. Friedlander's witty and intelligent blog posts are a must read not only for editors, book designers, and graphic artists, but for any aspiring or professional author.

Myers concludes that… paraphrased from Karen Myers, "How to Use CreateSpace and Ingram Spark Together," *Alliance of Independent Authors*: http://selfpublishingadvice.org/how-to-use-createspace-and-ingram-spark-together/ [Accessed 03 June 2016].

Use CreateSpace for… paraphrased from Amy Collins' post "Why You Need IngramSpark and CreateSpace–Updated," *New Shelves*: http://www.newshelves.com/2016/05/21/why-you-need-lightning-source-and-createspace/ [Accessed: 05 June 2016].

27 | The Quintessential Quail

the illustration of… David Pelletier, *The Graphic Alphabet*, back matter.

Not since Milton… Zena Sutherland, (ed.), *The Best in Children's Books*, p. 30.

29 | A Sngglement of String

here's a list… I've long been a fan of Alistair Reid's work. His sense of wordplay is impeccable and is displayed in no better fashion than in *Ounce Dice Trice*, a book that can engage the reader—young and old—for hours upon end.

domestically-raised Kobe… Lunch Menu, Hackney's Printers Row: http://www.hackneysprintersrow.net/menu/ [accessed 15 June 2016].

30 | This Is Going to Cost Me

Fabrizio, a book… Avi, *Murder at Midnight*, p. 31. The quotation comes at the end of a dialogue between Mangus the Magician and his assistant, Fabrizio. Here is the full conversation found on pages 30–31:

Fabrizio tried to think of something that might engage Mangus. "Master, I've heard it said that reading deadens the soul."

"Nonsense," snapped Mangus. "If you are not well read, you might as well *be* dead."

"But, Master, some suggest that too much reading causes blindness."

Mangust looked up. "The wise person knows that reading books is the best way to see the world."

"I give thanks, then," said Fabrizio, "that you have all the books in the world. As soon as I get through yours, I'll never have to read another."

"There can never be enough books," said Mangus. "The pity is it takes years to create each one."

"Is that true?" said the surprised boy.

"Fabrizio, a book must first be written. To do so, the writer exchanges days for words, months for paragraphs, and years for chapters—time turned into books. There's your magic."

Nikola, I got... Tom Fox, personal correspondence.

32 | Time Present, Time Past
Time present and... T. S. Eliot, *Four Quartets*, p. 13.

34 | Street Views
The clouds below... David Wolman, *A Left-hand Turn Around the World*, p. 25.

I'm wearing the... Ibid., p. 147.

For a few... Dava Sobel, *Longitude*, p. 178.

Part IV

39 | Dear Mr. Pirsig
On a cycle... Robert Pirsig, *Zen & the Art of Motorcycle Maintenance*, p. 12.

They were like... Ibid., p. 34.

40 | What Jane Yolen Said
Babe Ruth? Why... W. Nikola-Lisa, unpublished manuscript. As much as I like my tongue-in-cheek look at the strange life of Babe Ruth, if you can only read one book on the Ruth make it Leigh Montville's *The Big Bam: The Life & Times of Babe Ruth*. Montville blends a thorough

understanding of Ruth's oversized personality with the cultural forces that helped shape him.

44 | Bicameral Mind

Having just finished... Edward Profitt, home page of the Julian Jaynes Society: http://www.julianjaynes.org/bicameralmind.php [accessed 11 August 2016].

With e-book sales... taken from Luke Graham, "Book Sales Are in Decline But Audio Books Are Thriving." *CNBC News*, 3 March 2016: http://www.cnbc.com [accessed 15 August 2016].

45 | Concord Dust

I'd like to... Robert Sullivan, *The Thoreau You Don't Know*, p. 1. Well, I was rather severe on Sullivan. I shouldn't be: there are gems sprinkled throughout the book, making it worth the read.

[Am] I not... Ibid., p. 112.

47 | Old Possum

is a poetic... Nikki Giovanni, *The Genie in the Jar*, inside front flap.

read it carefully... Ibid., inside front flap.

The history of... Richard de la Mare, *A Publisher on Book Production: The Sixth Dent Memorial Lecture*. London: J. M. Dent & Sons LTD, 1936, p. 41.

These playful verses... T. S. Eliot, *Old Possum's Book of Practical Cats*, inside front flap.

48 | Cease and Desist

Gyroscope Books™ is... W. Nikola-Lisa, home page of Gyroscope Books: http://gyroscopebooks.com/ [accessed 12 October 2016]. It's the Gemini thing—having two websites. But, recently, commonsense won out and I've moved most of the content on the Gyroscope Books website to the Nikola Books website. ("Whew!" is all my wife can say.)

52 | So Many Books

So many books… Frank Zappa, op cit.

Selected Bibliography

Aldersey-Williams, Hugh. *Periodic Tales: A Cultural History of the Elements, from Arsenic to Zinc*. New York: Viking, 2011.

Alexander, Jonathan. *Medieval Illuminators and Their Methods of Work*. New Haven: Yale University Press, 1992.

Alexie, Sherman. *The Absolutely True Diary of a Part-Time Indian*. Boston: Little, Brown and Company, 2007.

Aliki. *A Medieval Feast*. New York: HarperCollins, 1983.

Anno, Mitsumasa. *Anno's Medieval World*. New York: Philomel, 1980.

Avi. *Murder at Midnight*. New York: Scholastic, 2009.

Bachelard, Gaston. *The Poetics of Space*. Maria Jolas, Trans. Boston: Beacon Press, 1969.

Basbanes, Nicholas. *On Paper: The Everything of Its Two-Thousand-Year History*. New York: Vintage Books, 2014.

Baskin, Leonard. *Hosie's Alphabet*. New York: Viking, 1972.

Behr, Caroline. *T. S. Eliot: A Chronology of his Life and Works*. London: Palgrave Macmillan, 1983.

Berner, David W. *Accidental Lessons*. Durham, CT: Strategic Book Publishing, 2009.

________. *Any Road Will Take You There*. Downers Grove, IL: Dream of Things, 2014.

________. *Night Radio*. Dunlo, PA: Cawing Crow Press, 2016.

Berry, James. *Rough Sketch Beginning*. Boston: Houghton Mifflin Harcourt, 1996.

Blanding, Michael. *The Map Thief.* New York: Gotham Books, 2014.

Brown, Michael. *Understanding Illuminated Manuscripts: A Guide to Technical Terms*. Los Angeles: The J. Paul Getty Museum, 1994.

Bryson, Bill. *The Life and Times of the Thunderbolt Kid: A Memoir*. New York: Broadway Books, 2007.

Burkert, Nancy Ekholm. *Valentine & Orson*. New York: Farrar, Straus and Giroux, 1989.

Carrick, Donald. *Harald and the Great Stag*. New York: Clarion, 1988.

Carroll, Lewis. *Alice's Adventures in Wonderland*. New York: MacMillan, 1943.

Cazelles, Raymond and Johannes Rathofer. *Illuminations of the Heaven and Earth: The Glories of the Tres Riches Heures Du Duc De Berry.* New York: Abrams, 1988.

Cline, Emily. *The Girls*. New York: Random House, 2016.

Cohen, Barbara. *Geoffrey Chaucer's Canterbury Tales*. New York: Lothrop, Lee & Shepard, 1988.

Collins, Marie and Virginia Davis. *A Medieval Book of Seasons*. New York: HarperCollins, 1992.

Creswick, Paul. *Robin Hood*. New York: Charles Scribner's Sons, 1984.

Cushman, Karen. *Catherine, Called Birdy*. New York: Clarion, 1994.

Dane, Joseph A. *Dogfish Memory: A Memoir*. Woodstock, VT: Countryman Press, 2011.

de Hamel, Christopher. *A History of Illuminated Manuscripts*. New York: Phaidon, 1994.

________. *Medieval Craftsmen: Scribes and Illuminators*. Toronto: University of Toronto Press, 1992.

________. *The British Library Guide to Manuscript Illumination: History and Techniques*. Toronto: University of Toronto Press, 2001.

Drogin, Marc. *Medieval Calligraphy: Its History and Technique*. New York: Dover, 1980.

Divry, Sophie. *The Library of Unrequited Love*. New York: Quercus, 2015.

Eliot, T. S. *Four Quartets*. New York: Harcourt, Brace & World, Inc., 1943.

Finnegan, William. *Barbarian Days: A Surfing Life*. New York: Penguin, 2015.

Foer, Jonathan Safran. *Here I Am*. New York: Farrar, Straus and Giroux, 2016.

Freethy, Barbara. *Daniel's Gift*. New York: Avon, 1996.

________. *The Way Back Home*. New York: Pocket Books, 2012.

Gantos, Jack. *Dead End in Norvelt*. New York: Farrar Straus and Giroux, 2011.

Gardner, Howard. *Multiple Intelligences: The Theory in Practice*. New York: Basic Books, 1993.

Gilbert, Henry. *Robin Hood & the Men of Greenwood*. London: Bracken Books, 1985.

Goodwin, Doris Kearns. *Wait Till Next Year: A Memoir*. New York: Simon & Schuster, 1998.

Grahame, Kenneth. *The Wind in the Willows*. New York: Dell Yearling, 1972.

Guarnieri, Paolo. *A Boy Named Giotto*. New York: Farrar, Straus and Giroux, 1999.

Haissen, Carl. *Razor Girl*. New York: Knopf, 2016.

Halberstam, David. *October 1964*. New York: Villard Books, 1994.

Harrison, Jim. *The River Swimmer*. New York: Grove Press, 1994.

Harvey, Miles. *The Island of the Lost Maps: A True Story of Cartographic Crime*. New York: Broadway Books. 2001.

Herbert, Susan. *Medieval Cats*. Boston: Bulfinch Press, 1995.

Hesse, Herman, *Narcissus and Goldmund*. Translated by Ursule Molinaro. New York: Farrar, Straus and Giroux, 1968.

Hesse, Karen. *Aleutian Sparrow*. New York: Margaret McElderry, 2003.

Hunt, Jonathan. *Illuminations*. New York: Simon & Schuster, 1989.

Jaynes, Julian. *The Origin of Consciousness in the Breakdown of the Bicameral Mind*. Boston: Houghton Mifflin, 1976.

Johnson, George. *Miss Leavitt's Stars*. New York: Atlas Books, 2005.

Jung, C. G. *Memories, Dreams, Reflections*. New York: Vintage, 1965.

Kahn, Roger. *The Boys of Summer*. New York: Harper Perennial Modern Classics, 2006.

Kalanithi, Paul. *When Breath Becomes Air*. New York: Random House, 2016.

Konigsburg, E. L. *A Proud Taste for Scarlet and Miniver*. New York: Atheneum, 1973.

Lamb, Harold. *Genghis Khan: The Emperor of All Men*. New York: McBride, 1928.

Larson, Erik. *Dead Wake: The Last Crossing of the Lusitania*. New York: Broadway Books, 2015.

________. *Isaac's Storm: A Man, a Time, and the Deadliest Hurricane in History*. New York: Crown Publishers, 1999.

________. *The Devil in the White City: Murder, Magic, and Madness at the Fair that Changed America*. New York: Crown Publishers, 2003.

________. *Thunderstruck*. New York: Broadway Books, 2007.

Lasker, Joe. *Merry Ever After*. New York: Viking, 1976.

Lawrence, Lucy. *Fly, Fly, Witchy*. Crystal Lake, IL: Rigby Literacy Series, 2000.

Leach, Amy. *Things That Are*. Minneapolis: Milkweed Editions, 2012.

Lithgow, John. *I Got Two Dogs*. New York: Simon & Schuster, 2008.

Manchester, William. *A World Lit Only by Fire: The Medieval Mind and the Renaissance*. Boston: Little, Brown, 1992.

Martin, Jr., Bill. *Brown Bear, Brown Bear, What do You See?* New York: Henry Holt, 1983.

________ and John Archambault. *Chicka Chicka Boom Boom*. New York: Simon & Schuster, 1989.

McKinley, Robin. *The Outlaws of Sherwood*. New York: Greenwillow, 1988.

McMillan Bruce. *Mary Had a Little Lamb*. New York: Scholastic, 1990.

Merriam, Eve. *Train Leaves the Station*. New York: Henry Holt, 1994.

Montville, Leigh. *The Big Bam: The Life & Times of Babe Ruth*. New York: Broadway Books, 2006. 2006.

Neill, A. S. *Summerhill: A Radical Approach to Child Rearing*. New York: Pocket Books, 1977.

Nelson, Kadir. *We Are the Ship*. New York: Hyperion/Jump at the Sun, 2008.

Nikola-Lisa, W. *1, 2, 3 Thanksgiving*. Chicago: Albert Whitman, 1991.

________. *America: A Book of Opposites*. New York: Lee & Low Books, 2001.

________. *Bein' With You This Way*. New York: Lee & Low Books, 1994.

________. *Dear Frank: Babe Ruth, the Red Sox, and the Great War*. Chicago: Gyroscope Books, 2011.

________. *Dragonfly: A Childhood Memoir*. Chicago: Gyroscope Books, 2010.

________. *Gaya Lives in a Blue House*. Chicago: Gyroscope Books, 2013.

________. *Hallelujah: A Christmas Celebration*. New York: Atheneum, 2000.

________. *Hey, Aren't You the Janitor? And Other Tales in the Life of a Children's Book Author*. Chicago: Gyroscope Books, 2011.

________. *How We Are Smart*. New York: Lee & Low Books, 2006.

________. *Magic in the Margins*. Boston: Houghton Mifflin, 2007.

________. *Night Is Coming*. New York: E. P. Dutton, 1991.

________. *No Babies Asleep.* New York: Atheneum, 1995.

________. *One Hole in the Road.* New York: Henry Holt, 1997.

________. *Setting the Turkeys Free.* New York: Jump at the Sun/ Hyperion, 2004.

________. *Shake Dem Halloween Bones.* Boston: Houghton Mifflin, 1997.

________. *Shark Man.* Chicago: Gyroscope Books, 2016.

________. *Storm.* New York: Atheneum, 1993.

________. *Summer Sun Risin'.* New York: Lee & Low Books, 2002.

________. *Tangletalk.* New York: E. P. Dutton, 1997.

________. *The Men Who Made the Yankees: The Odyssey of the World's Greatest Baseball Team from Baltimore to the Bronx.* Chicago: Gyroscope Books, 2014.

________. *Till Year's Good End.* New York: Atheneum, 1997.

________. *To Hear the Angles Sing.* New York: Holiday House, 2002.

Noad, Timothy and Patricia Seligman. *The Illuminated Alphabet.* Philadelphia: Running Press, 1994.

Pachett, Ann. *Commonwealth.* New York: Harper, 2016.

Pelletier, David. *The Graphic Alphabet.* New York: Orchard Books, 1996.

Pirsig, Robert. *Zen and the Art of Motorcycle Maintenance.* New York: Morrow, 1974.

Pyle, Howard. *The Merry Adventures of Robin Hood.* New York: Charles Scribner's Sons, 1946.

Raschka, Chris. *Charlie Parker played be-bop.* New York: Orchard, 1997.

Reid, Alistair. *Ounce Dice Trice*. Boston: Atlantic Monthly Press, 1958.

Robertson, Bruce. *Marguerite Makes a Book*. Los Angeles: The J. Paul Getty Museum, 1999.

Robinson, Marilynne. *Gilead.* New York: Picador, 2006.

________. *Home*. New York: Picador, 2009.

________. *Lila*. New York: Picador, 2015.

Rybczynski, Witold. *One Good Turn: A Natural History of the Screwdriver and the Screw*. New York: Scribner, 2000.

Saller, Carol Fisher. *Eddie's War*. South Hampton, NH: namelos, 2011.

Sandburg, Carl. "Fog." *Carl Sandburg: Selected Poems*. New York: Mariner Books, 1996.

Sandler, Martin W. *Trapped in Ice!* New York: Scholastic, 2006.

Saramago, José. *Small Memories: A Memoir*. London: Vintage, 2010.

Schultz, Philip. *failure: poems*. Boston: Mariner Books, 2007.

Sedaris, David. *Me Talk Pretty One Day*. New York: Back Bay Books, 2001.

Shailor, Barbara. *The Medieval Book*. Toronto: University of Toronto Press, 2002.

Shaw, Charles. *It Looked Like Spilt Milk*. New York: Harper Collins, 1988.

Singer, Isaac Bashevis. "Naftali the Storyteller & His Horse, Sus." *Stories for Children*. New York: Farrar, Straus and Giroux, 1984.

Smith, Clayton. *Anomaly Flats: A Novel.* Chicago: Dapper Press, 2015.

Sobel, Dava. *Galileo's Daughter: A Historical Memoir of Science, Faith, and Love.* New York: Penguin, 2000,

________. *Longitude: The True Story of a Lone Genius Who Solved the Greatest Scientific Problem of His Time.* New York: Bloomsbury, 2007.

Steinbeck, John. *Of Mice and Men.* New York: Covici Freide, 1937; Penguin Reissue, 1993.

Steiner, Rudolf. *The Child's Changing Consciousness as the Basis of Pedagogical Practice.* London: Rudolf Steiner Press, 1988.

________. *The Education of the Child in the Light of Anthroposophy.* London: Rudolf Steiner Press, 1981.

Sullivan, Robert. *The Thoreau You Don't Know: The Father of Nature Writers on the Importance of Cities, Finance, and Fooling Around.* New York: Harper Perennial, 2011.

Sutherland, Zena (ed.). *The Best in Children's Books: The University of Chicago Guide to Children's Literature, 1973–1978.* Chicago: The University of Chicago Press, 1980.

Temple, Frances. *The Ramsay Scallop.* New York: Orchard, 1994.

Thompson, Tommy. *Basic Layout Design.* New York: Studio Publications, 1950.

________. *How to Render Roman Letter Forms.* New York: American Studio Books, 1946.

________. *The ABC of Our Alphabet:* New York: Studio Publications, 1942.

Thurlby, Paul. *Paul Thurlby's Alphabet.* Somerville, MA: Templar Books, 2011.

Tolkien, J. R. R. *The Hobbit or There and Back Again, 50th Anniversary Edition*. Boston: Houghton Mifflin, 1966.

Towles, Amor. *A Gentleman in Moscow.* New York: Viking, 2016.

Tuchman, Barbara. *A Distant Mirror: The Calamitous 14th Century*. New York: Random House, 1987.

Van Allsburg, Chris. *The Mysteries of Harris Burdick*. Boston: Houghton Mifflin, 1984.

Vecchione, Patrice. *Step Into Nature: Nurturing Imagination and Spirit in Everyday Life*. New York: Atria, 2015.

Waldegrave, Katie. *The Poets' Daughters: Dora Wordsworth and Sara Coleridge*. London: Windmill Books, 2013.

Watson, Fred. *Stargazer: The Life and Times of the Telescope*. New York: Da Capo Press, 2005.

Weinstein, Krystyna. *The Art of Medieval Manuscripts*. San Diego: Laurel Glen Publishing, 1997.

Westwood, J. O. *The Art of Illuminated Manuscripts: Illustrated Sacred Texts.* New York: Arch Cape Press1988.

Whitehead, Colson. *The Underground Railroad*. New York: Doubleday, 2016.

Wilson, Elizabeth B. *Bibles and Bestiaries: A Guide to Illuminated Manuscripts*. New York: Farrar, Straus and Giroux, 1994.

White, E. B. *Charlotte's Web*. New York: Harper and Row, 1973.

Wolman, David. *A Left-Hand Turn Around the World: Chasing the Mystery and Meaning of All Things Southpaw.* New York: Da Capo Press, 2006.

Yolen, Jane. *Owl Moon*. New York: Philomel, 1987.

About The Author

W. Nikola-Lisa is the author of over two-dozen books for readers young and old. His writing for young readers has garnered several awards: *Bein' With You This Way* was a runner-up for the 1995 Jane Addams Book Award. *Shake Dem Halloween Bones* won the 2001 Golden Archer Award. In 2007, *How We Are Smart* won a Christopher Award and was a runner-up for the Gustavus Myers Outstanding Book Award.

Mr. Nikola-Lisa's books for older readers have also won acclaim. *The Men Who Made the Yankees* won the 2015 Literary Classics Lumen Award and the Society of Children's Book Writers and Illustrators' 2nd Annual Spark Award. And *Dear Frank: Babe Ruth, the Red Sox, and the Great War* won a gold medal from Literary Classics for best historical fiction for young adult readers.

For more information about the author, his books, and his school and library programs, visit him on the web at www.nikola-books.com.

If You Liked This Book

Tweet about it, send a shout-out to your Facebook friends, give it a thumbs up on Goodreads, blog about it, post the front cover on Pinterest, and/or review it on Amazon, Barnes & Noble, or another one of your favorite online booksellers. As you know, this is how the world works in the digital age. This is how we let our friends know what we're reading and thinking about. This is how we shine a light on the things we like. So, if you enjoyed this book, please give a shout-out and let the world know.

www.ingramcontent.com/pod-product-compliance
Lightning Source LLC
Chambersburg PA
CBHW031128120726
47905CB00006B/1610

* 9 7 8 0 9 9 7 2 5 2 4 4 6 *